SPIDER-MAN

EVERYDAY HERO

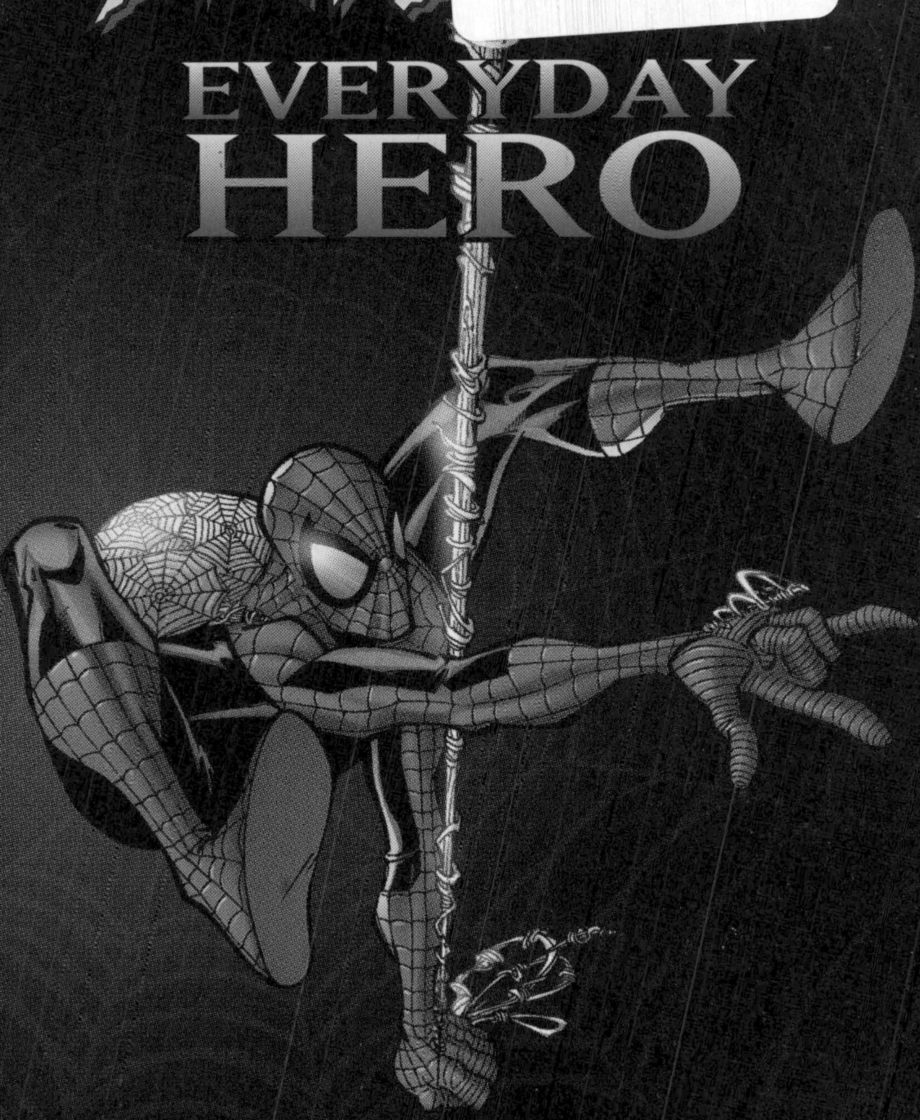

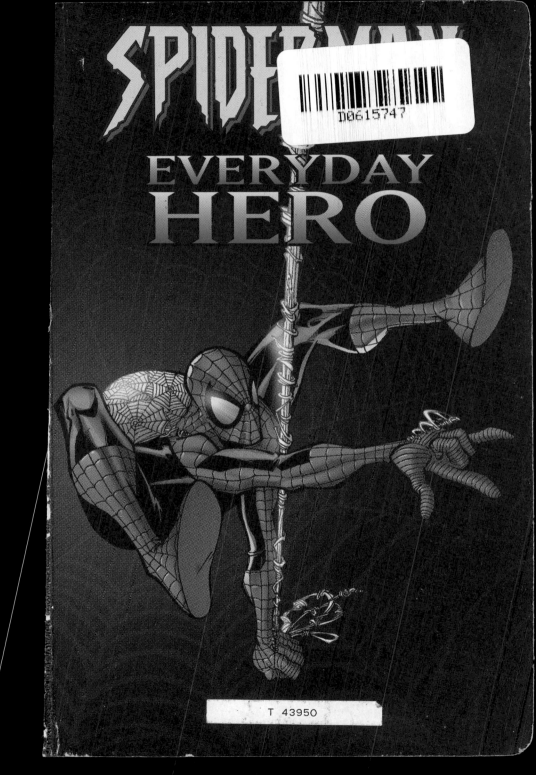

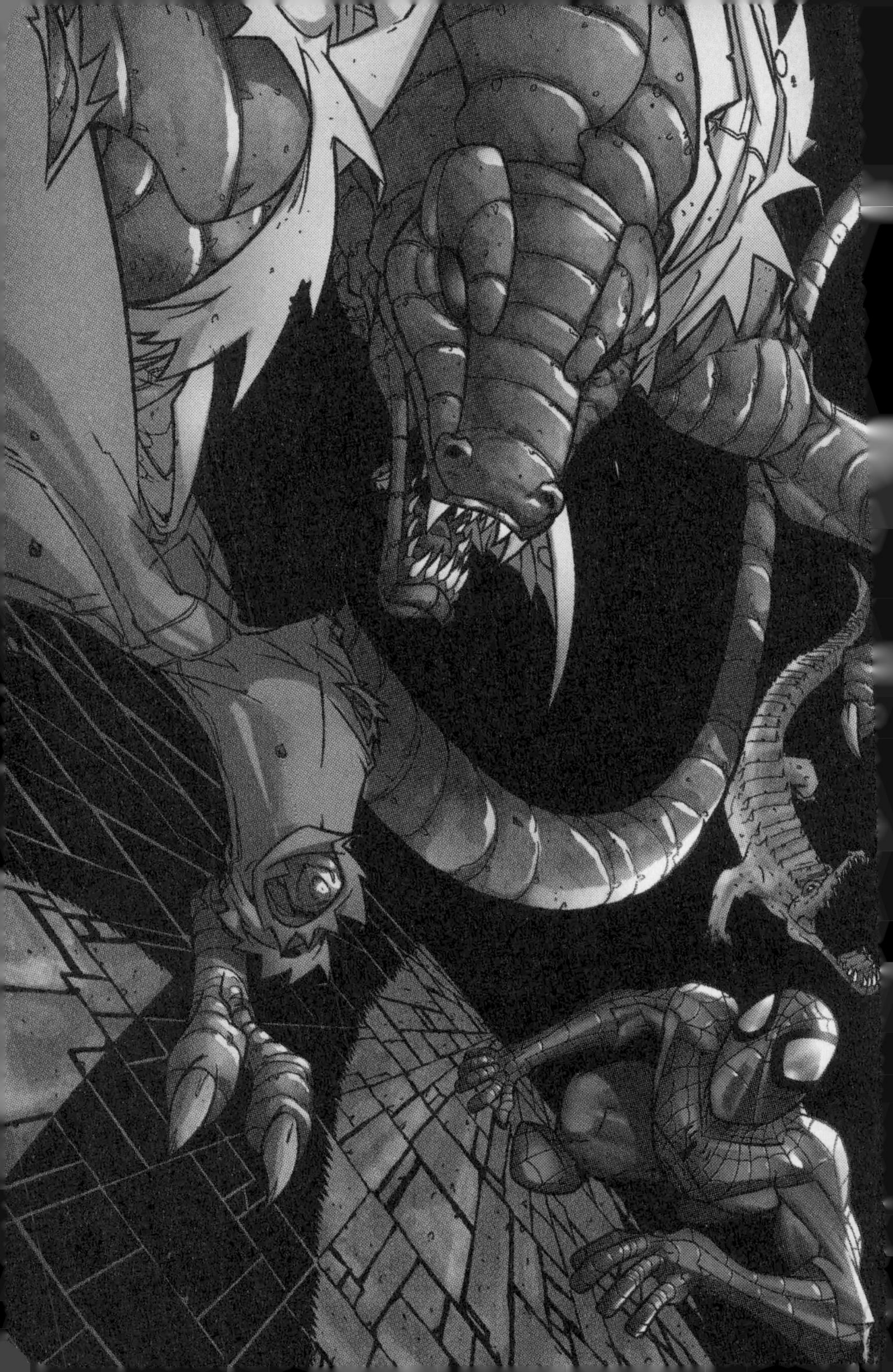

SPIDER-MAN

EVERYDAY HERO

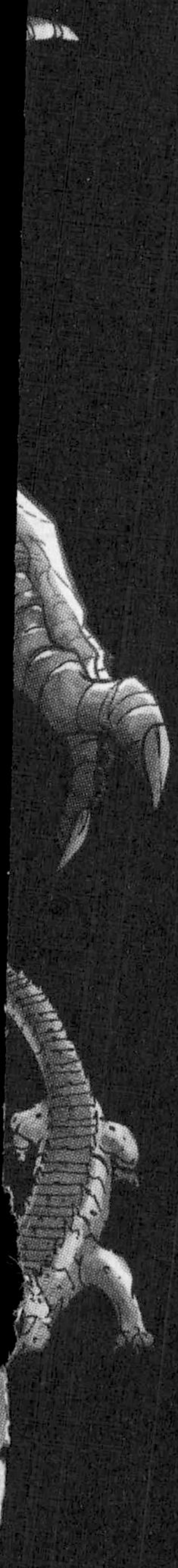

Writers:
Daniel Quantz & Todd Dezago

Pencils:
Mark Brooks, Jonboy Meyers & Michael O'Hare

Inks:
UDON, Pat Davidson & Derek Fridolfs

Colors:
UDON's Danimation and Lary Molinar

Letters:
Virtual Calligraphy's Randy Gentile & Cory Petit

Assistant Editor:
MacKenzie Cadenhead

Editor:
C.B. Cebulski

Consulting Editor:
Ralph Macchio

Collections Editor:
Jeff Youngquist

Assistant Editor:
Jennifer Grünwald

Book Designer:
Carrie Beadle

Editor in Chief:
Joe Quesada

Publisher:
Dan Buckley

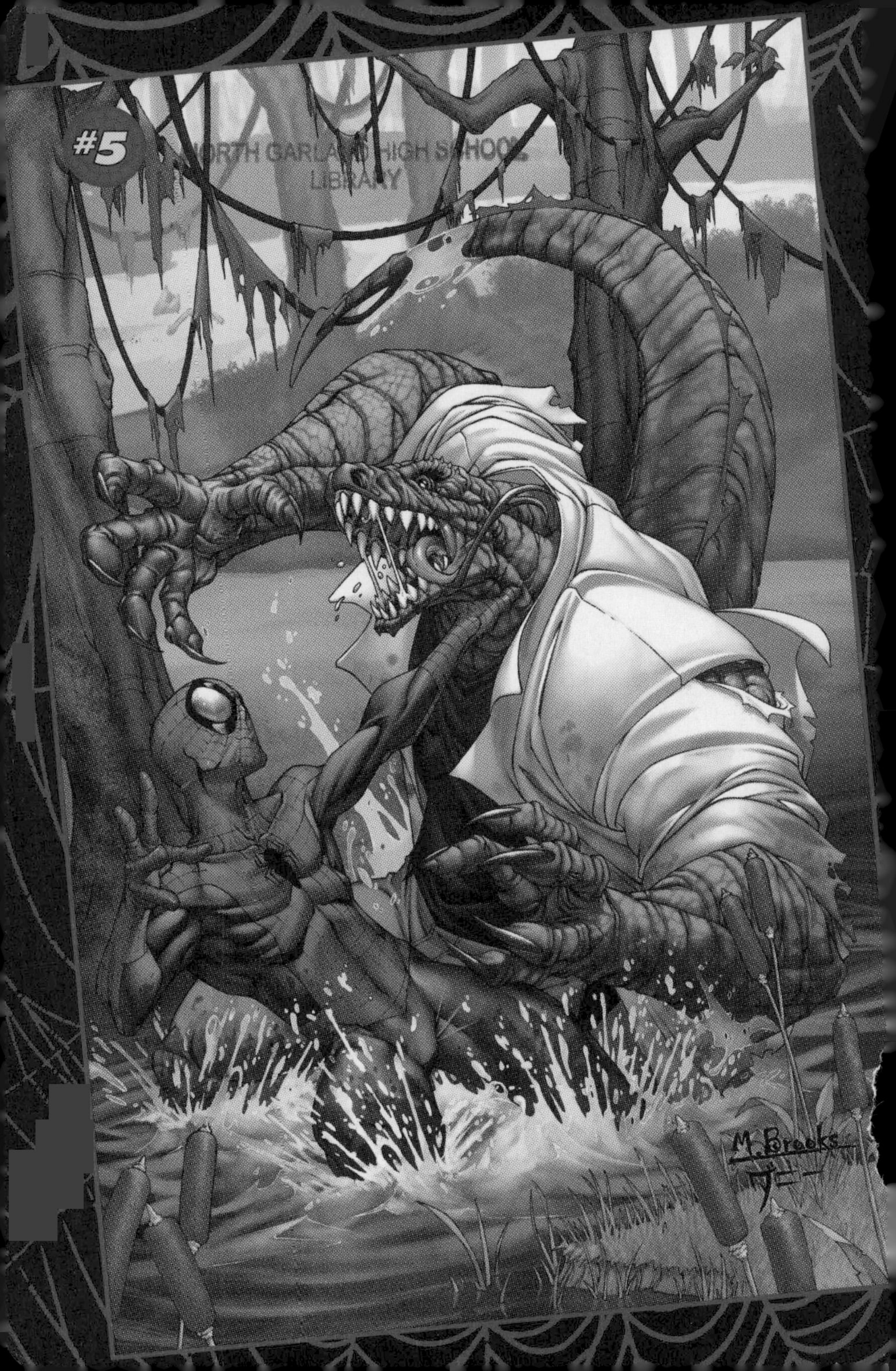
#5
M. Brooks

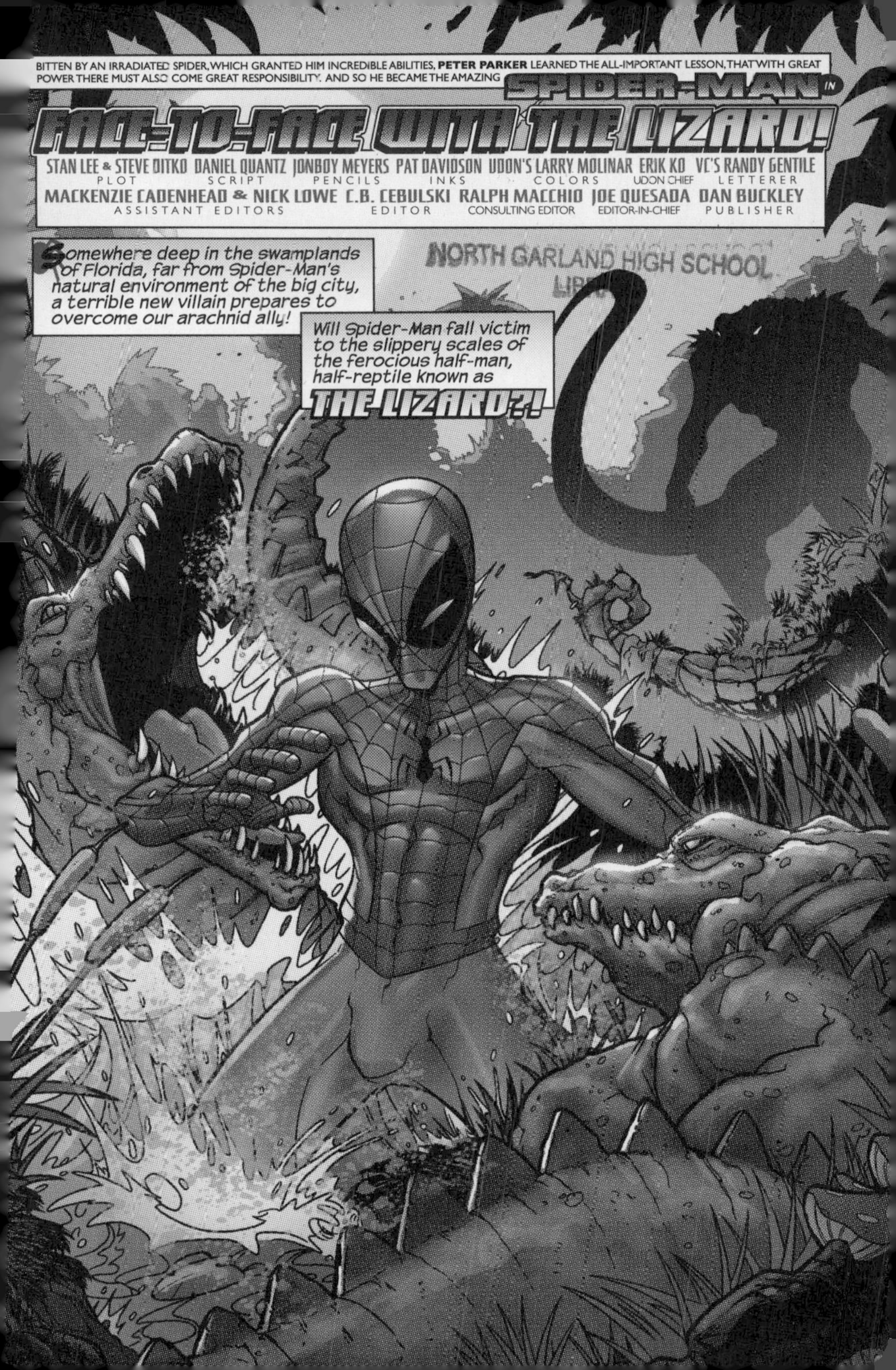
BITTEN BY AN IRRADIATED SPIDER, WHICH GRANTED HIM INCREDIBLE ABILITIES, PETER PARKER LEARNED THE ALL-IMPORTANT LESSON, THAT WITH GREAT POWER THERE MUST ALSO COME GREAT RESPONSIBILITY. AND SO HE BECAME THE AMAZING SPIDER-MAN IN
FACE-TO-FACE WITH THE LIZARD!
STAN LEE & STEVE DITKO PLOT
DANIEL QUANTZ SCRIPT
JONBOY MEYERS PENCILS
PAT DAVIDSON INKS
UDON'S LARRY MOLINAR COLORS
ERIK KO UDON CHIEF
VC'S RANDY GENTILE LETTERER
MACKENZIE CADENHEAD & NICK LOWE ASSISTANT EDITORS
C.B. CEBULSKI EDITOR
RALPH MACCHIO CONSULTING EDITOR
JOE QUESADA EDITOR-IN-CHIEF
DAN BUCKLEY PUBLISHER
Somewhere deep in the swamplands of Florida, far from Spider-Man's natural environment of the big city, a terrible new villain prepares to overcome our arachnid ally!
Will Spider-Man fall victim to the slippery scales of the ferocious half-man, half-reptile known as THE LIZARD?!

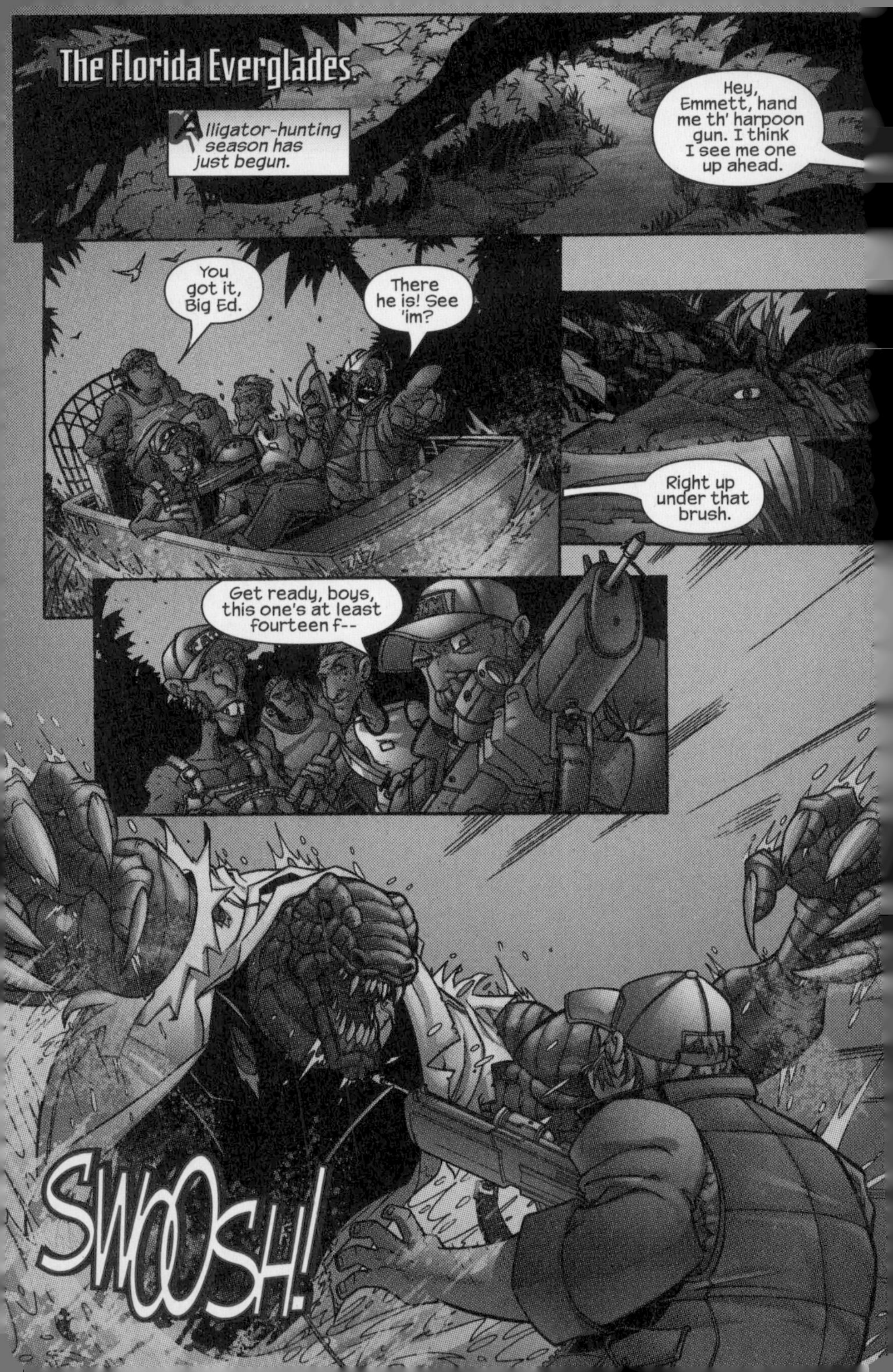
The Florida Everglades.
Alligator-hunting season has just begun.
Hey, Emmett, hand me th' harpoon gun. I think I see me one up ahead.
You got it, Big Ed.
There he is! See 'im?
Right up under that brush.
Get ready, boys, this one's at least fourteen f--
SWOOSH!

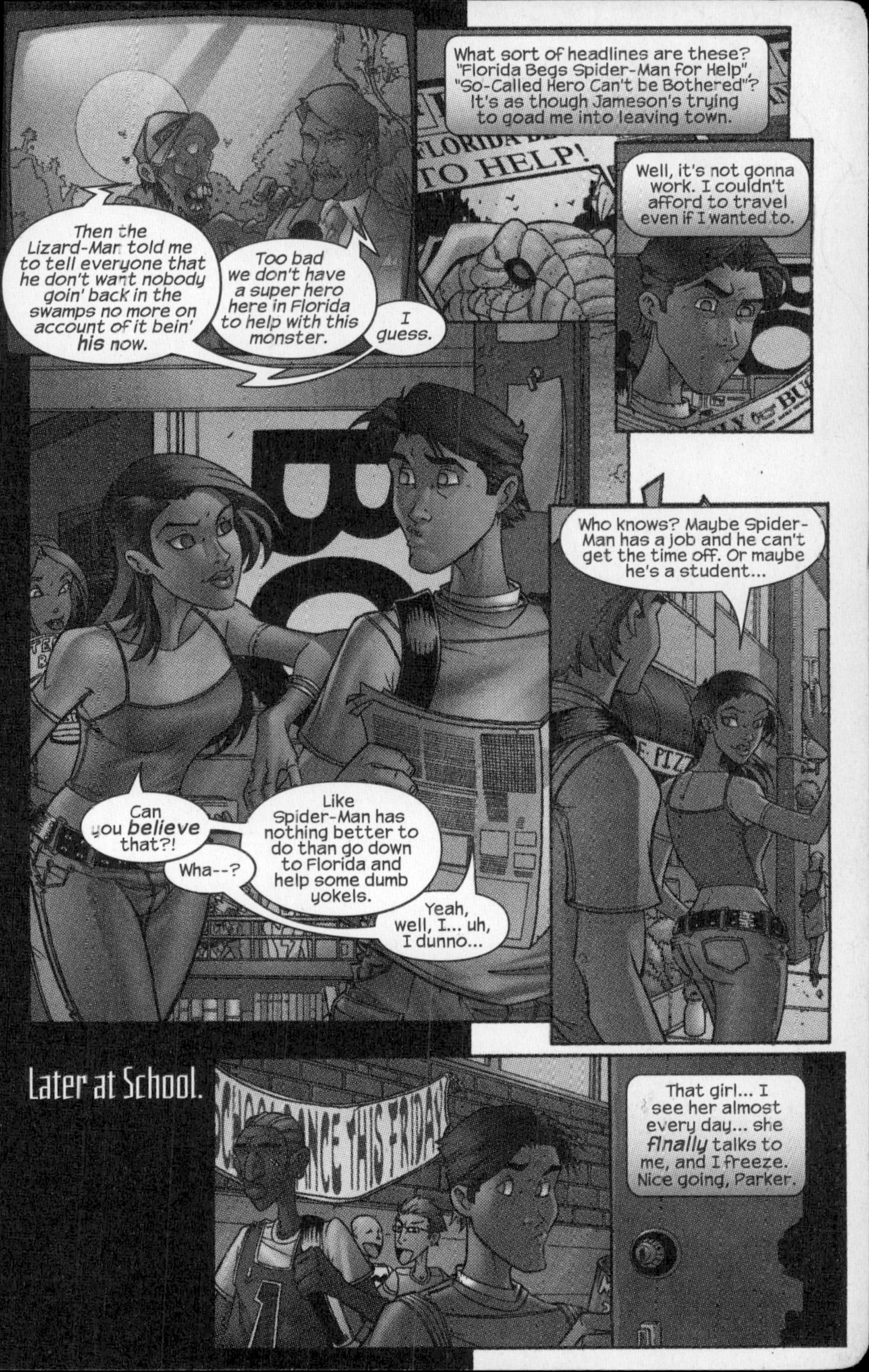

Then the Lizard-Man told me to tell everyone that he don't want nobody goin' back in the swamps no more on account of it bein' his now.
Too bad we don't have a super hero here in Florida to help with this monster.
I guess.
What sort of headlines are these? "Florida Begs Spider-Man for Help", "So-Called Hero Can't be Bothered"? It's as though Jameson's trying to goad me into leaving town.
TO HELP!
Well, it's not gonna work. I couldn't afford to travel even if I wanted to.
Can you believe that?!
Wha--?
Like Spider-Man has nothing better to do than go down to Florida and help some dumb yokels.
Yeah, well, I... uh, I dunno...
Who knows? Maybe Spider-Man has a job and he can't get the time off. Or maybe he's a student...
Later at School.
That girl... I see her almost every day... she finally talks to me, and I freeze. Nice going, Parker.

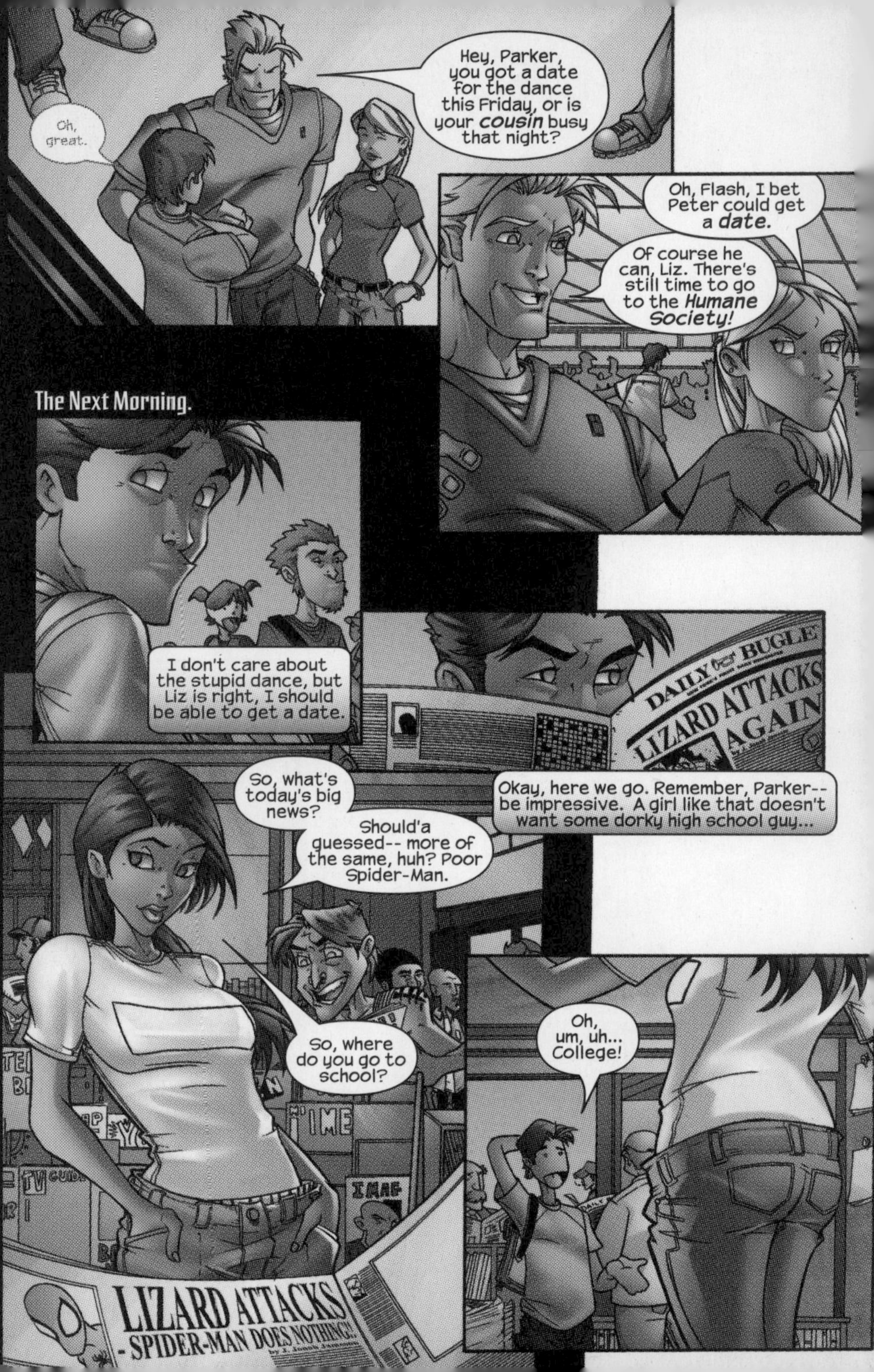
Oh, great.
Hey, Parker, you got a date for the dance this Friday, or is your *cousin* busy that night?
Oh, Flash, I bet Peter could get a *date.*
Of course he can, Liz. There's still time to go to the *Humane Society!*
The Next Morning.
I don't care about the stupid dance, but Liz is right, I should be able to get a date.
DAILY BUGLE
LIZARD ATTACKS AGAIN
So, what's today's big news?
Should'a guessed-- more of the same, huh? Poor Spider-Man.
Okay, here we go. Remember, Parker-- be impressive. A girl like that doesn't want some dorky high school guy...
So, where do you go to school?
Oh, um, uh... College!
LIZARD ATTACKS - SPIDER-MAN DOES NOTHING!!

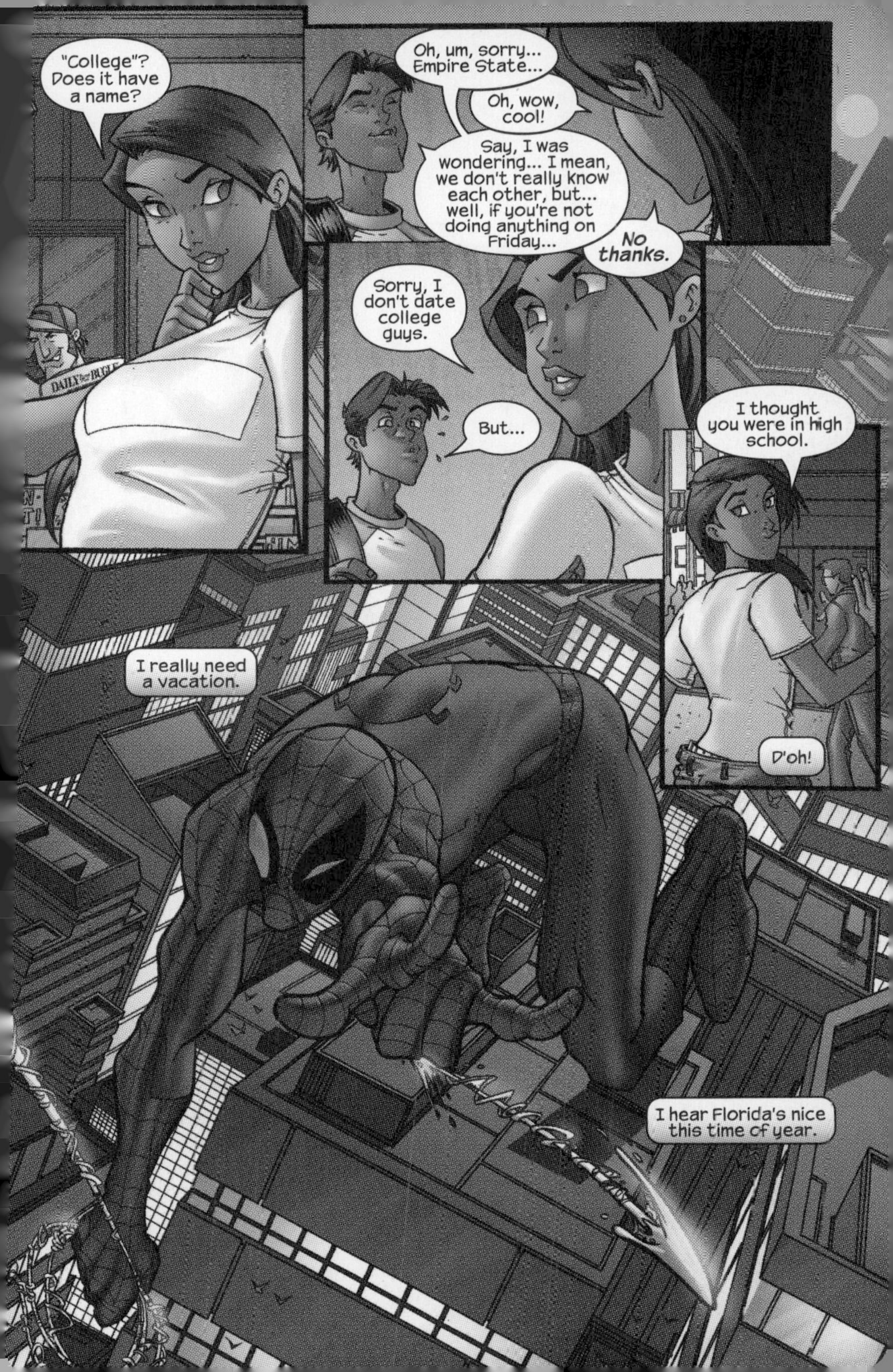
"College"? Does it have a name?
Oh, um, sorry... Empire State...
Oh, wow, cool!
Say, I was wondering... I mean, we don't really know each other, but... well, if you're not doing anything on Friday...
No thanks.
Sorry, I don't date college guys.
But...
I thought you were in high school.
D'oh!
I really need a vacation.
I hear Florida's nice this time of year.

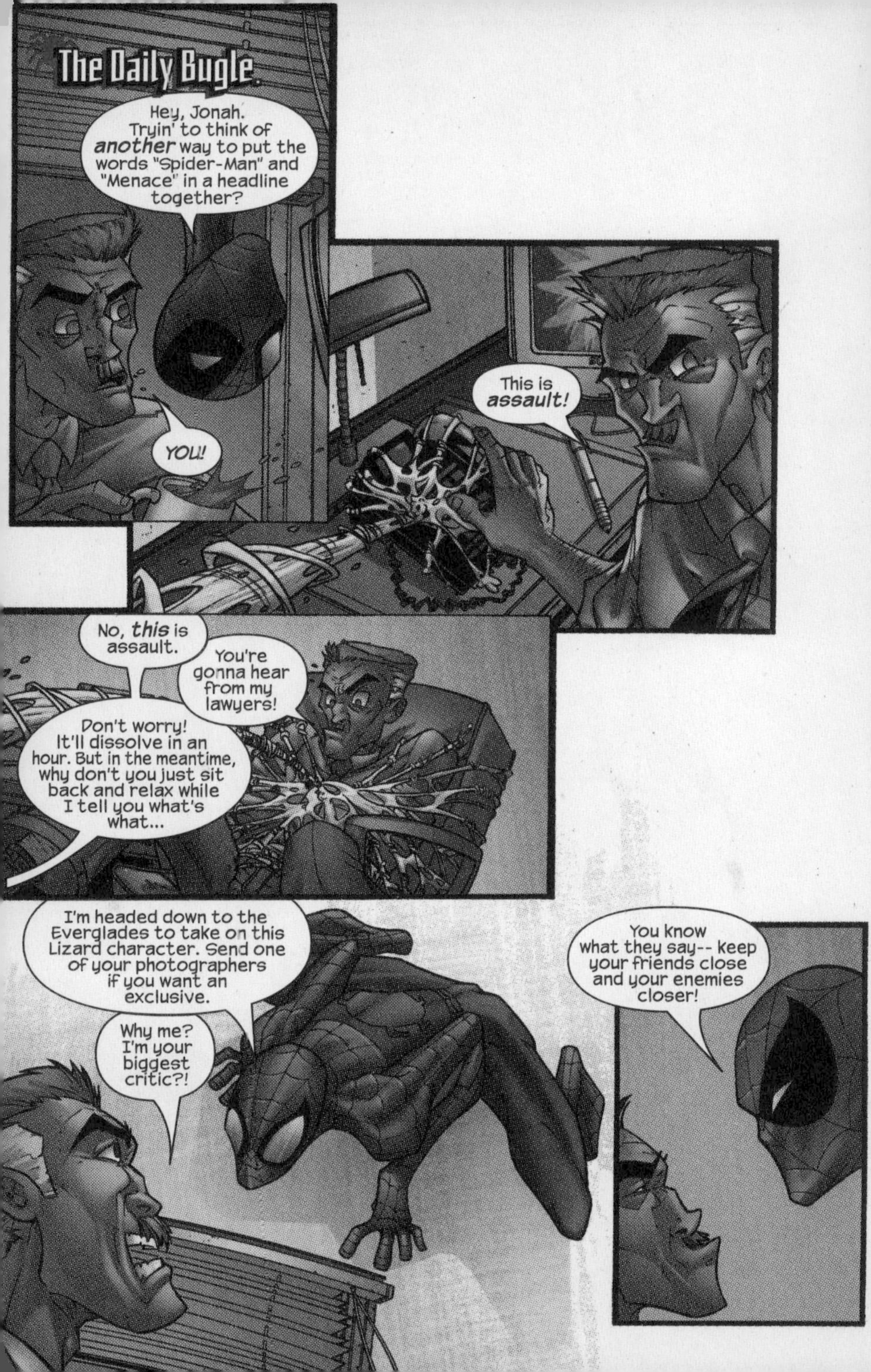
The Daily Bugle.
Hey, Jonah. Tryin' to think of another way to put the words "Spider-Man" and "Menace" in a headline together?
YOU!
This is assault!
No, this is assault.
You're gonna hear from my lawyers!
Don't worry! It'll dissolve in an hour. But in the meantime, why don't you just sit back and relax while I tell you what's what...
I'm headed down to the Everglades to take on this Lizard character. Send one of your photographers if you want an exclusive.
Why me? I'm your biggest critic?!
You know what they say-- keep your friends close and your enemies closer!

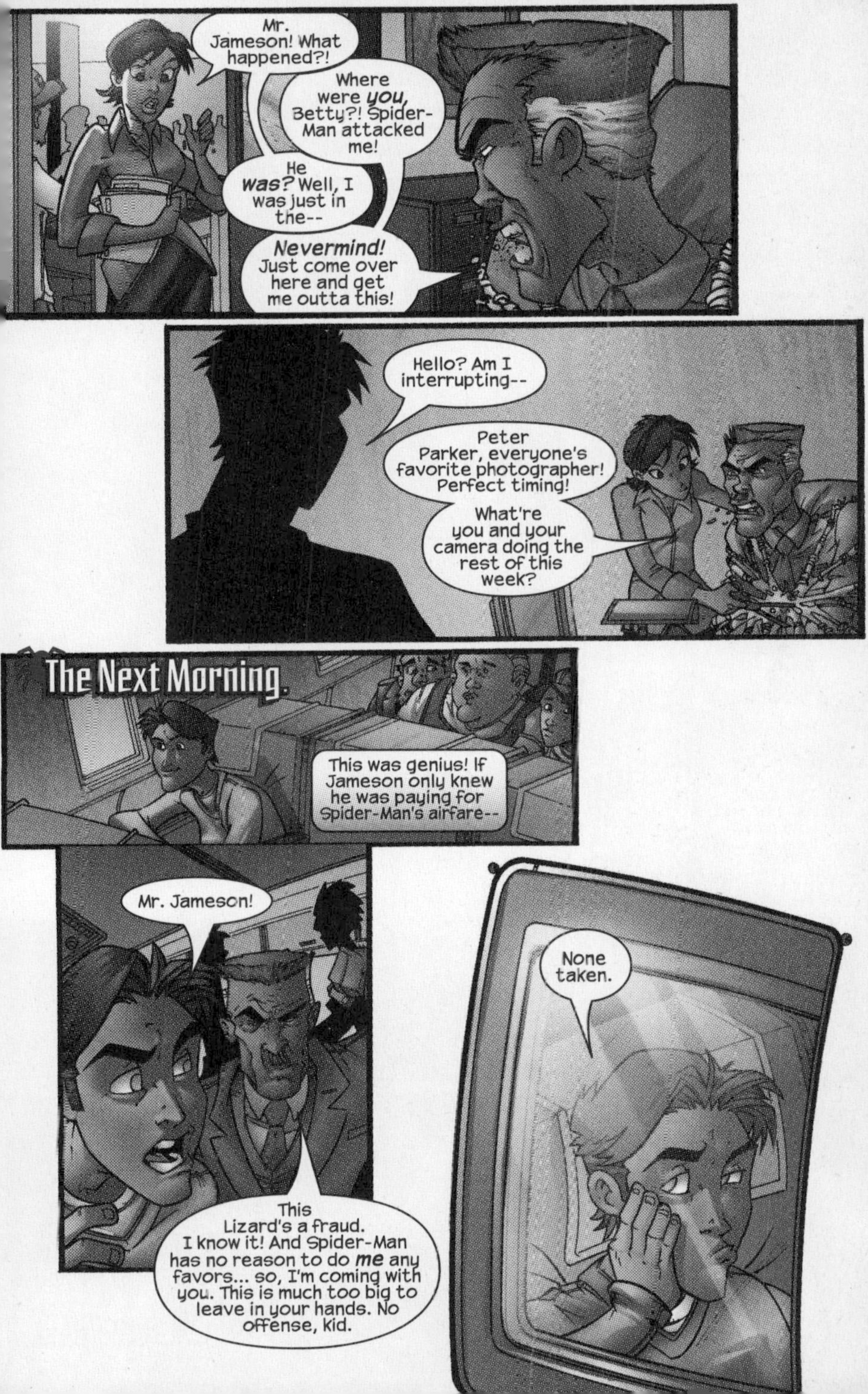
Mr. Jameson! What happened?!
Where were *you*, Betty?! Spider-Man attacked me!
He *was?* Well, I was just in the--
Nevermind! Just come over here and get me outta this!
Hello? Am I interrupting--
Peter Parker, everyone's favorite photographer! Perfect timing!
What're you and your camera doing the rest of this week?
The Next Morning.
This was genius! If Jameson only knew he was paying for Spider-Man's airfare--
Mr. Jameson!
This Lizard's a fraud. I know it! And Spider-Man has no reason to do *me* any favors... so, I'm coming with you. This is much too big to leave in your hands. No offense, kid.
None taken.

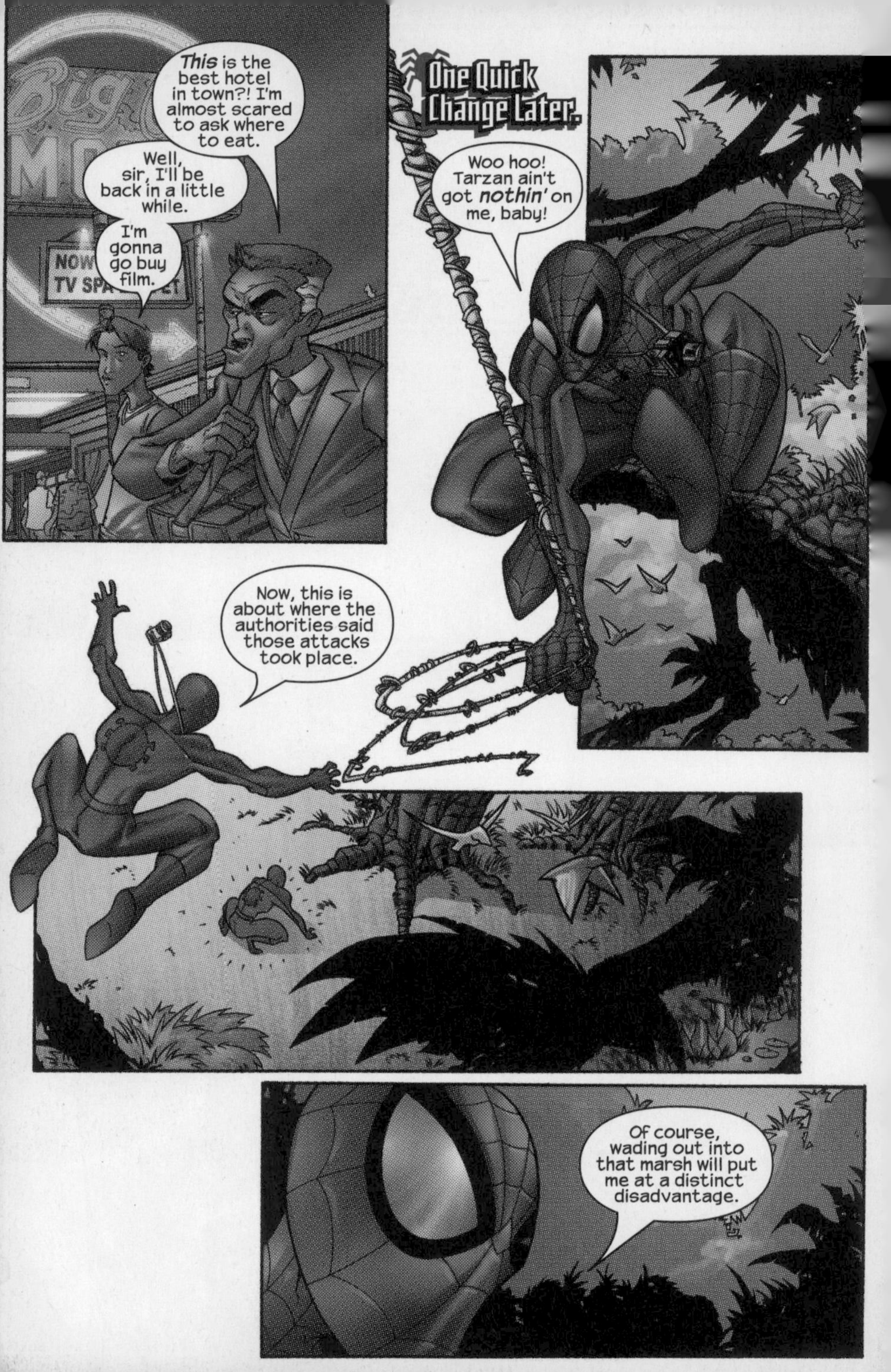

This is the best hotel in town?! I'm almost scared to ask where to eat.
Well, sir, I'll be back in a little while.
I'm gonna go buy film.
One Quick Change Later.
Woo hoo! Tarzan ain't got nothin' on me, baby!
Now, this is about where the authorities said those attacks took place.
Of course, wading out into that marsh will put me at a distinct disadvantage.

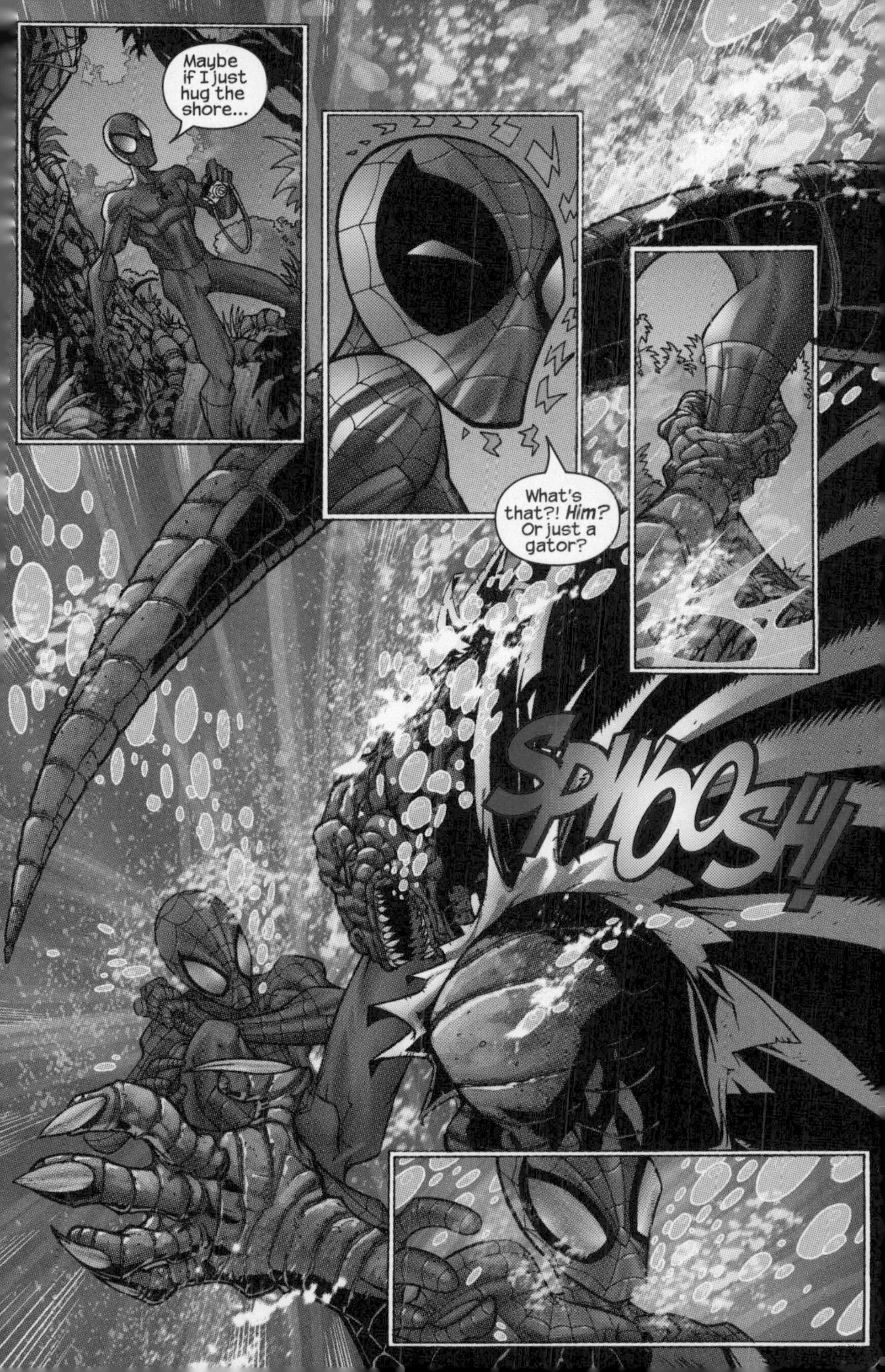
Maybe if I just hug the shore...
What's that?! *Him?* Or just a gator?
SPLOOSH!

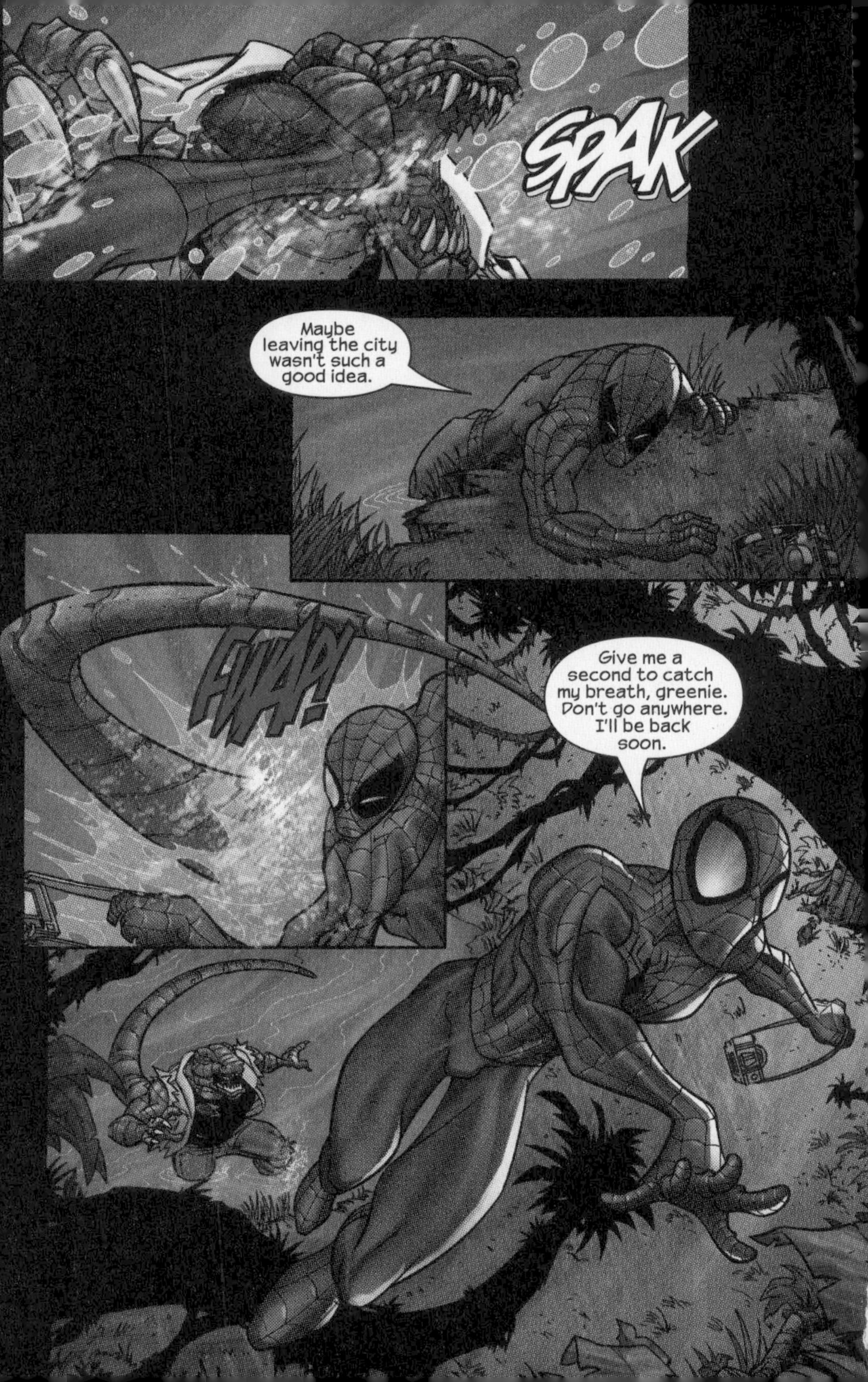
SPAK
Maybe leaving the city wasn't such a good idea.
FWAP!
Give me a second to catch my breath, greenie. Don't go anywhere. I'll be back soon.

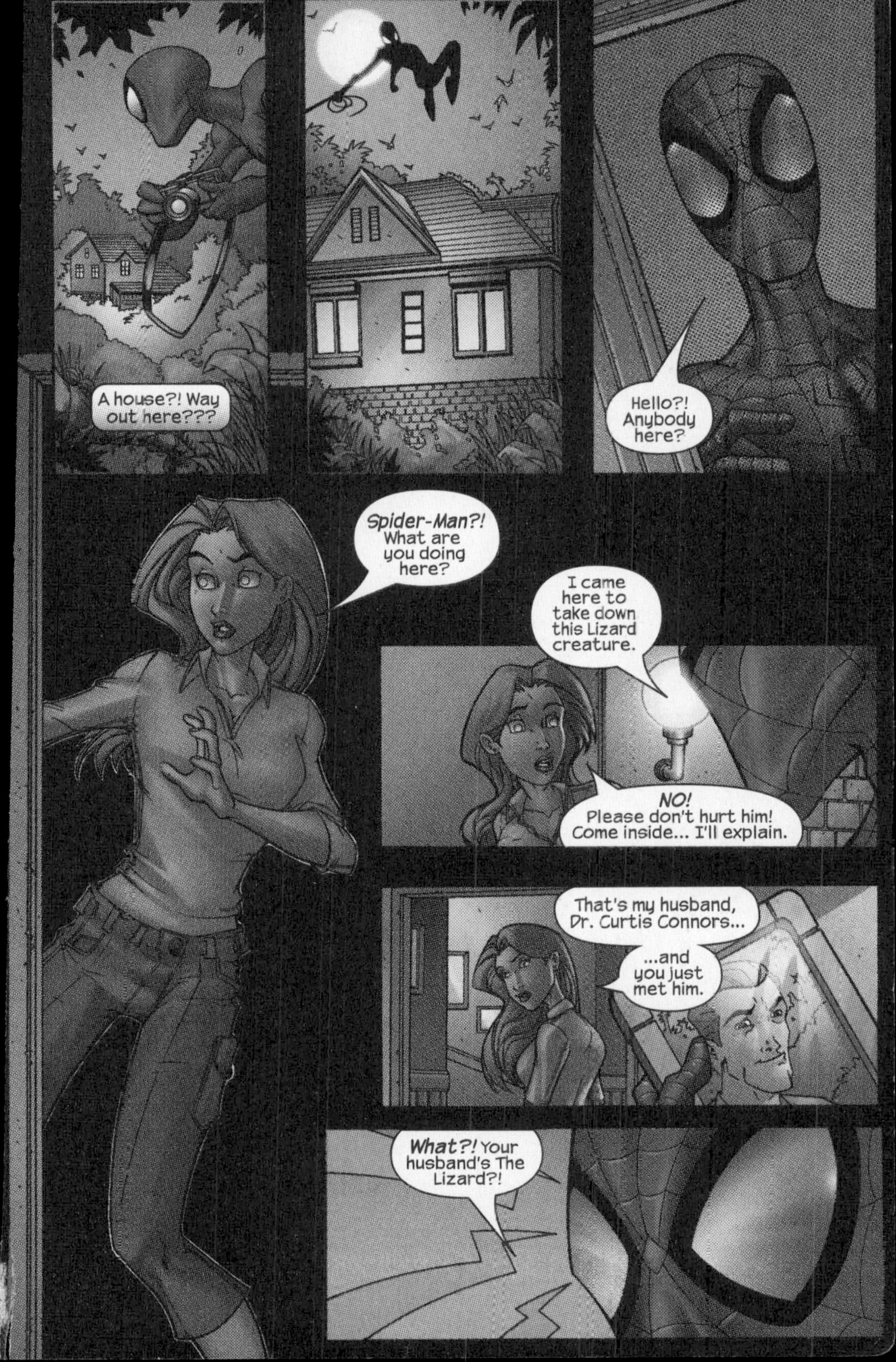
A house?! Way out here???
Hello?! Anybody here?
Spider-Man?! What are you doing here?
I came here to take down this Lizard creature.
NO! Please don't hurt him! Come inside... I'll explain.
That's my husband, Dr. Curtis Connors...
...and you just met him.
What?! Your husband's The Lizard?!

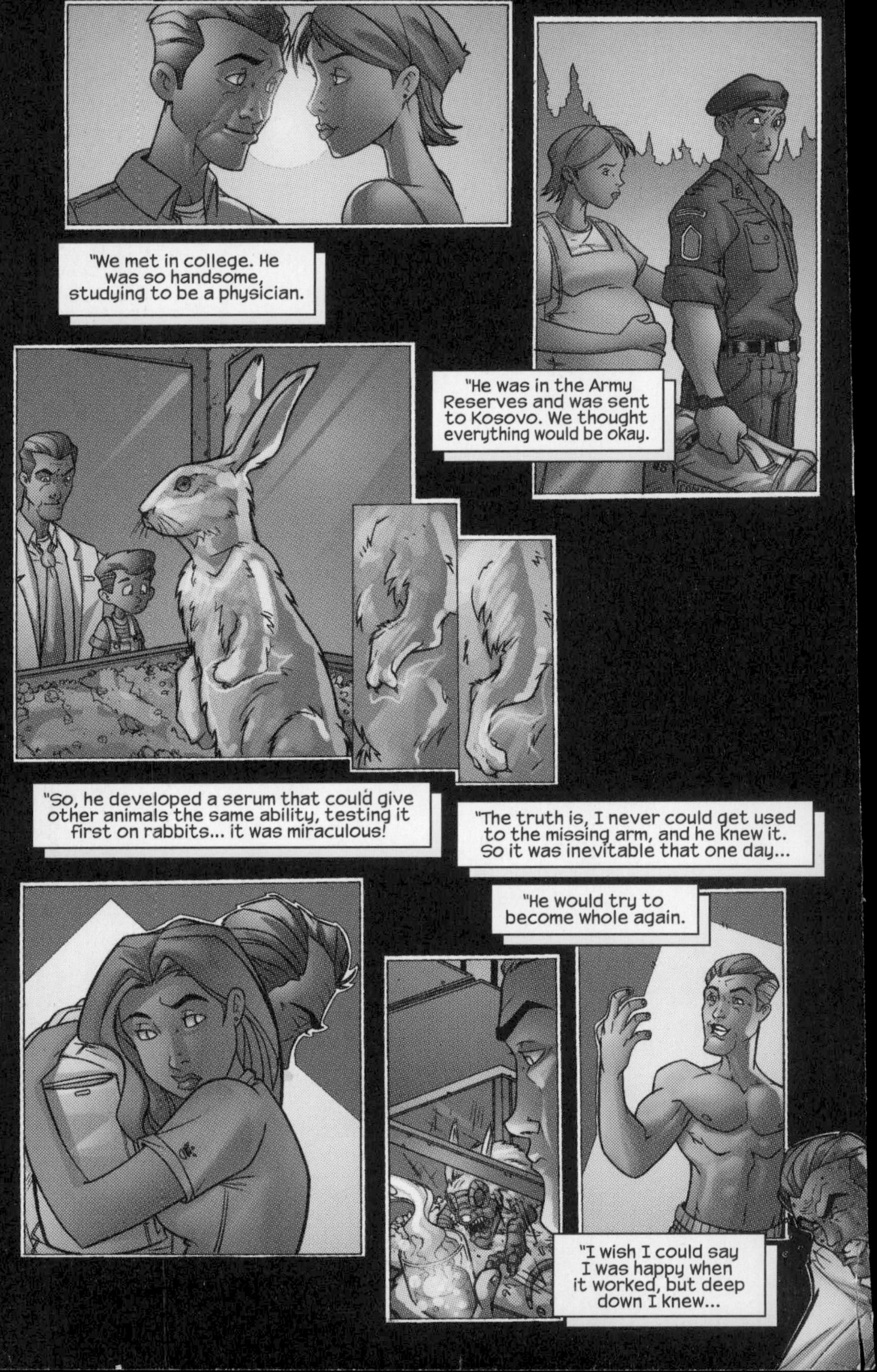
"We met in college. He was so handsome, studying to be a physician.
"He was in the Army Reserves and was sent to Kosovo. We thought everything would be okay.
"So, he developed a serum that could give other animals the same ability, testing it first on rabbits... it was miraculous!
"The truth is, I never could get used to the missing arm, and he knew it. So it was inevitable that one day...
"He would try to become whole again.
"I wish I could say I was happy when it worked, but deep down I knew...

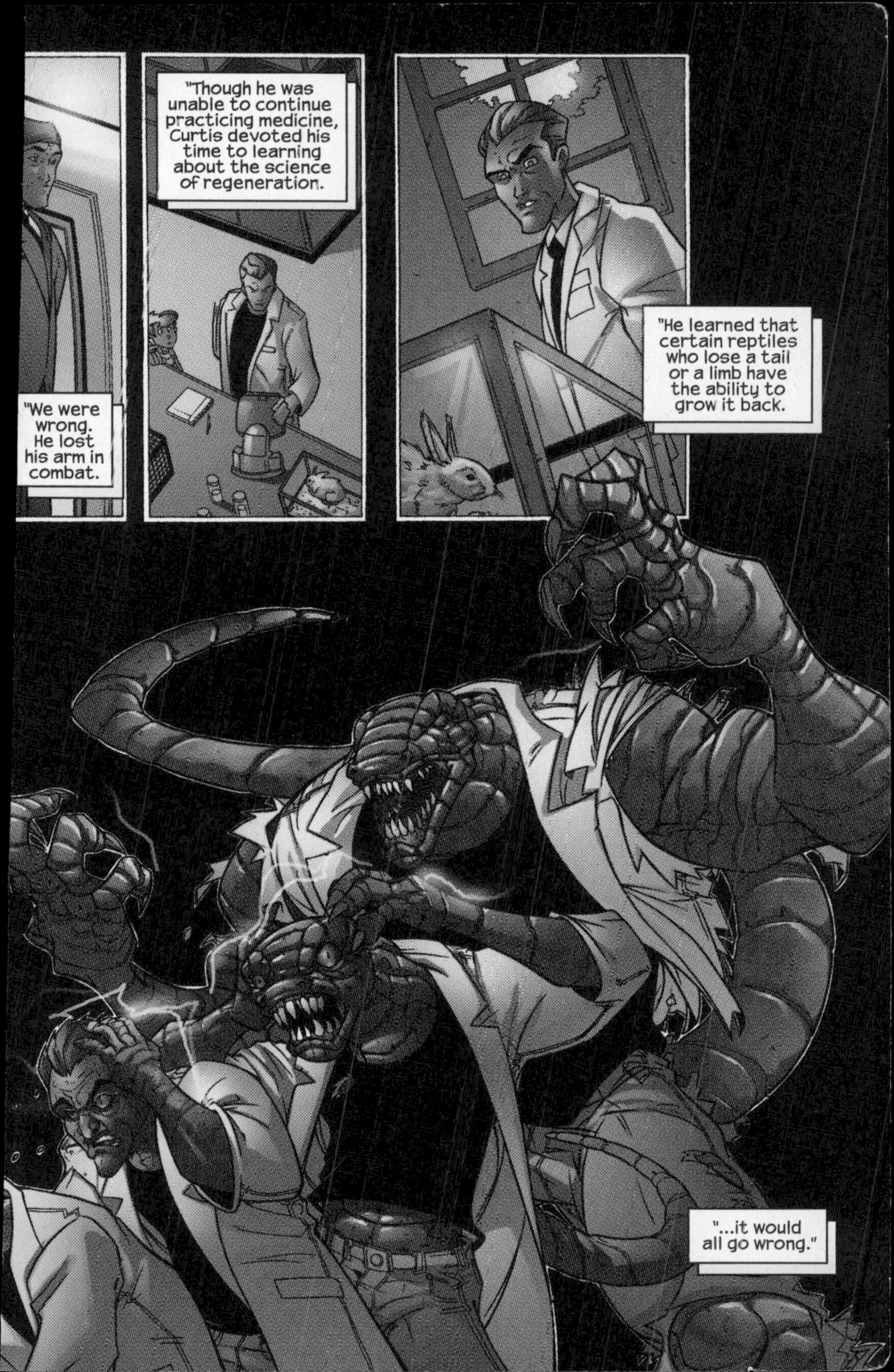
"We were wrong. He lost his arm in combat.
"Though he was unable to continue practicing medicine, Curtis devoted his time to learning about the science of regeneration.
"He learned that certain reptiles who lose a tail or a limb have the ability to grow it back.
"...it would all go wrong."

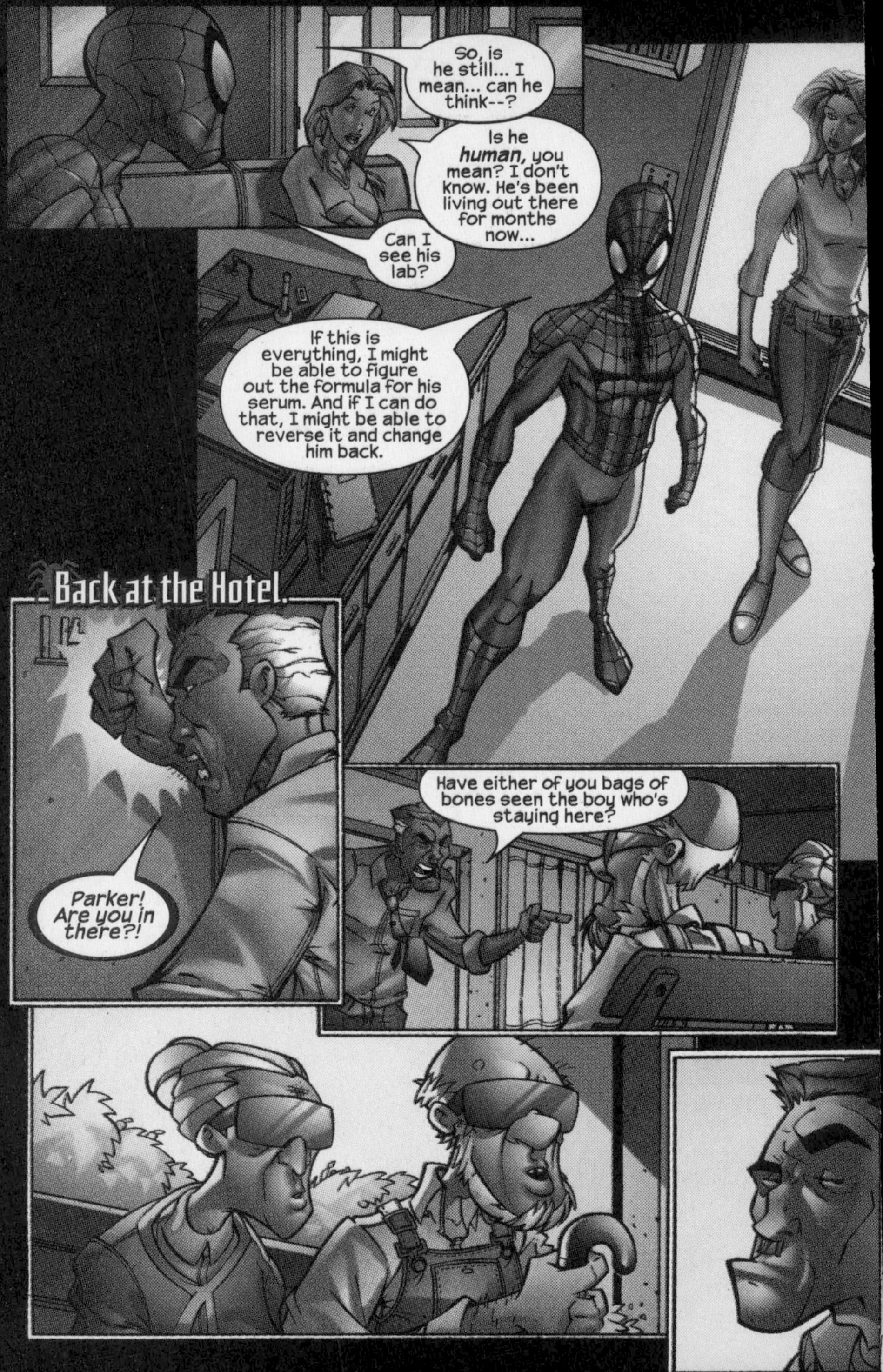

So, is he still... I mean... can he think--?
Is he human, you mean? I don't know. He's been living out there for months now...
Can I see his lab?
If this is everything, I might be able to figure out the formula for his serum. And if I can do that, I might be able to reverse it and change him back.
Back at the Hotel.
Parker! Are you in there?!
Have either of you bags of bones seen the boy who's staying here?

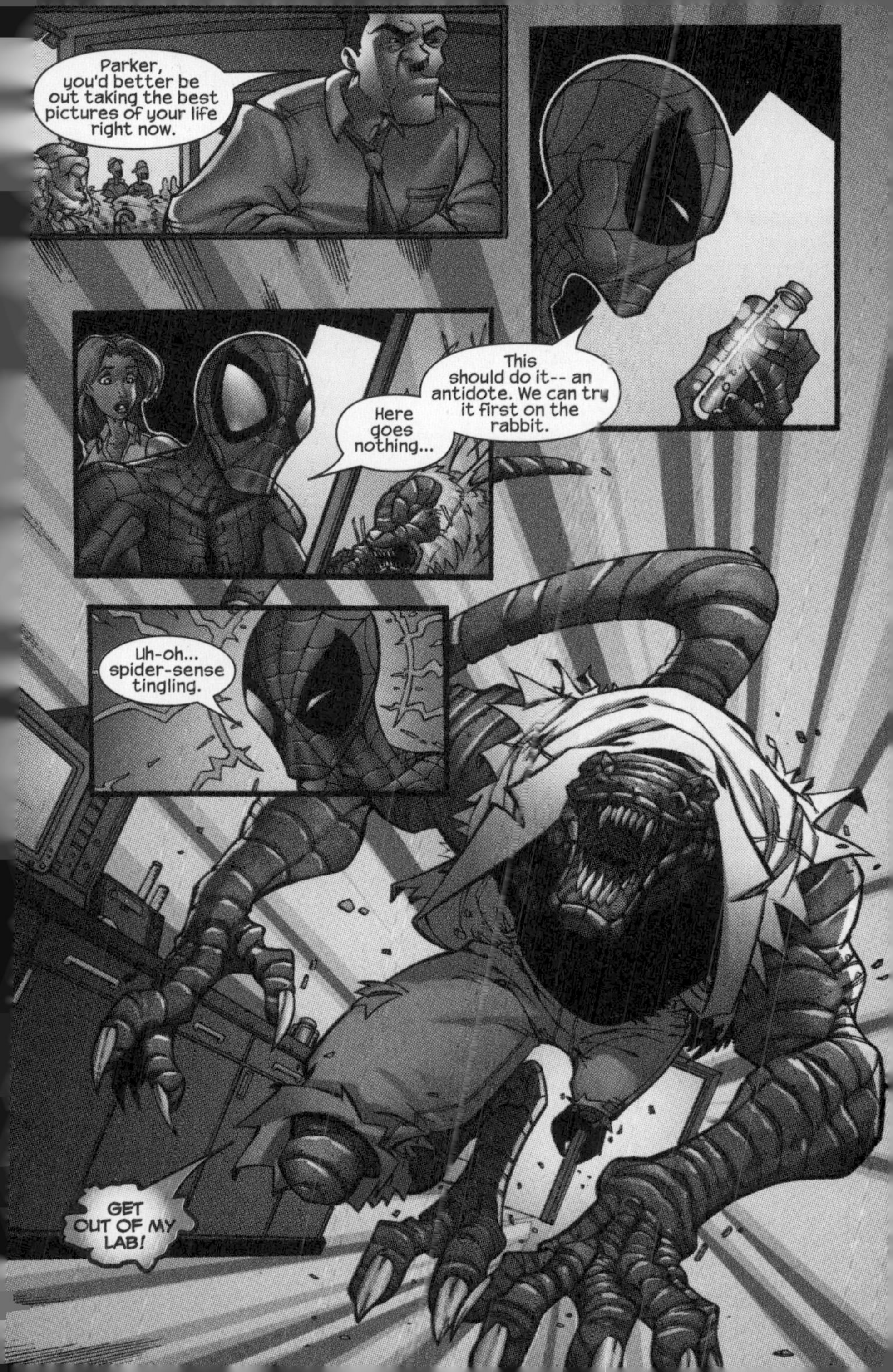
Parker, you'd better be out taking the best pictures of your life right now.
This should do it-- an antidote. We can try it first on the rabbit.
Here goes nothing...
Uh-oh... spider-sense tingling.
GET OUT OF MY LAB!

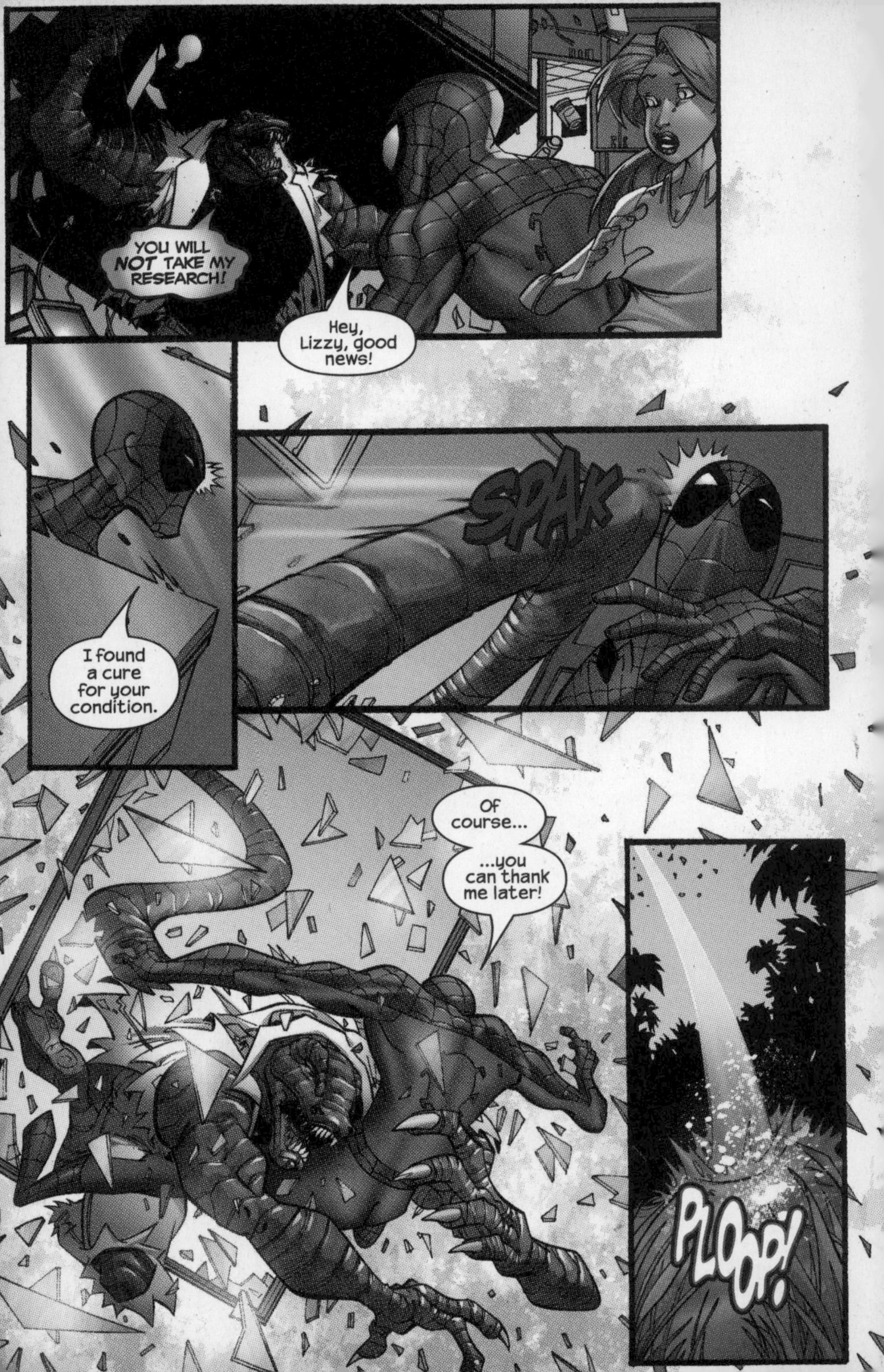

YOU WILL NOT TAKE MY RESEARCH!
Hey, Lizzy, good news!
I found a cure for your condition.
SPAK
Of course...
...you can thank me later!
PLOOP!

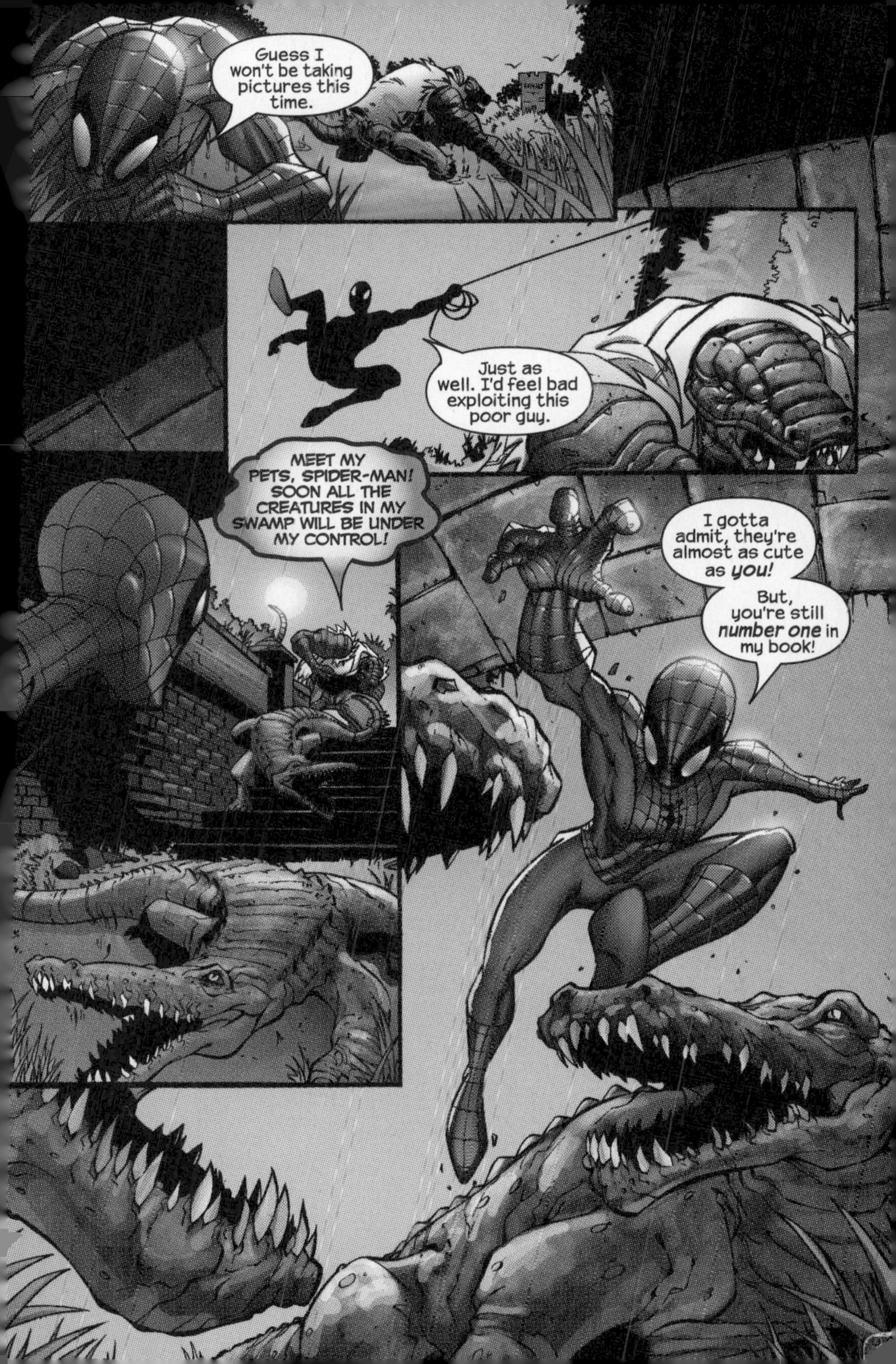
Guess I won't be taking pictures this time.
Just as well. I'd feel bad exploiting this poor guy.
MEET MY PETS, SPIDER-MAN! SOON ALL THE CREATURES IN MY SWAMP WILL BE UNDER MY CONTROL!
I gotta admit, they're almost as cute as *you!*
But, you're still *number one* in my book!

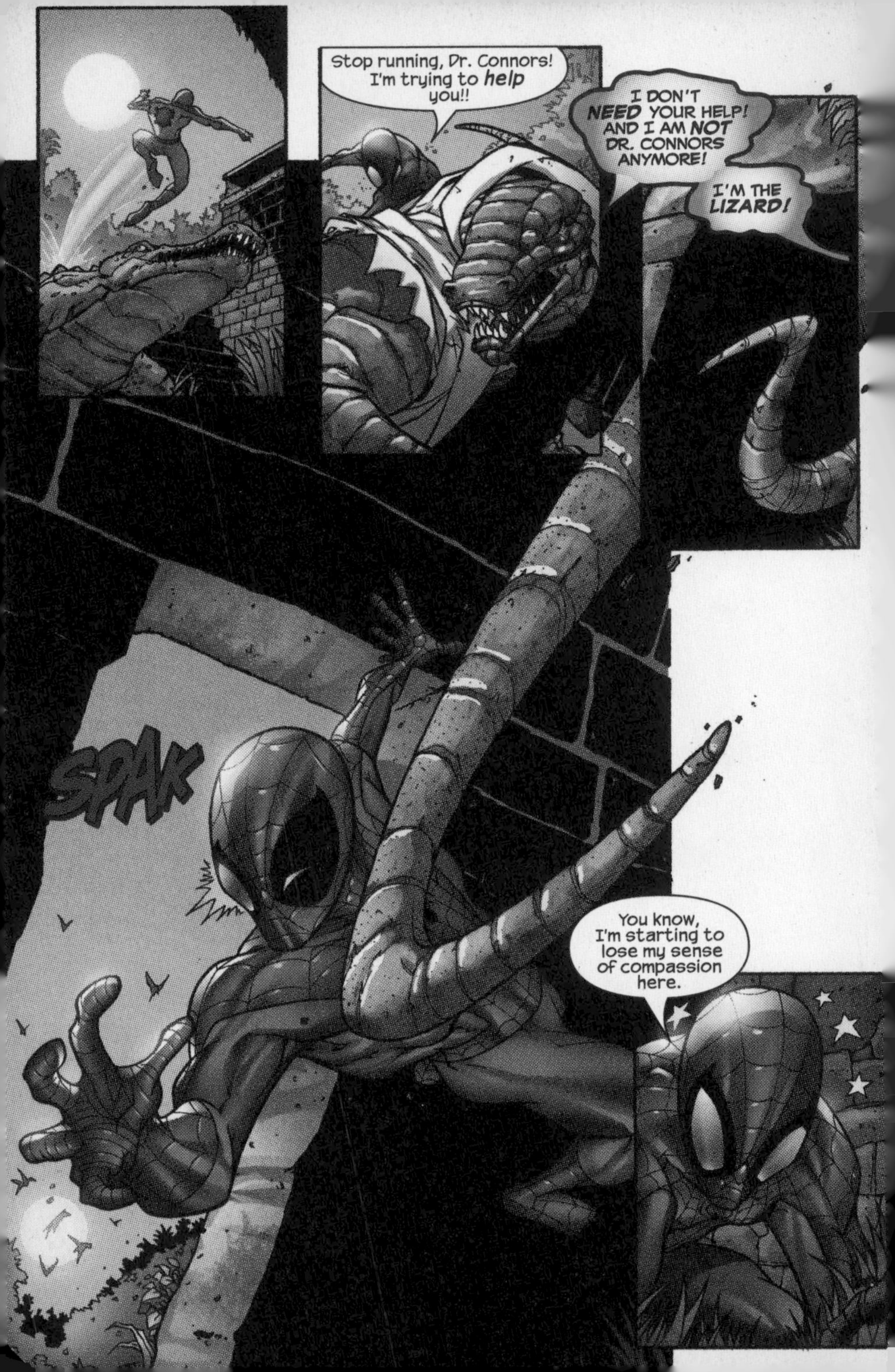
Stop running, Dr. Connors! I'm trying to help you!!
I DON'T NEED YOUR HELP! AND I AM NOT DR. CONNORS ANYMORE!
I'M THE LIZARD!
SPAK
You know, I'm starting to lose my sense of compassion here.

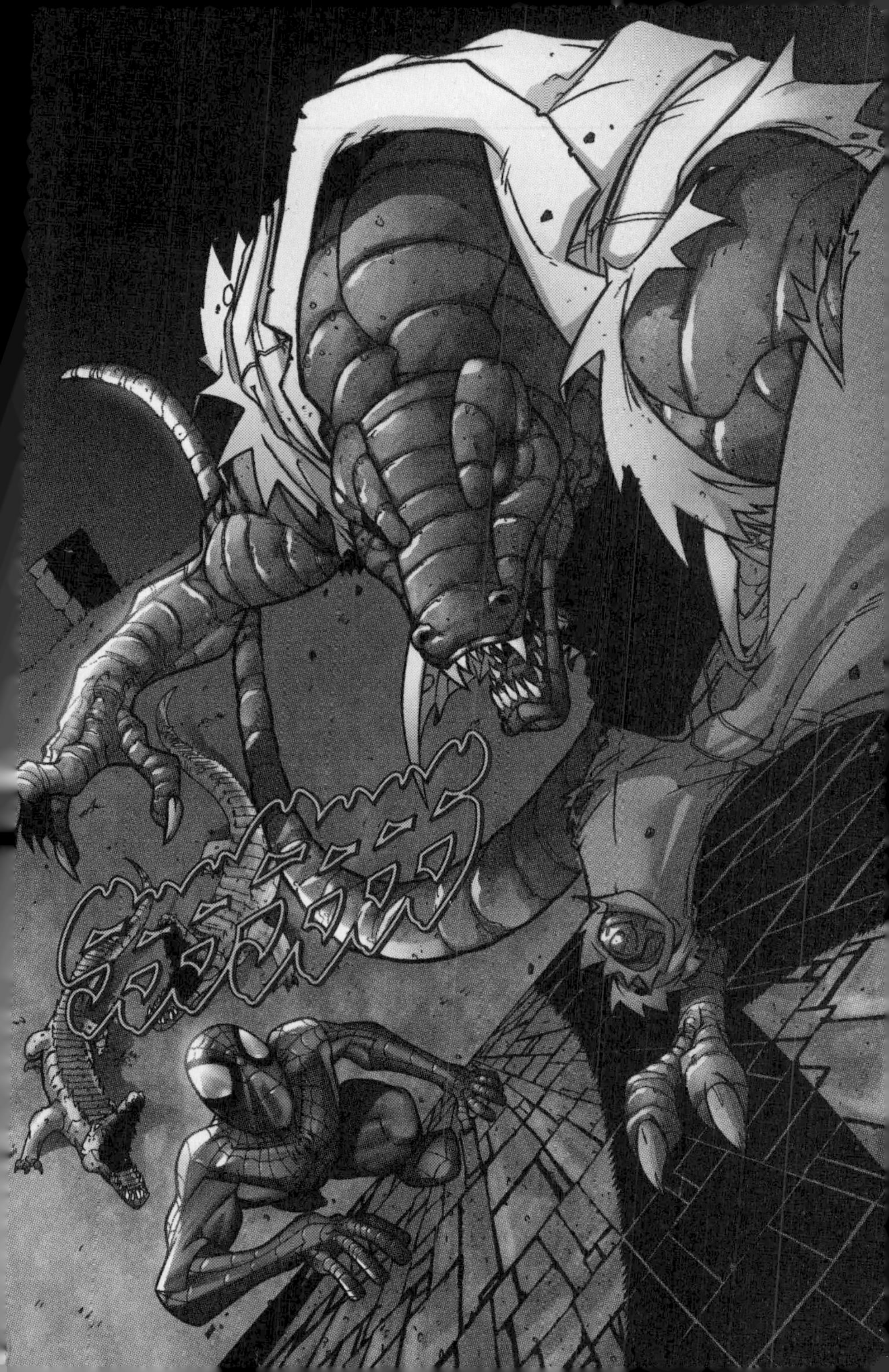

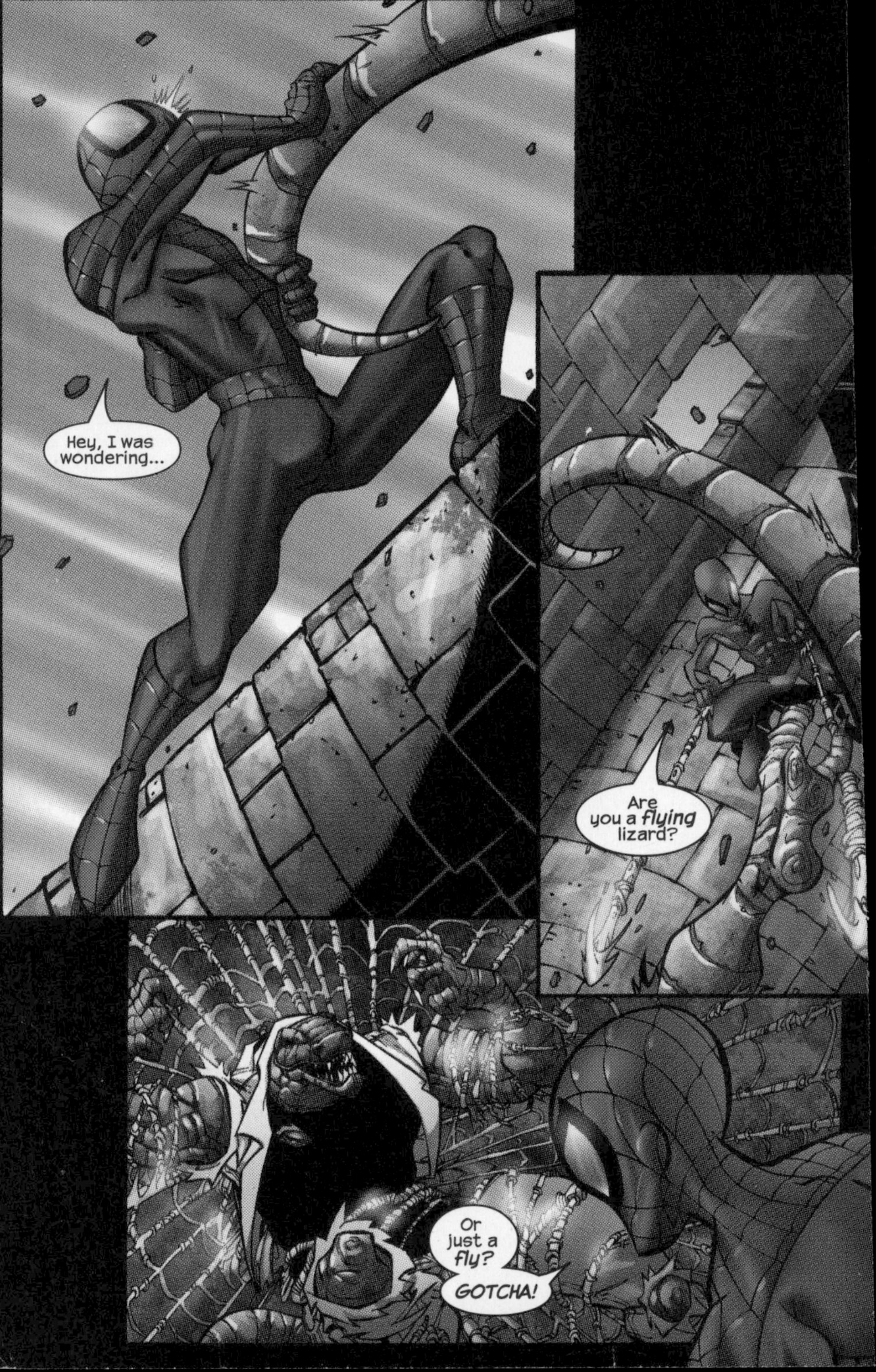

Hey, I was wondering...
Are you a *flying* lizard?
Or just a *fly?*
GOTCHA!

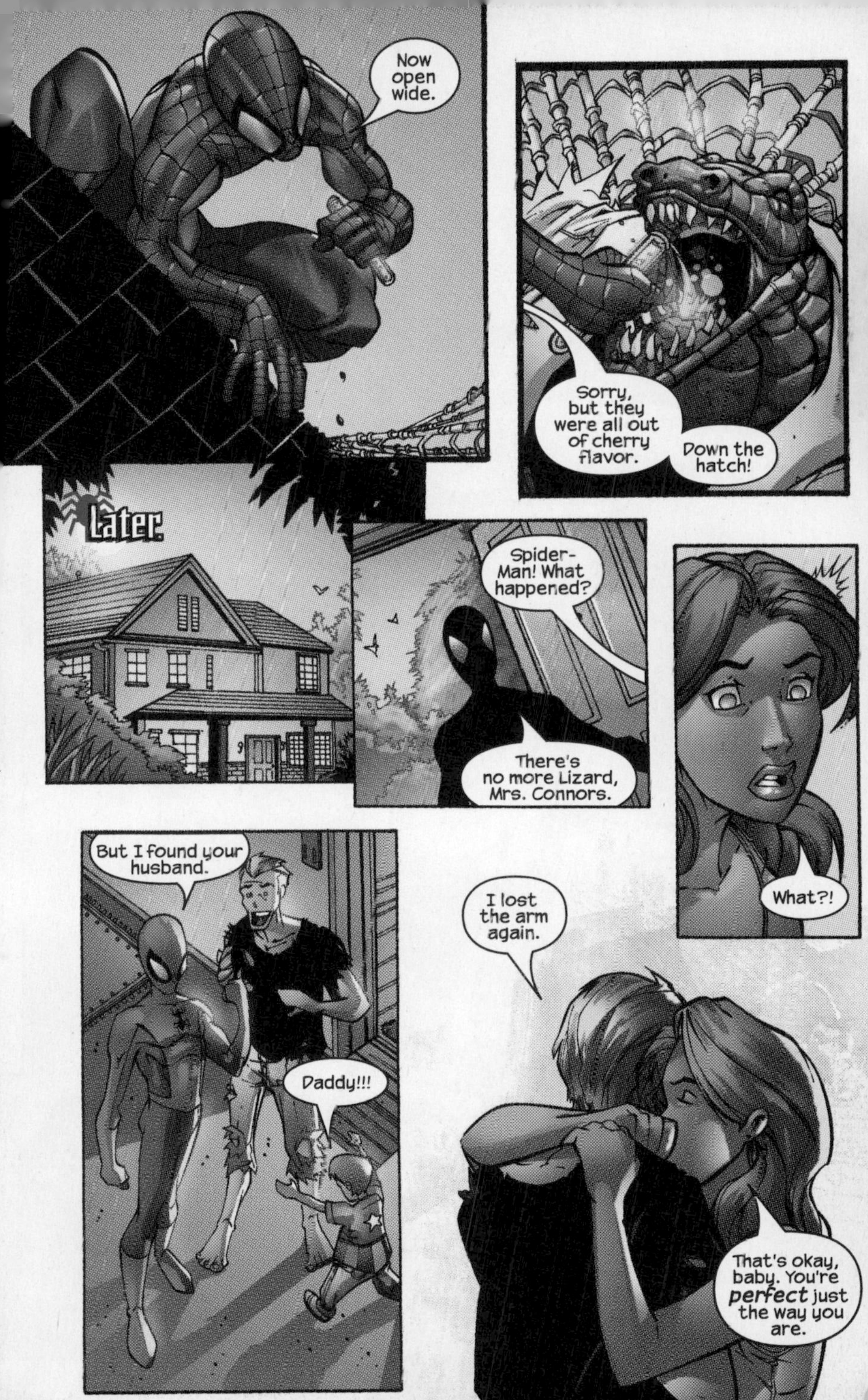
Now open wide.
Sorry, but they were all out of cherry flavor.
Down the hatch!
Later.
Spider-Man! What happened?
There's no more Lizard, Mrs. Connors.
What?!
But I found your husband.
Daddy!!!
I lost the arm again.
That's okay, baby. You're *perfect* just the way you are.

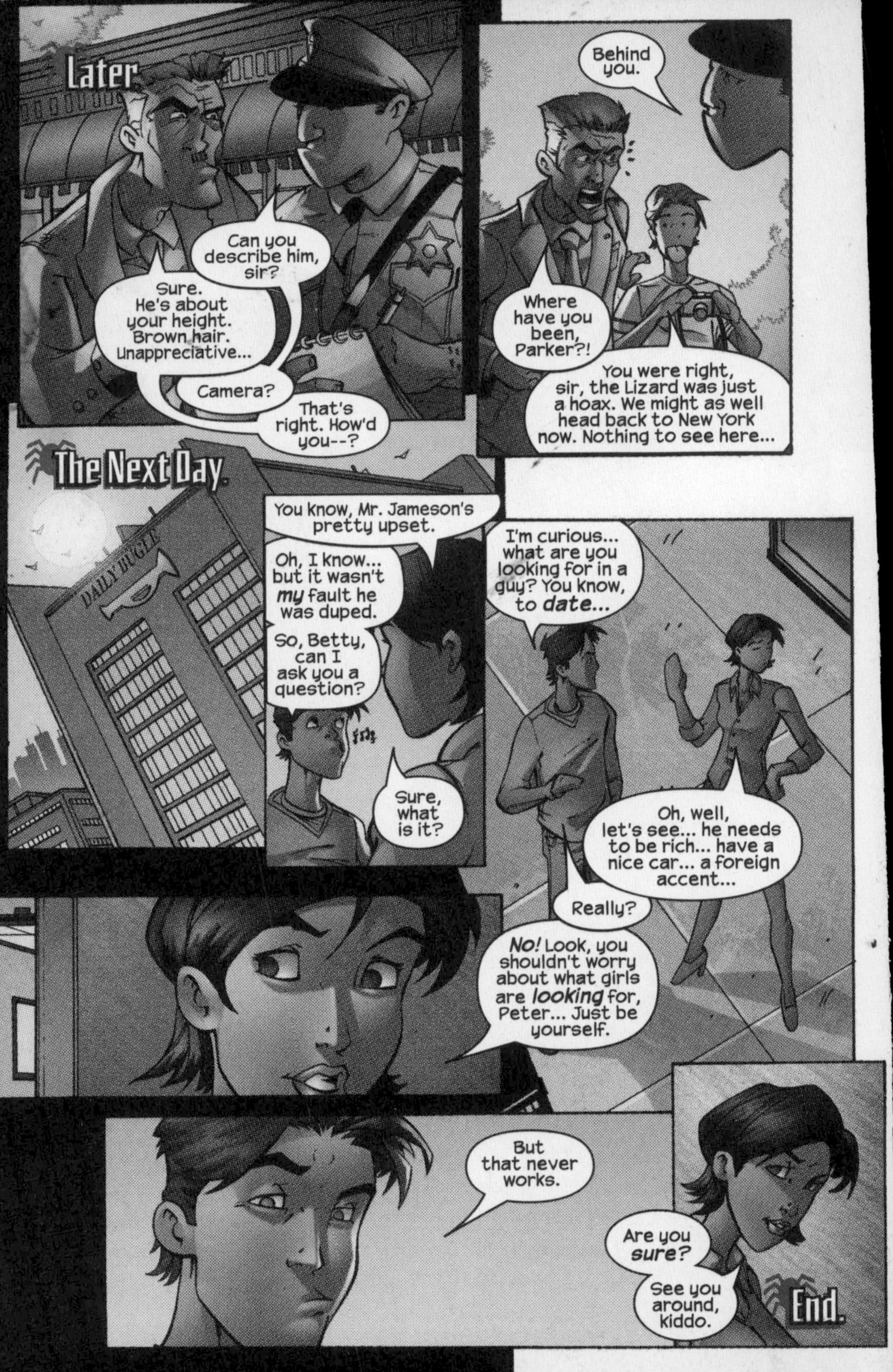
Later
Can you describe him, sir?
Sure. He's about your height. Brown hair. Unappreciative...
Camera?
That's right. How'd you--?
Behind you.
Where have you been, Parker?!
You were right, sir, the Lizard was just a hoax. We might as well head back to New York now. Nothing to see here...
The Next Day
DAILY BUGLE
You know, Mr. Jameson's pretty upset.
Oh, I know... but it wasn't *my* fault he was duped.
So, Betty, can I ask you a question?
Sure, what is it?
I'm curious... what are you looking for in a guy? You know, to *date*...
Oh, well, let's see... he needs to be rich... have a nice car... a foreign accent...
Really?
No! Look, you shouldn't worry about what girls are *looking* for, Peter... Just be yourself.
But that never works.
Are you *sure*?
See you around, kiddo.
End.

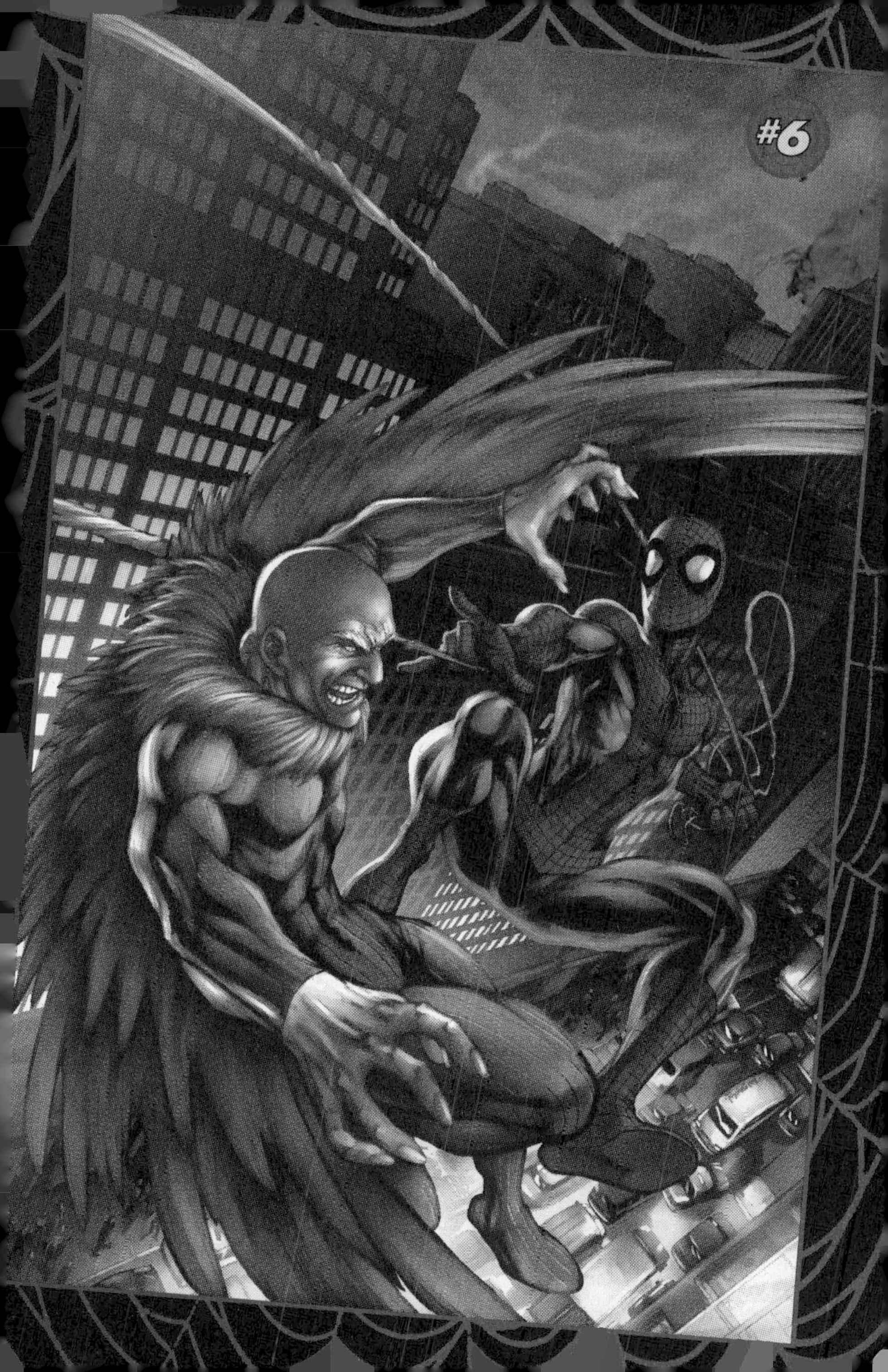
#6

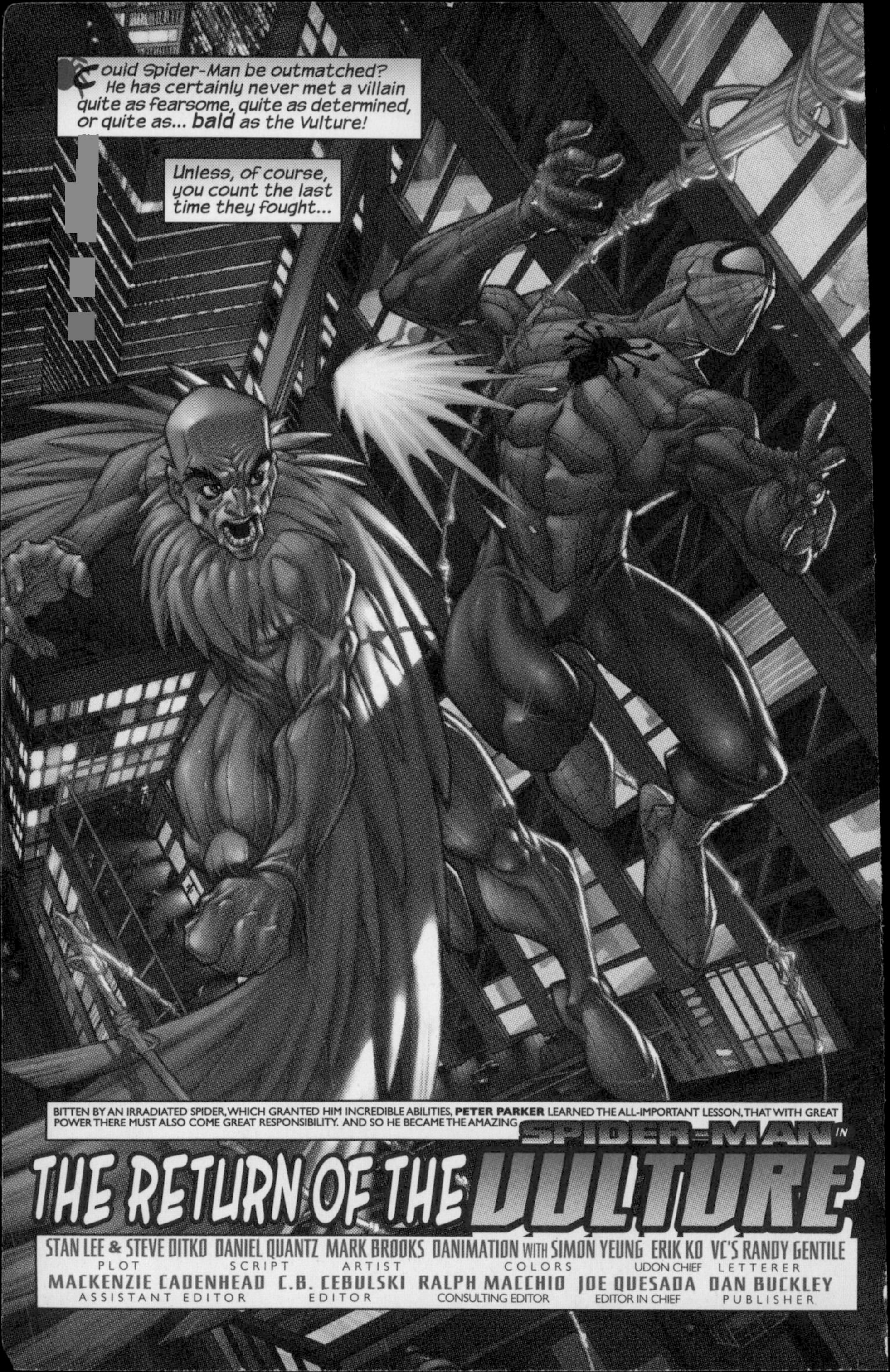
Could Spider-Man be outmatched? He has certainly never met a villain quite as fearsome, quite as determined, or quite as... **bald** as the Vulture!
Unless, of course, you count the last time they fought...

BITTEN BY AN IRRADIATED SPIDER, WHICH GRANTED HIM INCREDIBLE ABILITIES, **PETER PARKER** LEARNED THE ALL-IMPORTANT LESSON, THAT WITH GREAT POWER THERE MUST ALSO COME GREAT RESPONSIBILITY. AND SO HE BECAME THE AMAZING SPIDER-MAN IN

THE RETURN OF THE VULTURE!

STAN LEE & STEVE DITKO PLOT
DANIEL QUANTZ SCRIPT
MARK BROOKS ARTIST
DANIMATION WITH SIMON YEUNG COLORS
ERIK KO UDON CHIEF
VC'S RANDY GENTILE LETTERER
MACKENZIE CADENHEAD ASSISTANT EDITOR
C.B. CEBULSKI EDITOR
RALPH MACCHIO CONSULTING EDITOR
JOE QUESADA EDITOR IN CHIEF
DAN BUCKLEY PUBLISHER

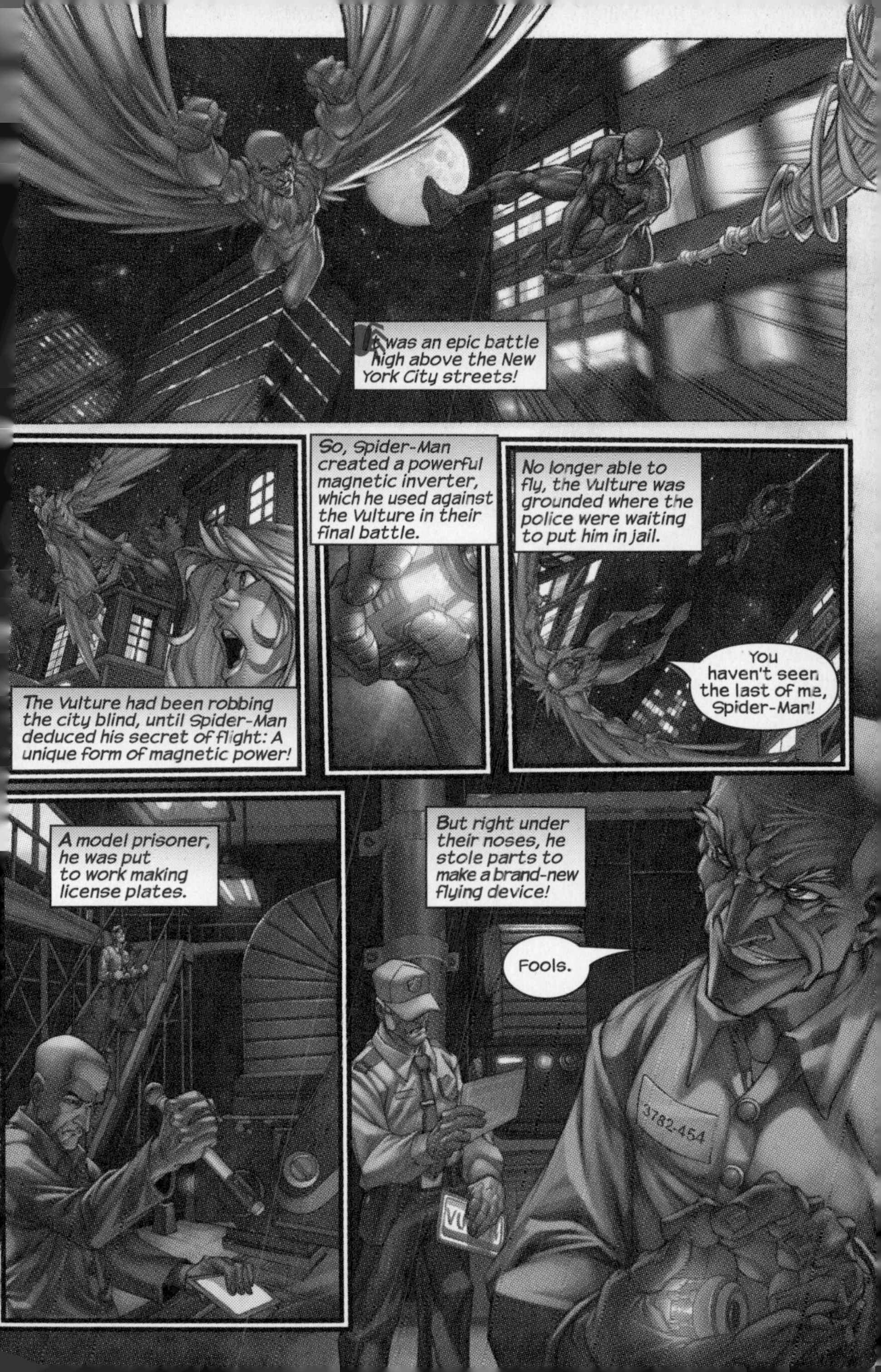
It was an epic battle high above the New York City streets!
The Vulture had been robbing the city blind, until Spider-Man deduced his secret of flight: A unique form of magnetic power!
So, Spider-Man created a powerful magnetic inverter, which he used against the Vulture in their final battle.
No longer able to fly, the Vulture was grounded where the police were waiting to put him in jail.
You haven't seen the last of me, Spider-Man!
A model prisoner, he was put to work making license plates.
But right under their noses, he stole parts to make a brand-new flying device!
Fools.
3782-454

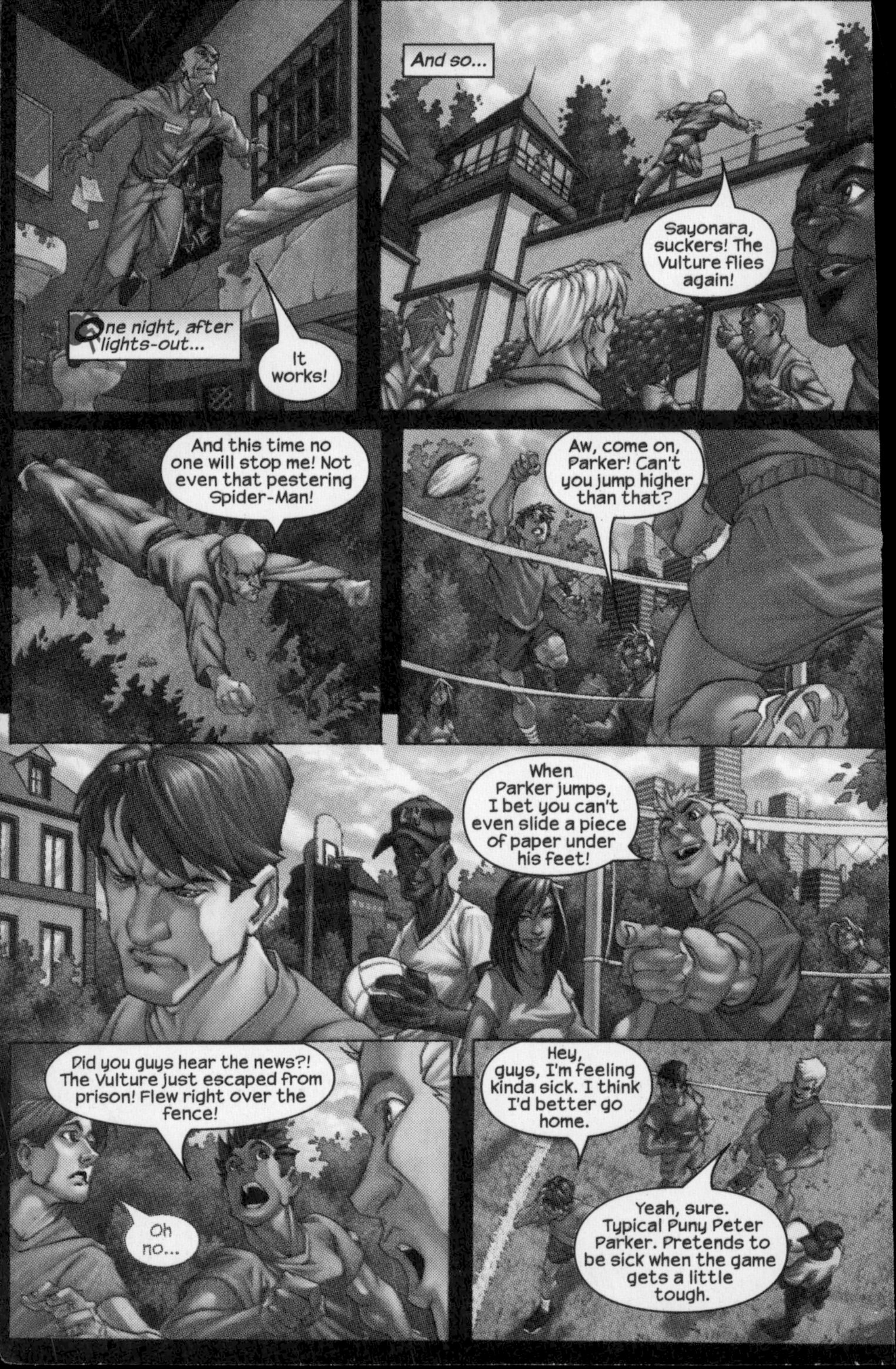
One night, after lights-out...
It works!
And so...
Sayonara, suckers! The Vulture flies again!
And this time no one will stop me! Not even that pestering Spider-Man!
Aw, come on, Parker! Can't you jump higher than that?
When Parker jumps, I bet you can't even slide a piece of paper under his feet!
Did you guys hear the news?! The Vulture just escaped from prison! Flew right over the fence!
Oh no...
Hey, guys, I'm feeling kinda sick. I think I'd better go home.
Yeah, sure. Typical Puny Peter Parker. Pretends to be sick when the game gets a little tough.

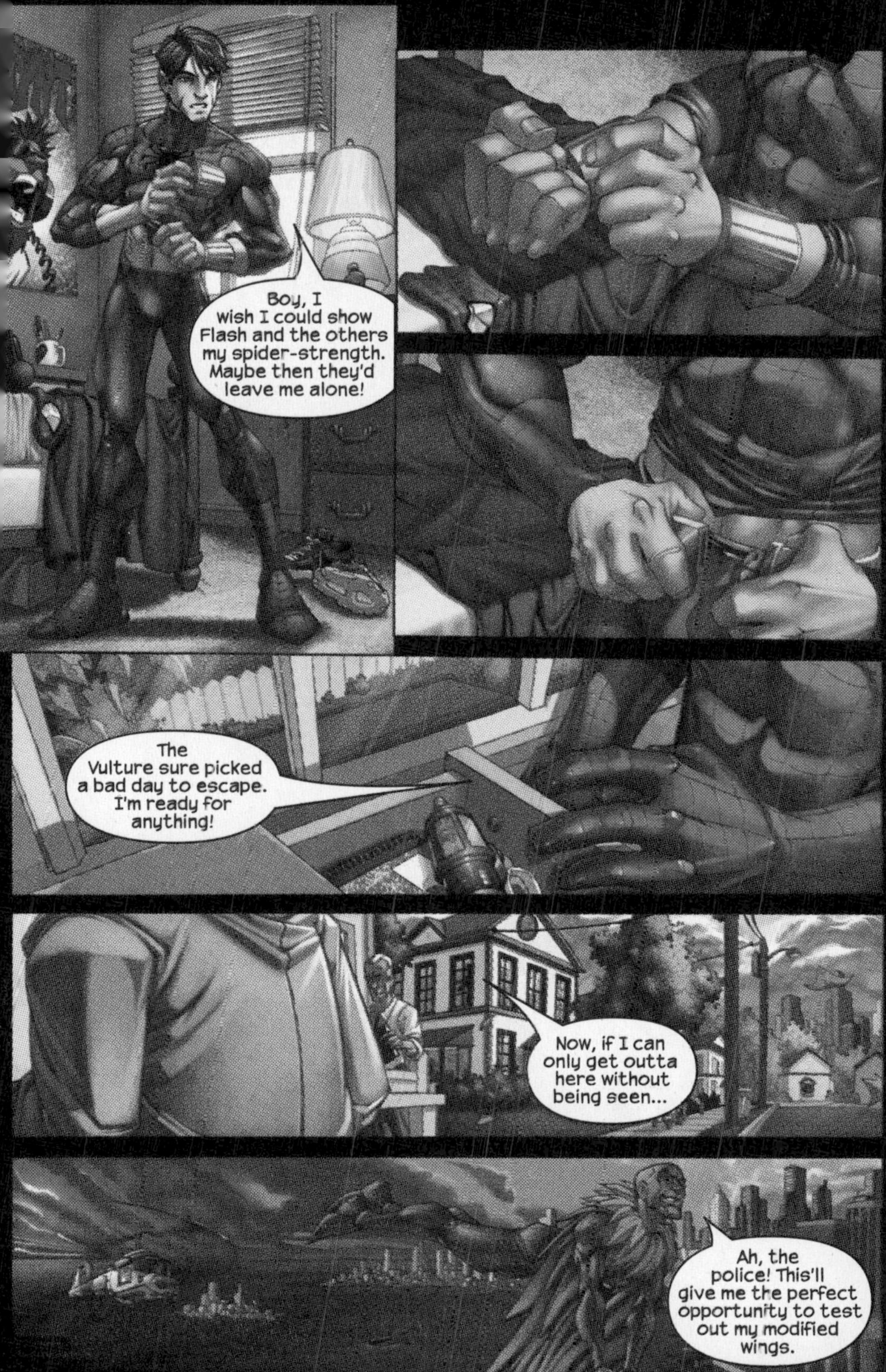
Boy, I wish I could show Flash and the others my spider-strength. Maybe then they'd leave me alone!
The Vulture sure picked a bad day to escape. I'm ready for anything!
Now, if I can only get outta here without being seen...
Ah, the police! This'll give me the perfect opportunity to test out my modified wings.

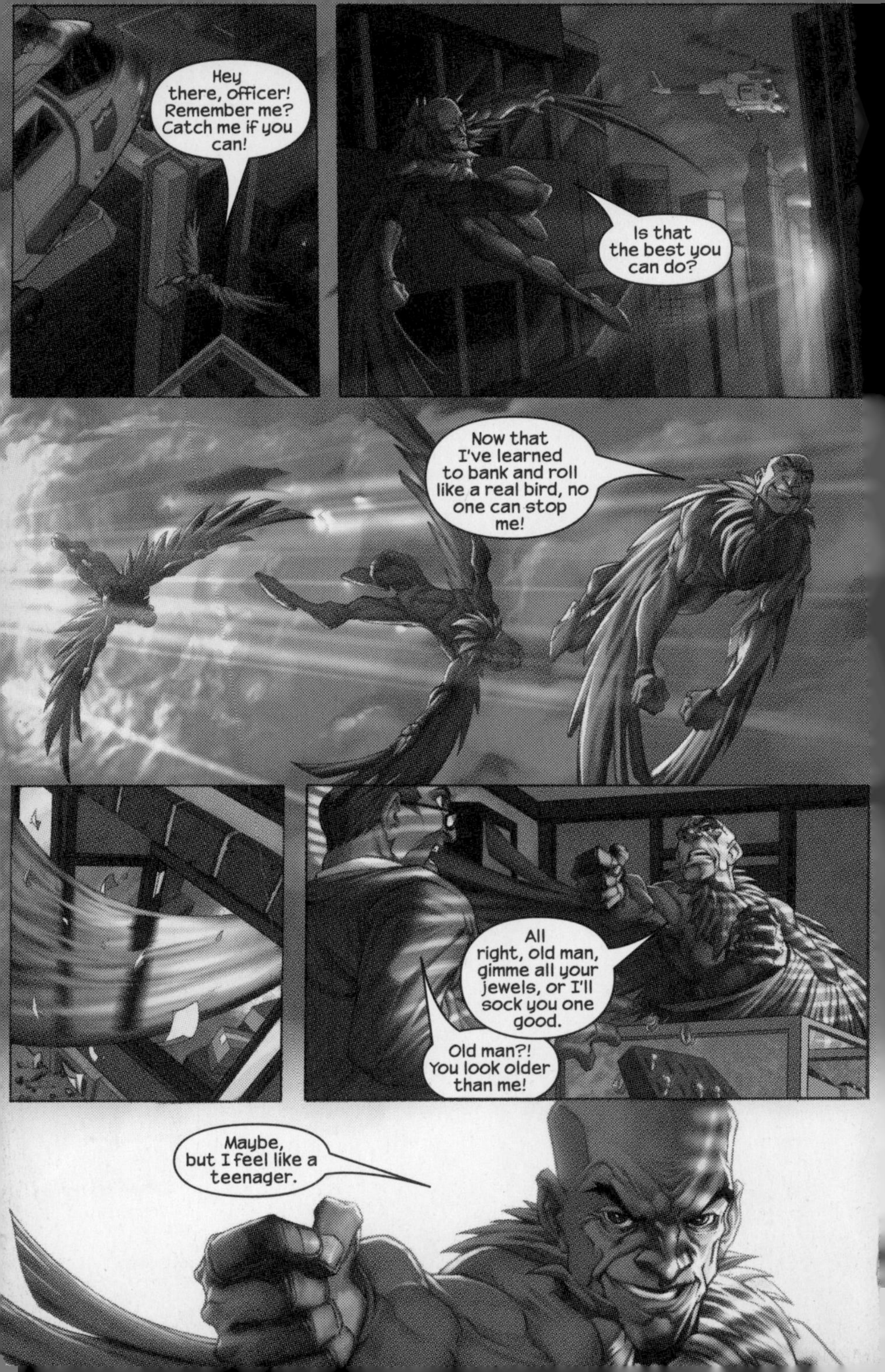
Hey there, officer! Remember me? Catch me if you can!
Is that the best you can do?
Now that I've learned to bank and roll like a real bird, no one can stop me!
All right, old man, gimme all your jewels, or I'll sock you one good.
Old man?! You look older than me!
Maybe, but I feel like a teenager.

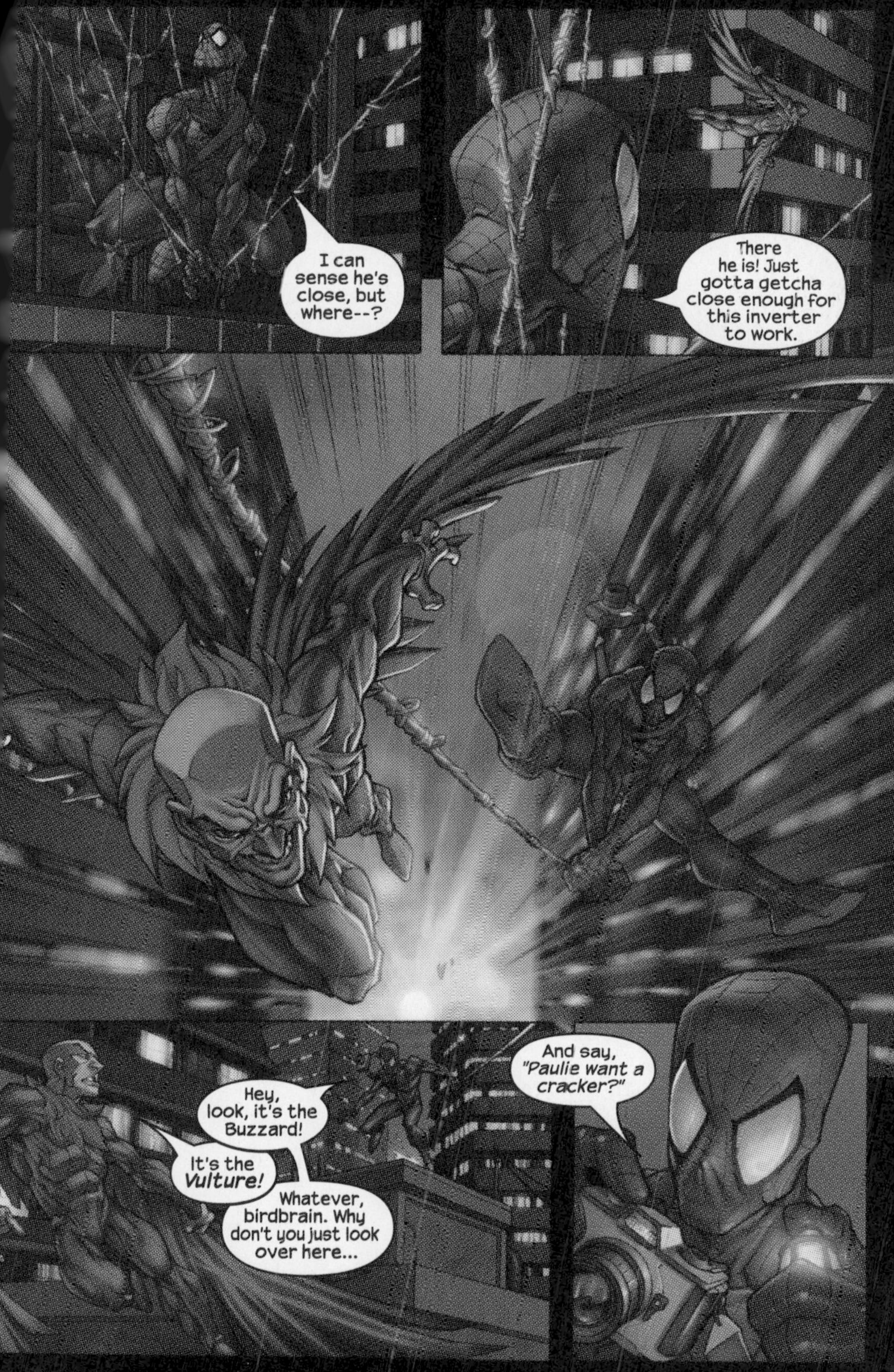
I can sense he's close, but where--?
There he is! Just gotta getcha close enough for this inverter to work.
Hey, look, it's the Buzzard!
It's the *Vulture!*
Whatever, birdbrain. Why don't you just look over here...
And say, "Paulie want a cracker?"

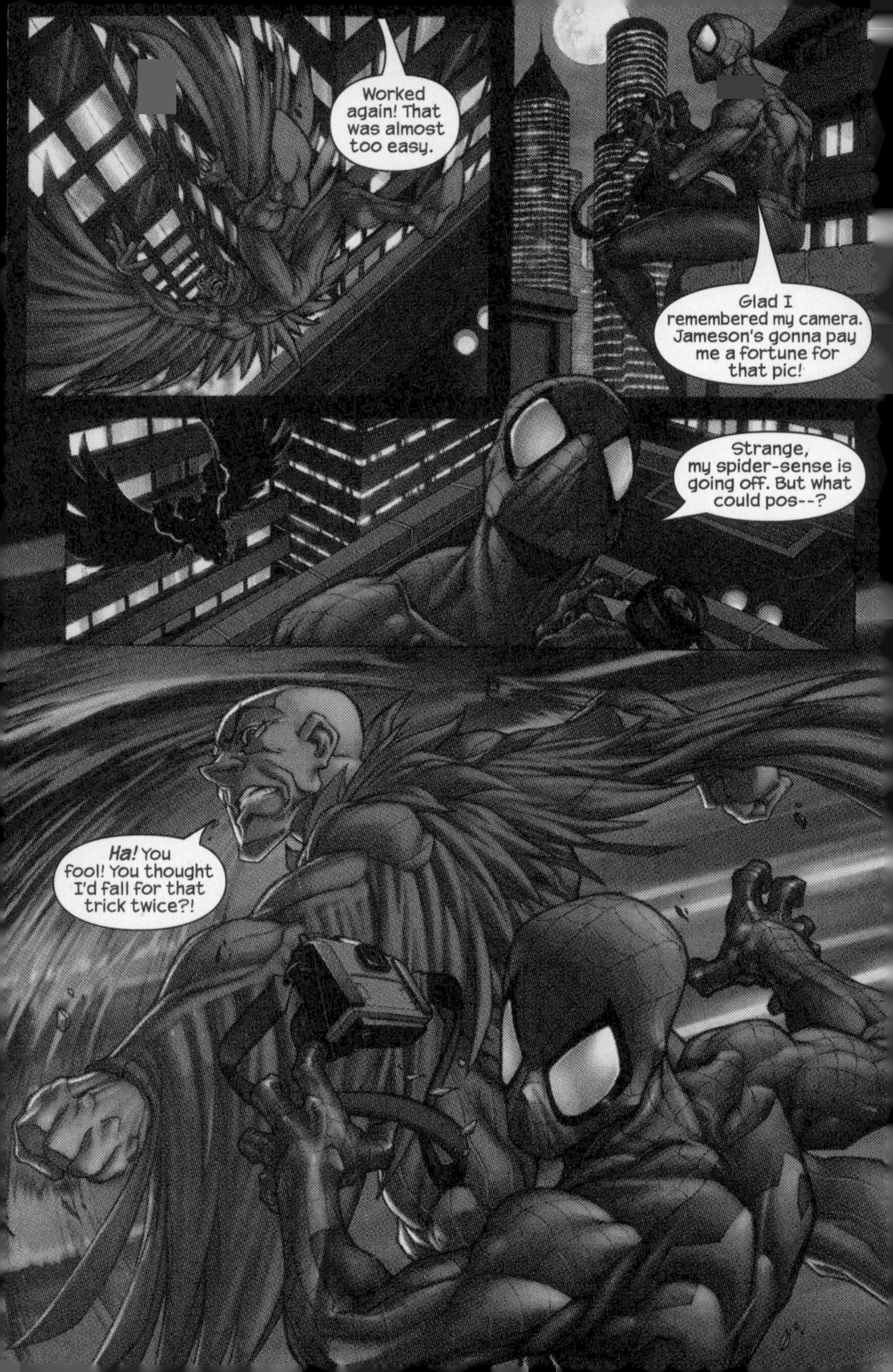
Worked again! That was almost too easy.
Glad I remembered my camera. Jameson's gonna pay me a fortune for that pic!
Strange, my spider-sense is going off. But what could pos--?
Ha! You fool! You thought I'd fall for that trick twice?!

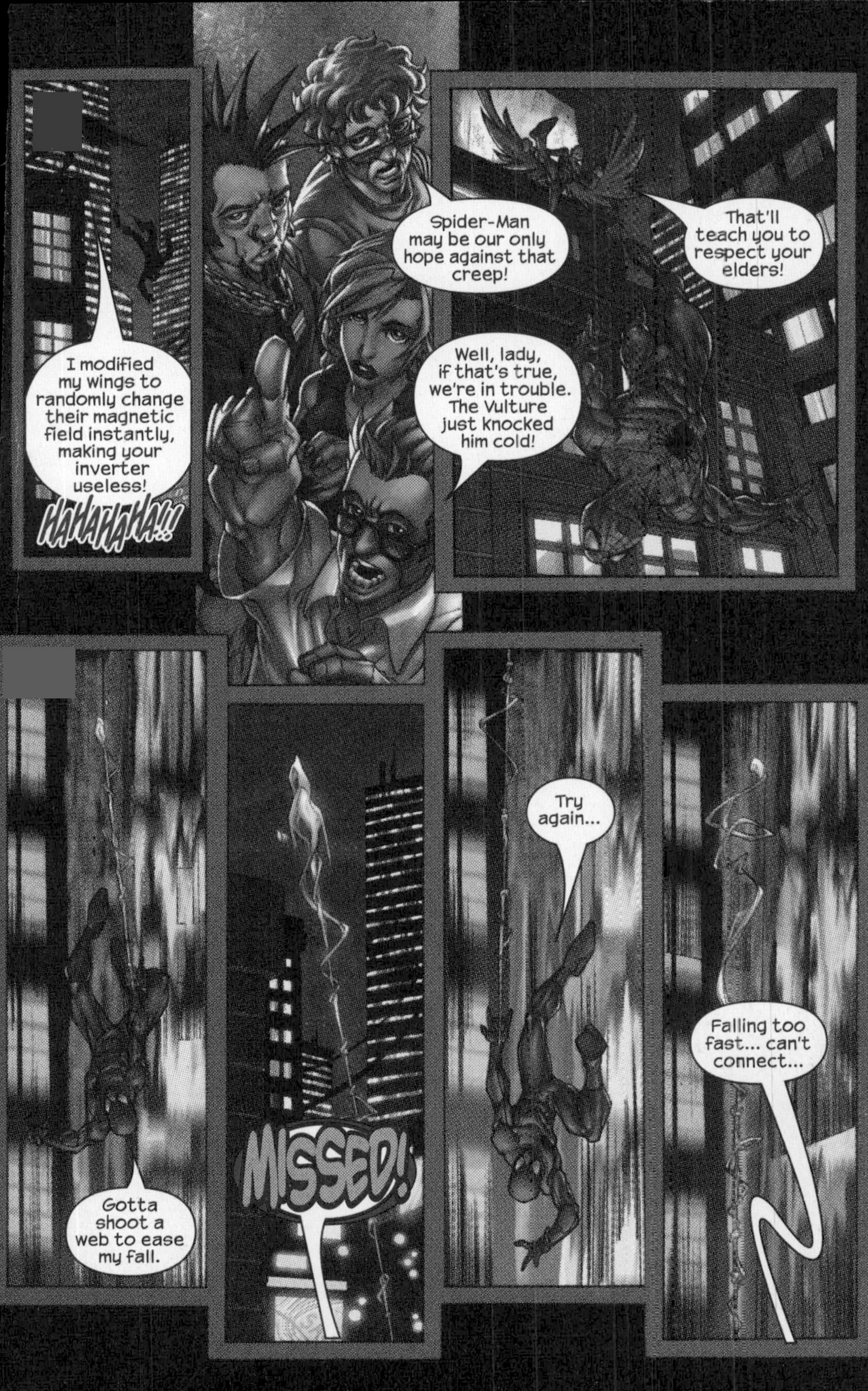
I modified my wings to randomly change their magnetic field instantly, making your inverter useless!
HAHAHAHA!!
Spider-Man may be our only hope against that creep!
Well, lady, if that's true, we're in trouble. The Vulture just knocked him cold!
That'll teach you to respect your elders!
Gotta shoot a web to ease my fall.
MISSED!
Try again...
Falling too fast... can't connect...

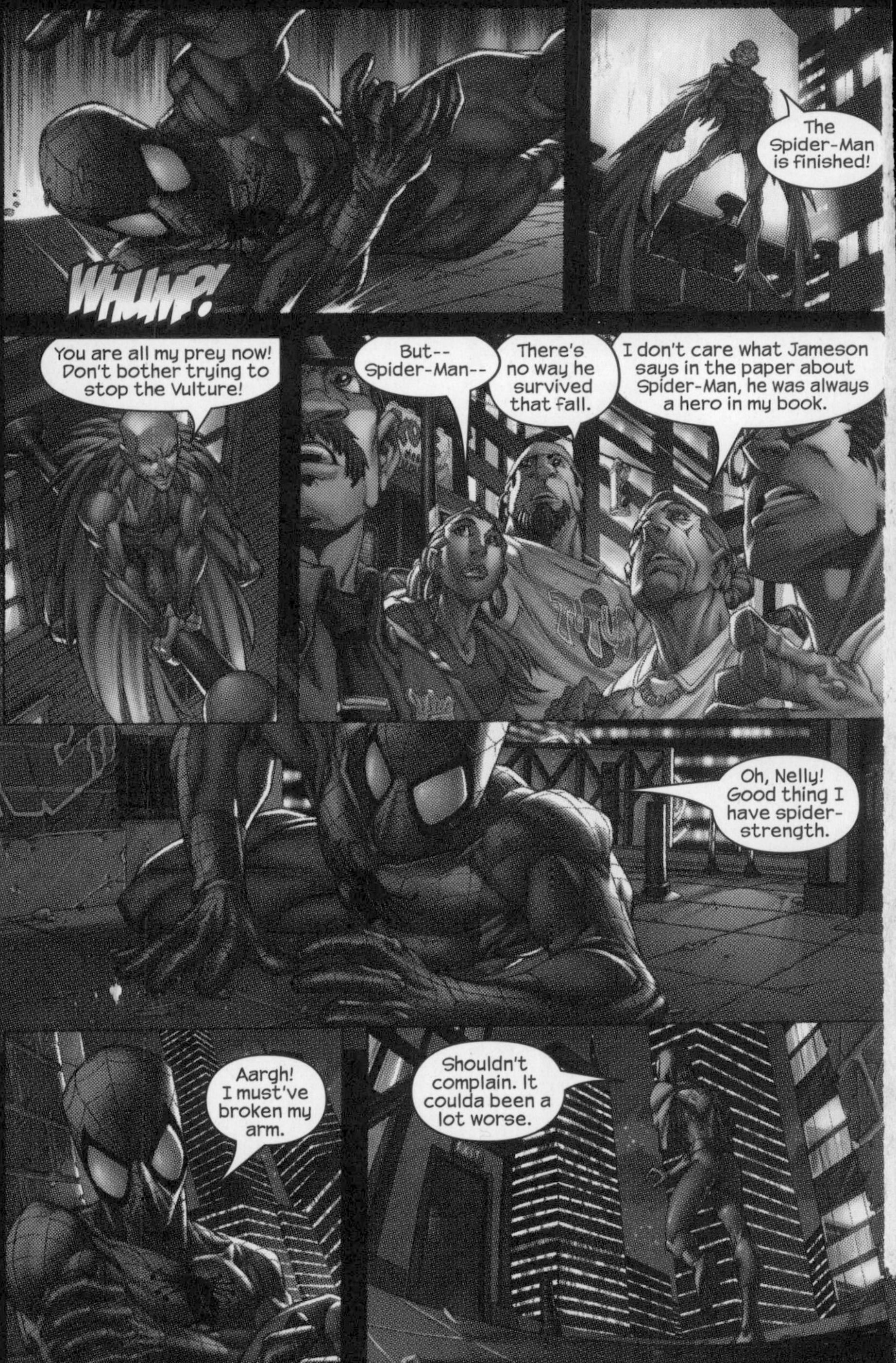
WHUMP!
The Spider-Man is finished!
You are all my prey now! Don't bother trying to stop the Vulture!
But-- Spider-Man--
There's no way he survived that fall.
I don't care what Jameson says in the paper about Spider-Man, he was always a hero in my book.
Oh, Nelly! Good thing I have spider-strength.
Aargh! I must've broken my arm.
Shouldn't complain. It coulda been a lot worse.

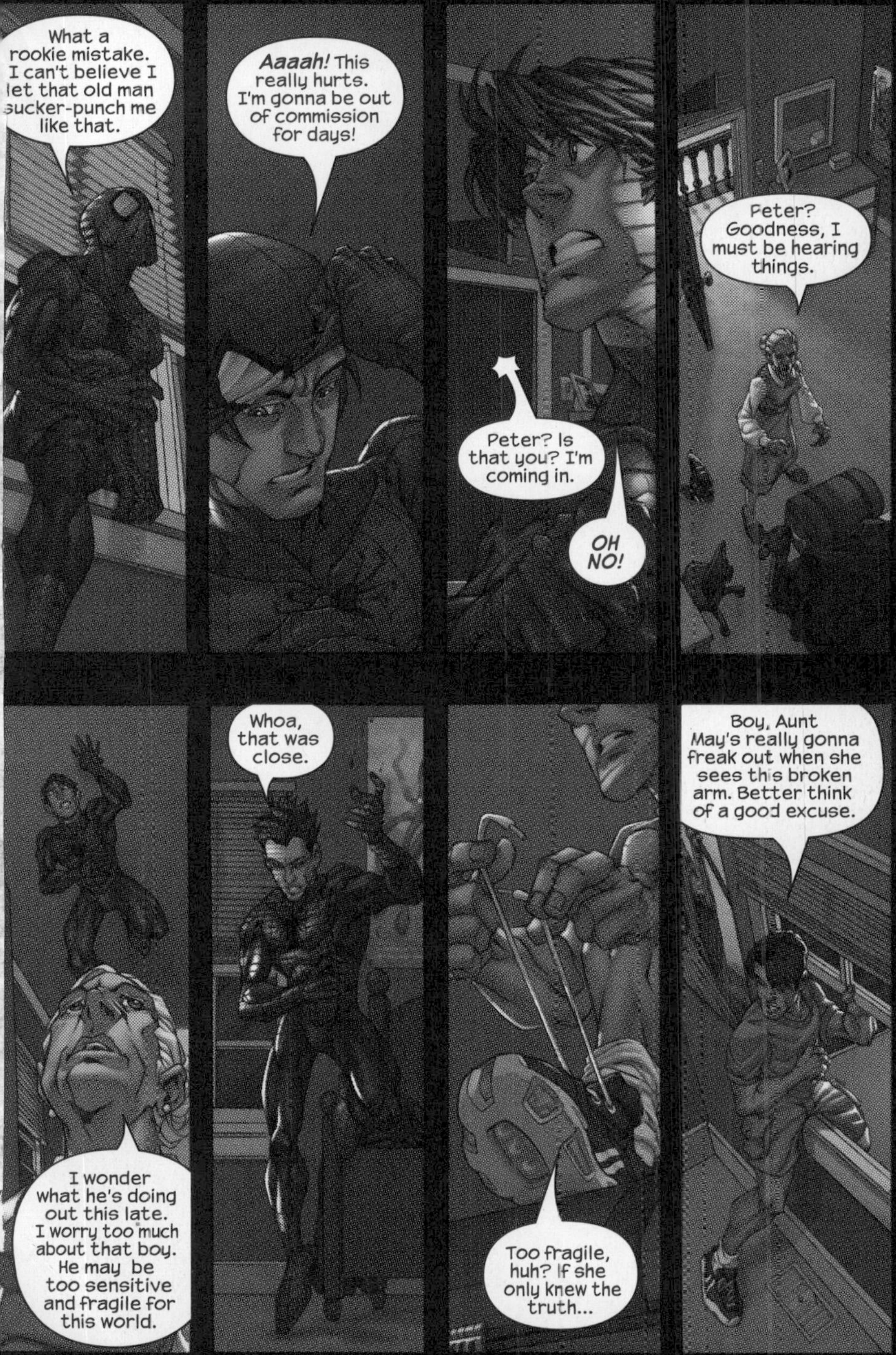

What a rookie mistake. I can't believe I let that old man sucker-punch me like that.
Aaaah! This really hurts. I'm gonna be out of commission for days!
Peter? Is that you? I'm coming in.
OH NO!
Peter? Goodness, I must be hearing things.
I wonder what he's doing out this late. I worry too much about that boy. He may be too sensitive and fragile for this world.
Whoa, that was close.
Too fragile, huh? If she only knew the truth...
Boy, Aunt May's really gonna freak out when she sees this broken arm. Better think of a good excuse.

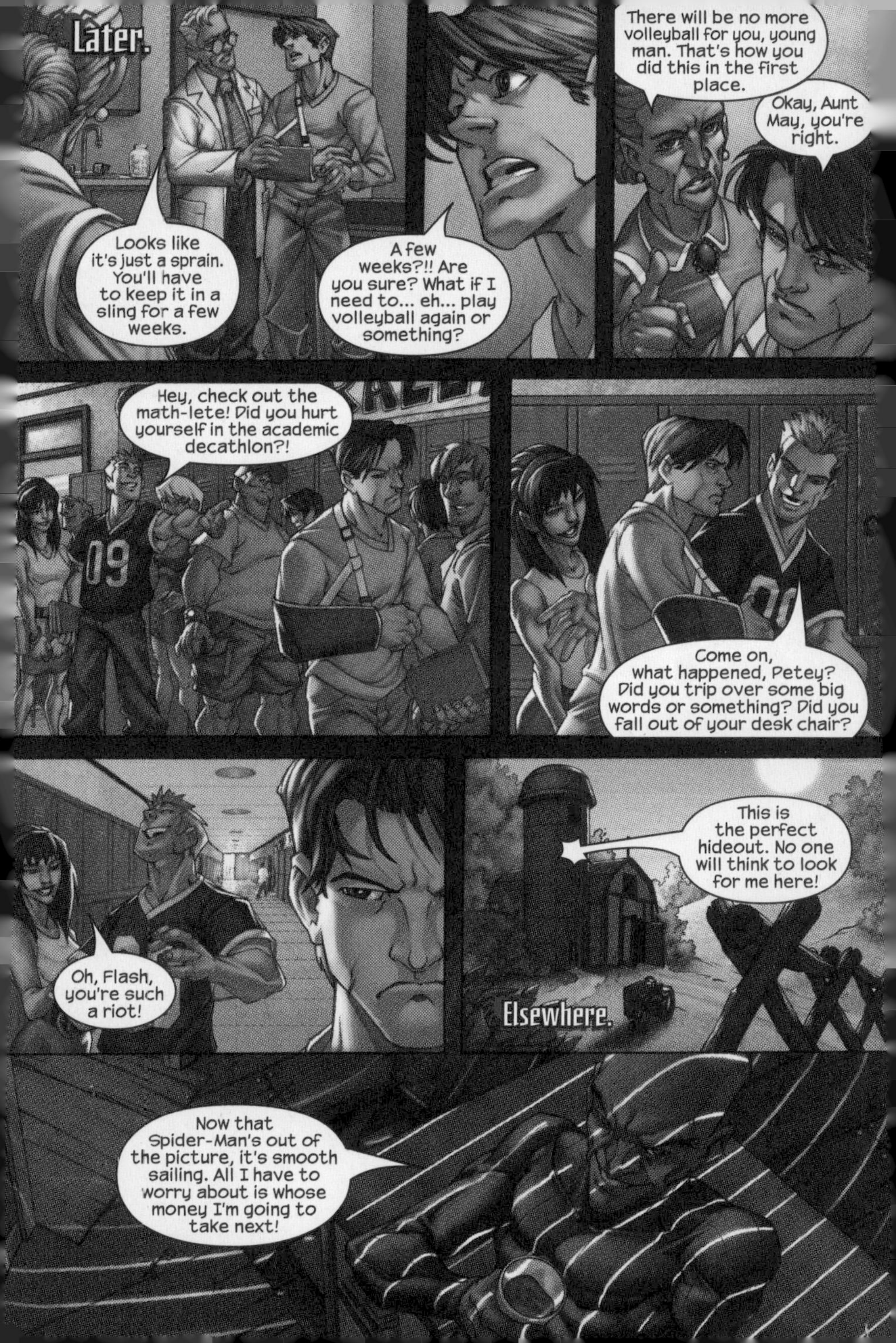
Later.
Looks like it's just a sprain. You'll have to keep it in a sling for a few weeks.
A few weeks?!! Are you sure? What if I need to... eh... play volleyball again or something?
There will be no more volleyball for you, young man. That's how you did this in the first place.
Okay, Aunt May, you're right.
Hey, check out the math-lete! Did you hurt yourself in the academic decathlon?!
Come on, what happened, Petey? Did you trip over some big words or something? Did you fall out of your desk chair?
Oh, Flash, you're such a riot!
Elsewhere.
This is the perfect hideout. No one will think to look for me here!
Now that Spider-Man's out of the picture, it's smooth sailing. All I have to worry about is whose money I'm going to take next!

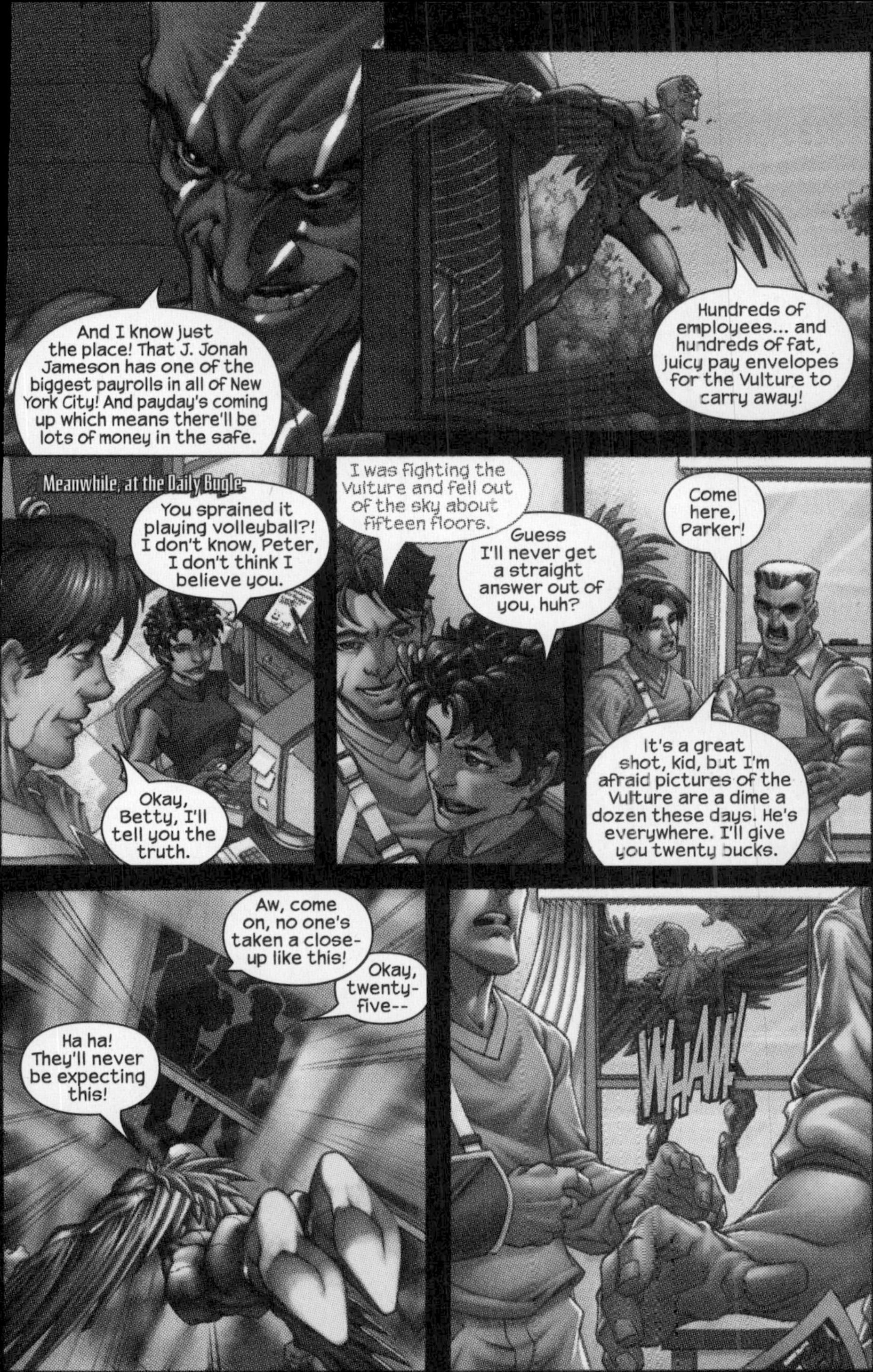
And I know just the place! That J. Jonah Jameson has one of the biggest payrolls in all of New York City! And payday's coming up which means there'll be lots of money in the safe.
Hundreds of employees... and hundreds of fat, juicy pay envelopes for the Vulture to carry away!
Meanwhile, at the Daily Bugle.
You sprained it playing volleyball?! I don't know, Peter, I don't think I believe you.
Okay, Betty, I'll tell you the truth.
I was fighting the Vulture and fell out of the sky about fifteen floors.
Guess I'll never get a straight answer out of you, huh?
Come here, Parker!
It's a great shot, kid, but I'm afraid pictures of the Vulture are a dime a dozen these days. He's everywhere. I'll give you twenty bucks.
Aw, come on, no one's taken a close-up like this!
Okay, twenty-five--
Ha ha! They'll never be expecting this!
WHAM!

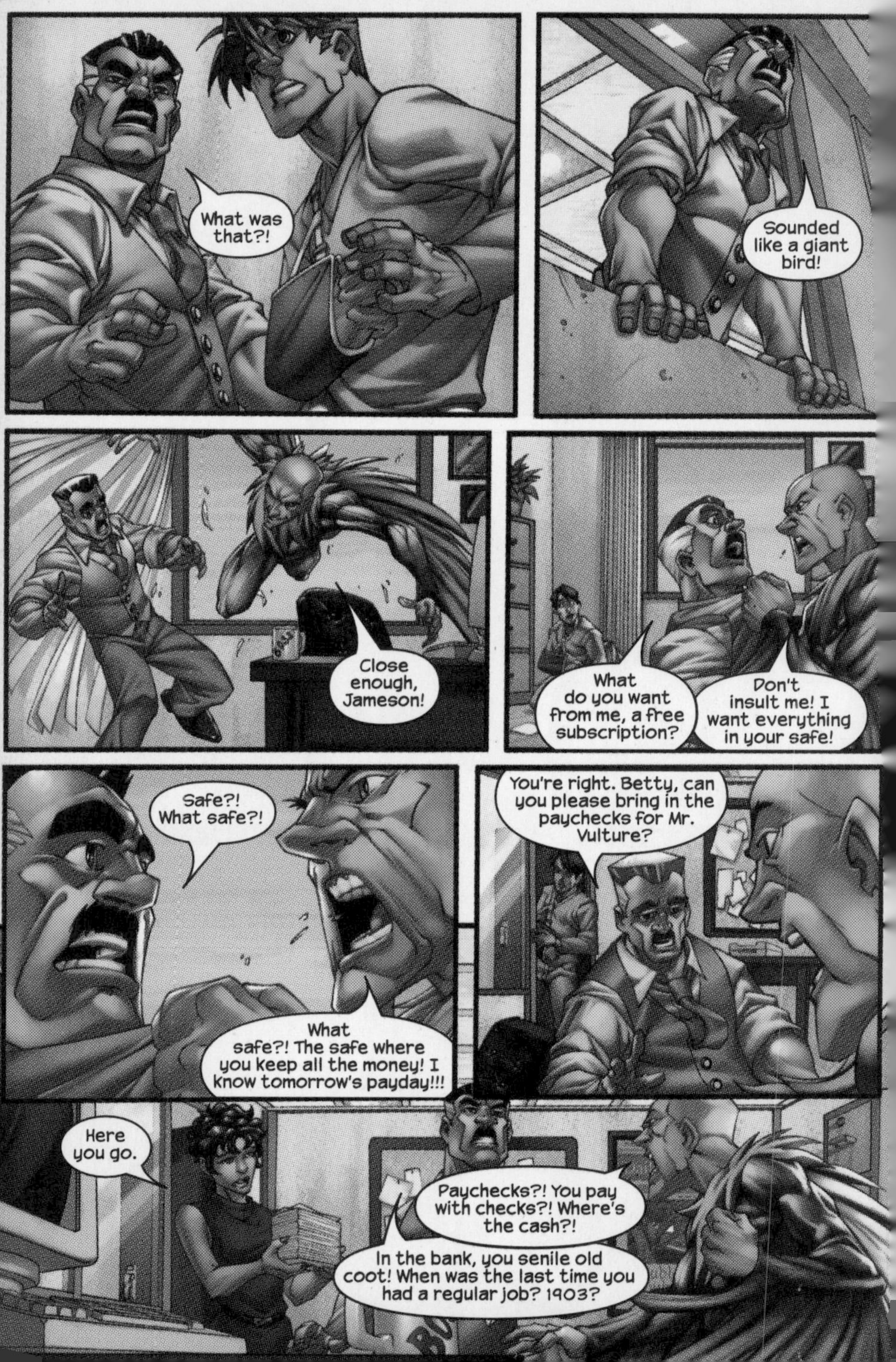
What was that?!
Sounded like a giant bird!
Close enough, Jameson!
What do you want from me, a free subscription?
Don't insult me! I want everything in your safe!
Safe?! What safe?!
What safe?! The safe where you keep all the money! I know tomorrow's payday!!!
You're right. Betty, can you please bring in the paychecks for Mr. Vulture?
Here you go.
Paychecks?! You pay with checks?! Where's the cash?!
In the bank, you senile old coot! When was the last time you had a regular job? 1903?

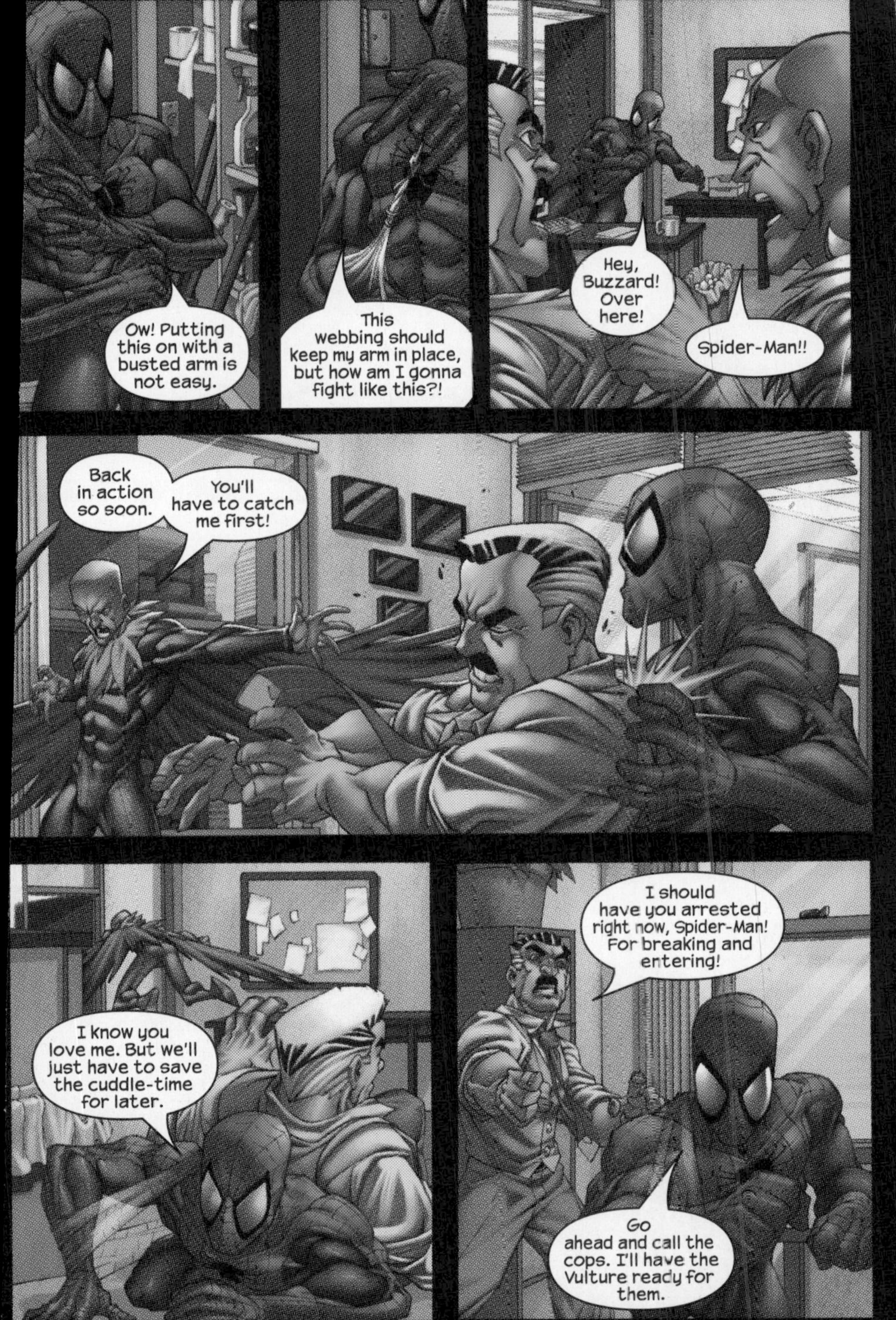
Ow! Putting this on with a busted arm is not easy.
This webbing should keep my arm in place, but how am I gonna fight like this?!
Hey, Buzzard! Over here!
Spider-Man!!
Back in action so soon.
You'll have to catch me first!
I know you love me. But we'll just have to save the cuddle-time for later.
I should have you arrested right now, Spider-Man! For breaking and entering!
Go ahead and call the cops. I'll have the Vulture ready for them.

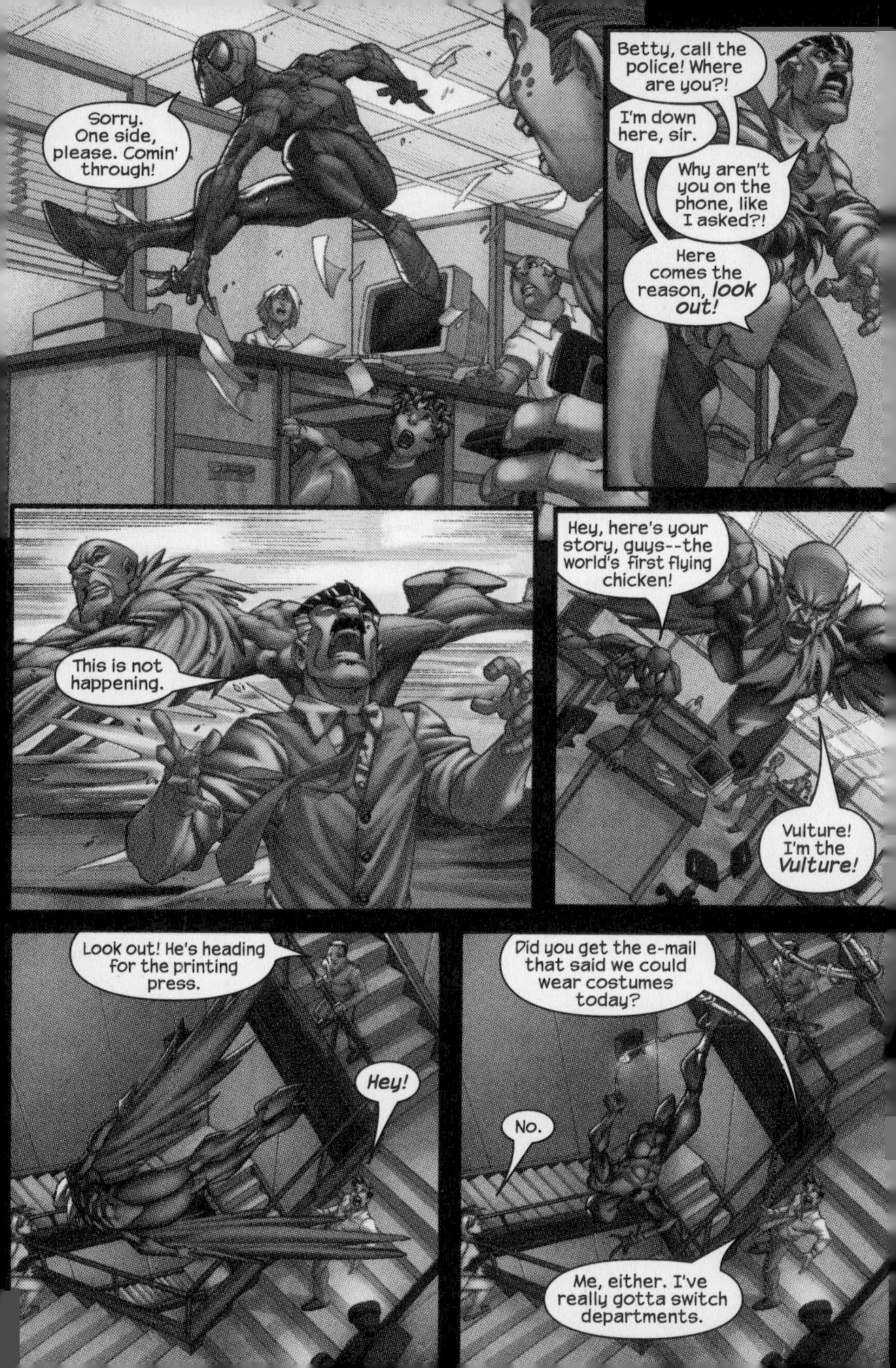
Sorry. One side, please. Comin' through!
Betty, call the police! Where are you?!
I'm down here, sir.
Why aren't you on the phone, like I asked?!
Here comes the reason, *look out!*
This is not happening.
Hey, here's your story, guys--the world's first flying chicken!
Vulture! I'm the *Vulture!*
Look out! He's heading for the printing press.
Hey!
Did you get the e-mail that said we could wear costumes today?
No.
Me, either. I've really gotta switch departments.

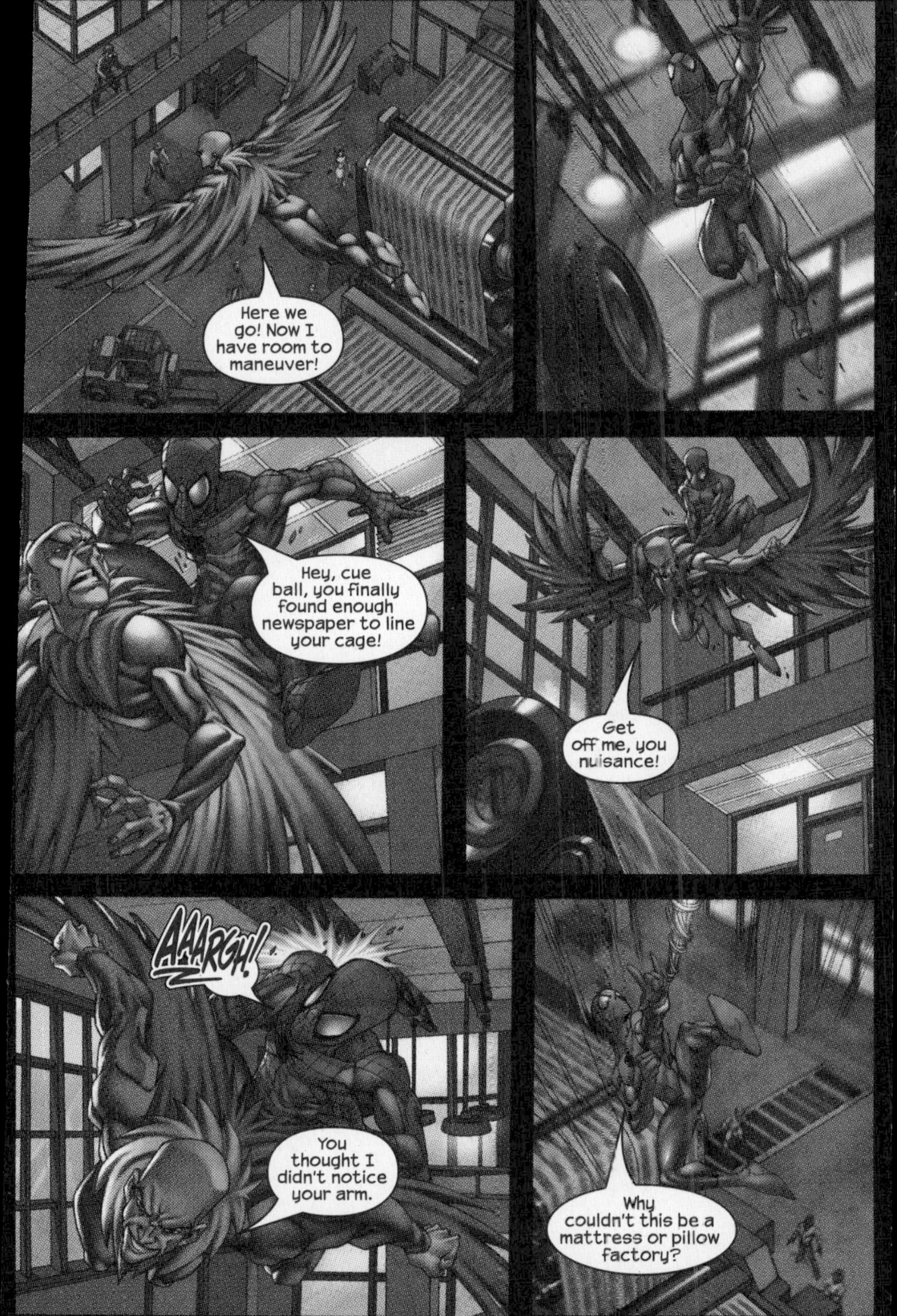
Here we go! Now I have room to maneuver!
Hey, cue ball, you finally found enough newspaper to line your cage!
Get off me, you nuisance!
AAARGH!
You thought I didn't notice your arm.
Why couldn't this be a mattress or pillow factory?

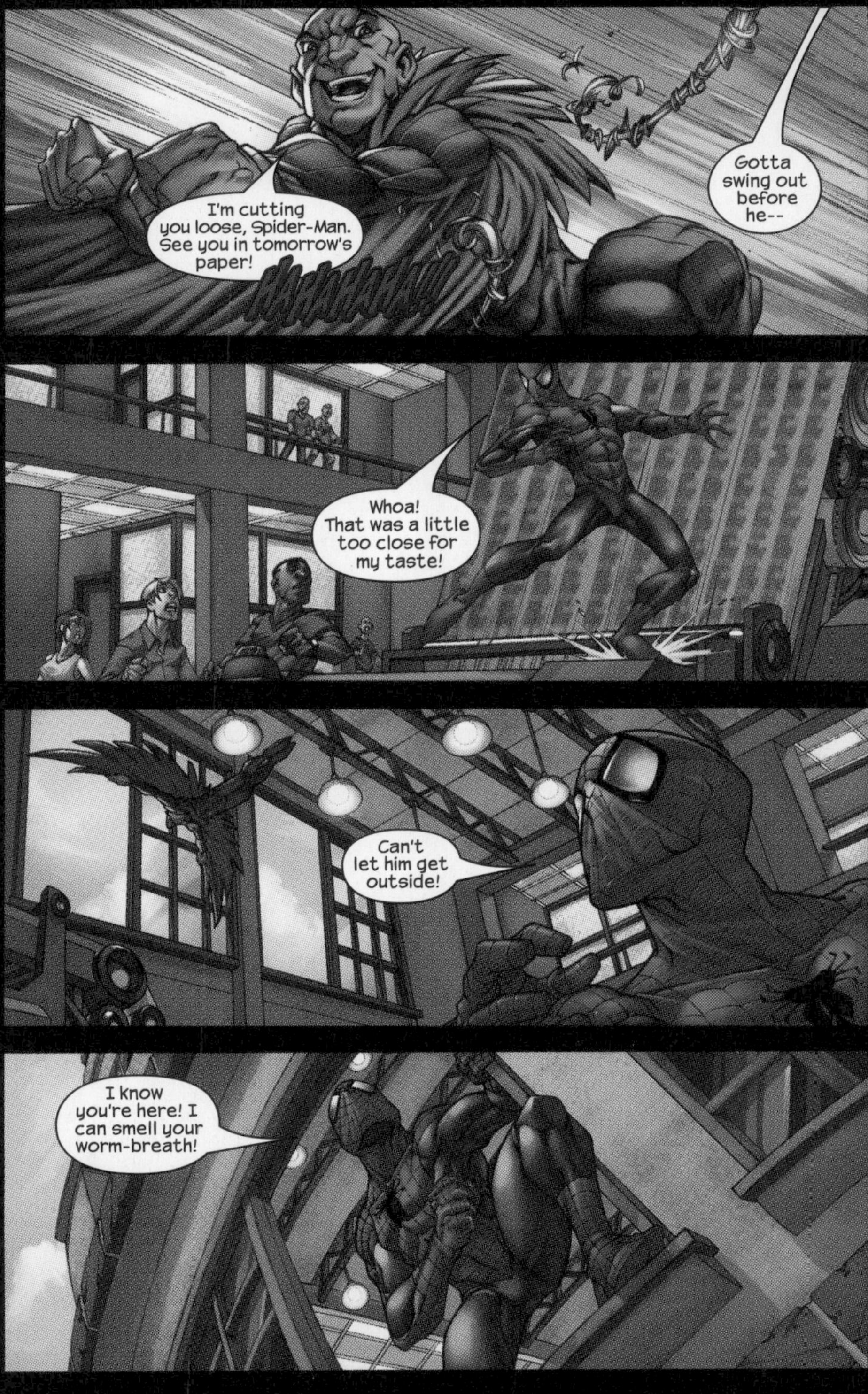
I'm cutting you loose, Spider-Man. See you in tomorrow's paper!
Gotta swing out before he--
Whoa! That was a little too close for my taste!
Can't let him get outside!
I know you're here! I can smell your worm-breath!

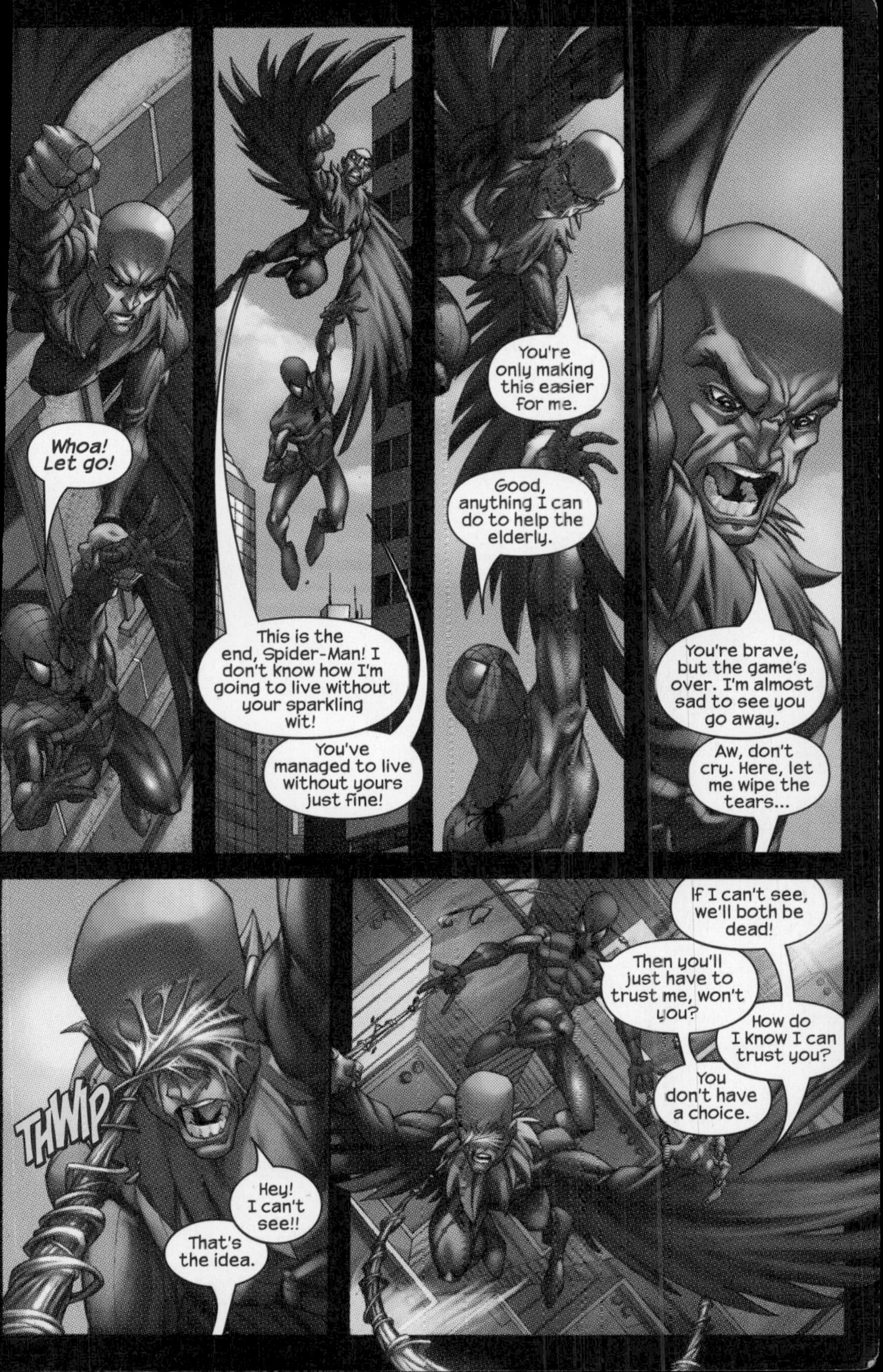
Whoa! Let go!
This is the end, Spider-Man! I don't know how I'm going to live without your sparkling wit!
You've managed to live without yours just fine!
You're only making this easier for me.
Good, anything I can do to help the elderly.
You're brave, but the game's over. I'm almost sad to see you go away.
Aw, don't cry. Here, let me wipe the tears...
THWIP
Hey! I can't see!!
That's the idea.
If I can't see, we'll both be dead!
Then you'll just have to trust me, won't you?
How do I know I can trust you?
You don't have a choice.

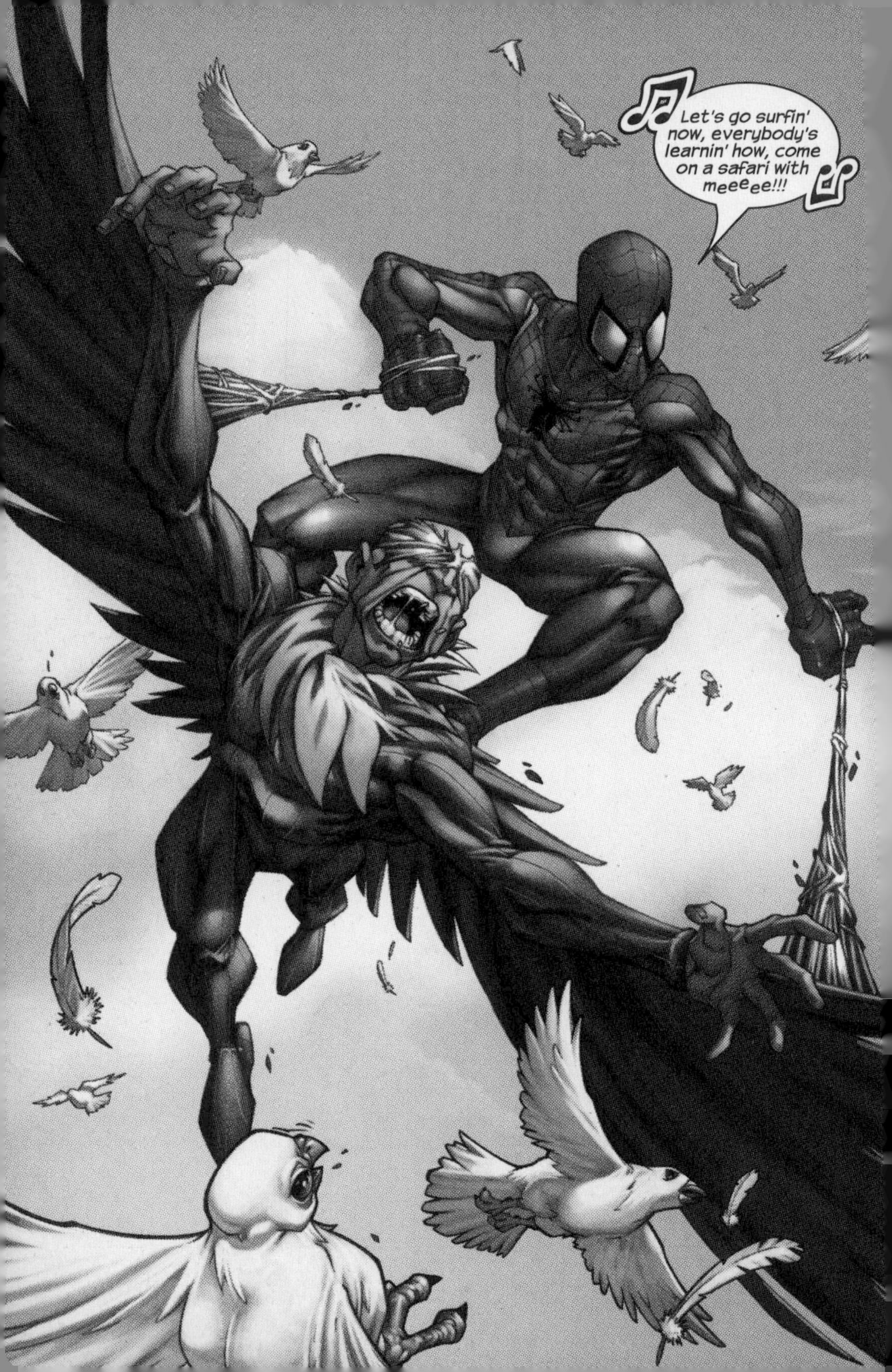
Let's go surfin' now, everybody's learnin' how, come on a safari with meeeeee!!!

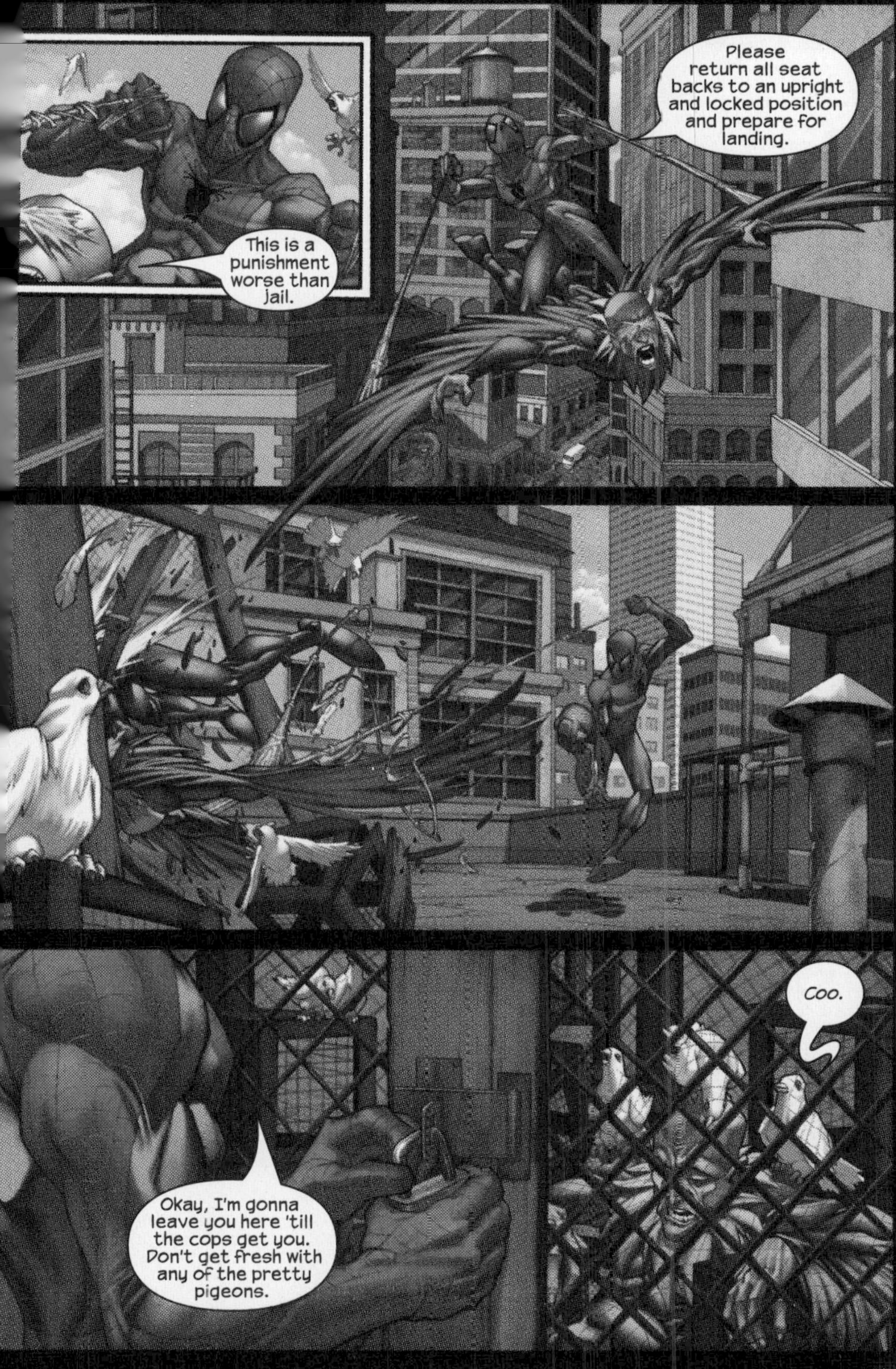
This is a punishment worse than jail.
Please return all seat backs to an upright and locked position and prepare for landing.
Okay, I'm gonna leave you here 'till the cops get you. Don't get fresh with any of the pretty pigeons.
Coo.

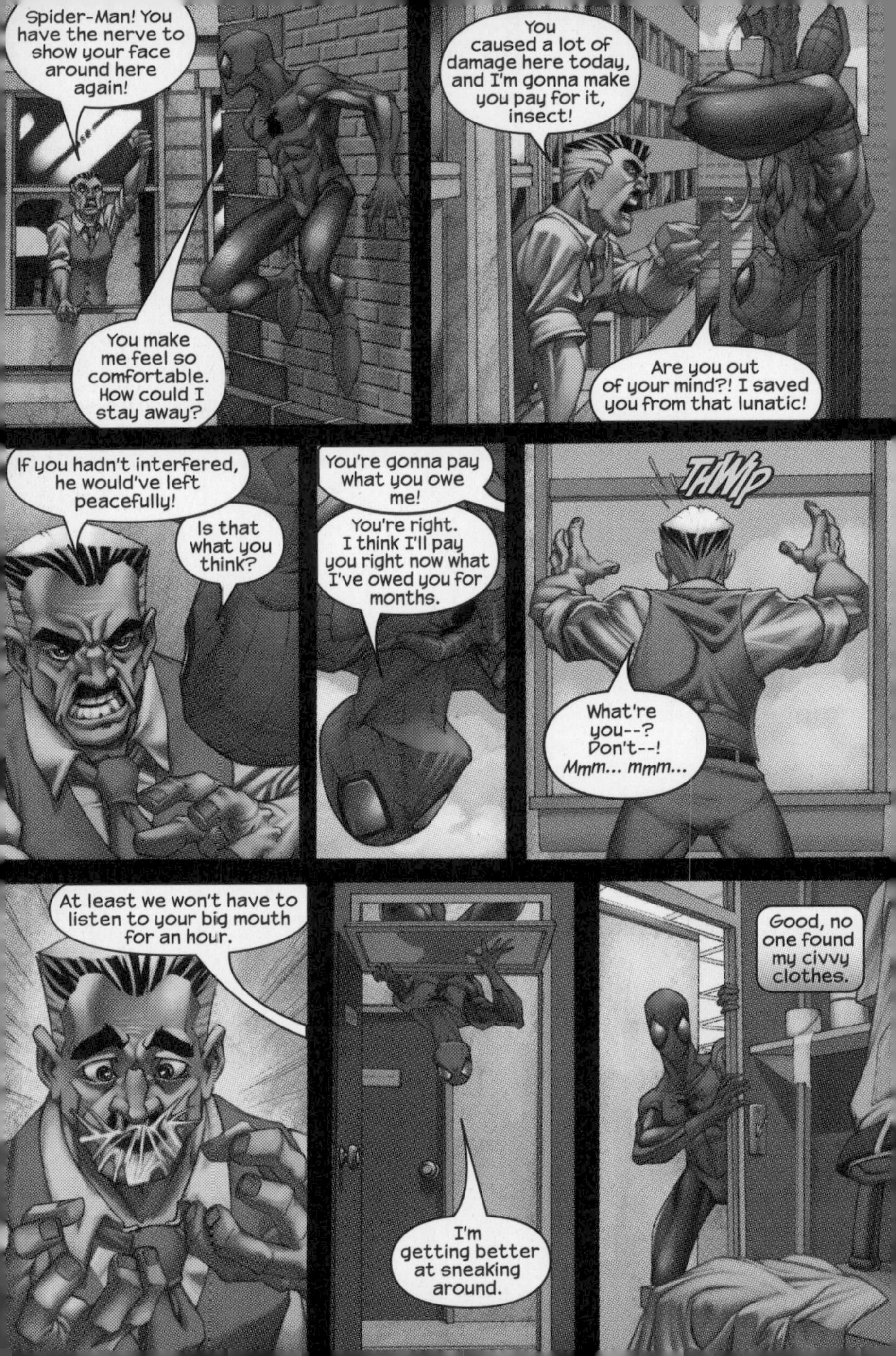
Spider-Man! You have the nerve to show your face around here again!
You make me feel so comfortable. How could I stay away?
You caused a lot of damage here today, and I'm gonna make you pay for it, insect!
Are you out of your mind?! I saved you from that lunatic!
If you hadn't interfered, he would've left peacefully!
Is that what you think?
You're gonna pay what you owe me!
You're right. I think I'll pay you right now what I've owed you for months.
THWIP
What're you--? Don't--! Mmm... mmm...
At least we won't have to listen to your big mouth for an hour.
I'm getting better at sneaking around.
Good, no one found my civvy clothes.

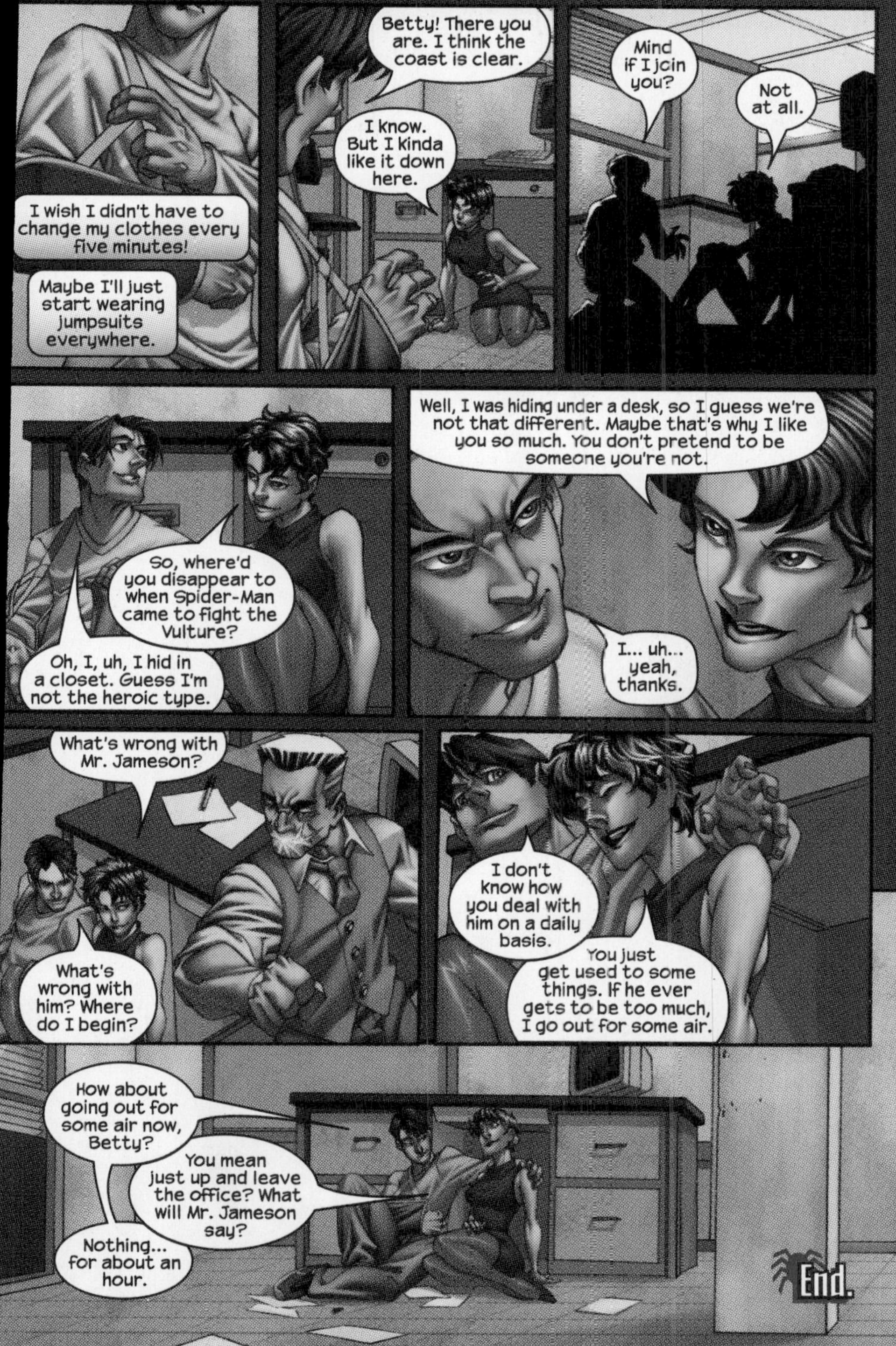
I wish I didn't have to change my clothes every five minutes!
Maybe I'll just start wearing jumpsuits everywhere.
Betty! There you are. I think the coast is clear.
I know. But I kinda like it down here.
Mind if I join you?
Not at all.
So, where'd you disappear to when Spider-Man came to fight the Vulture?
Oh, I, uh, I hid in a closet. Guess I'm not the heroic type.
Well, I was hiding under a desk, so I guess we're not that different. Maybe that's why I like you so much. You don't pretend to be someone you're not.
I... uh... yeah, thanks.
What's wrong with Mr. Jameson?
What's wrong with him? Where do I begin?
I don't know how you deal with him on a daily basis.
You just get used to some things. If he ever gets to be too much, I go out for some air.
How about going out for some air now, Betty?
You mean just up and leave the office? What will Mr. Jameson say?
Nothing... for about an hour.
End.

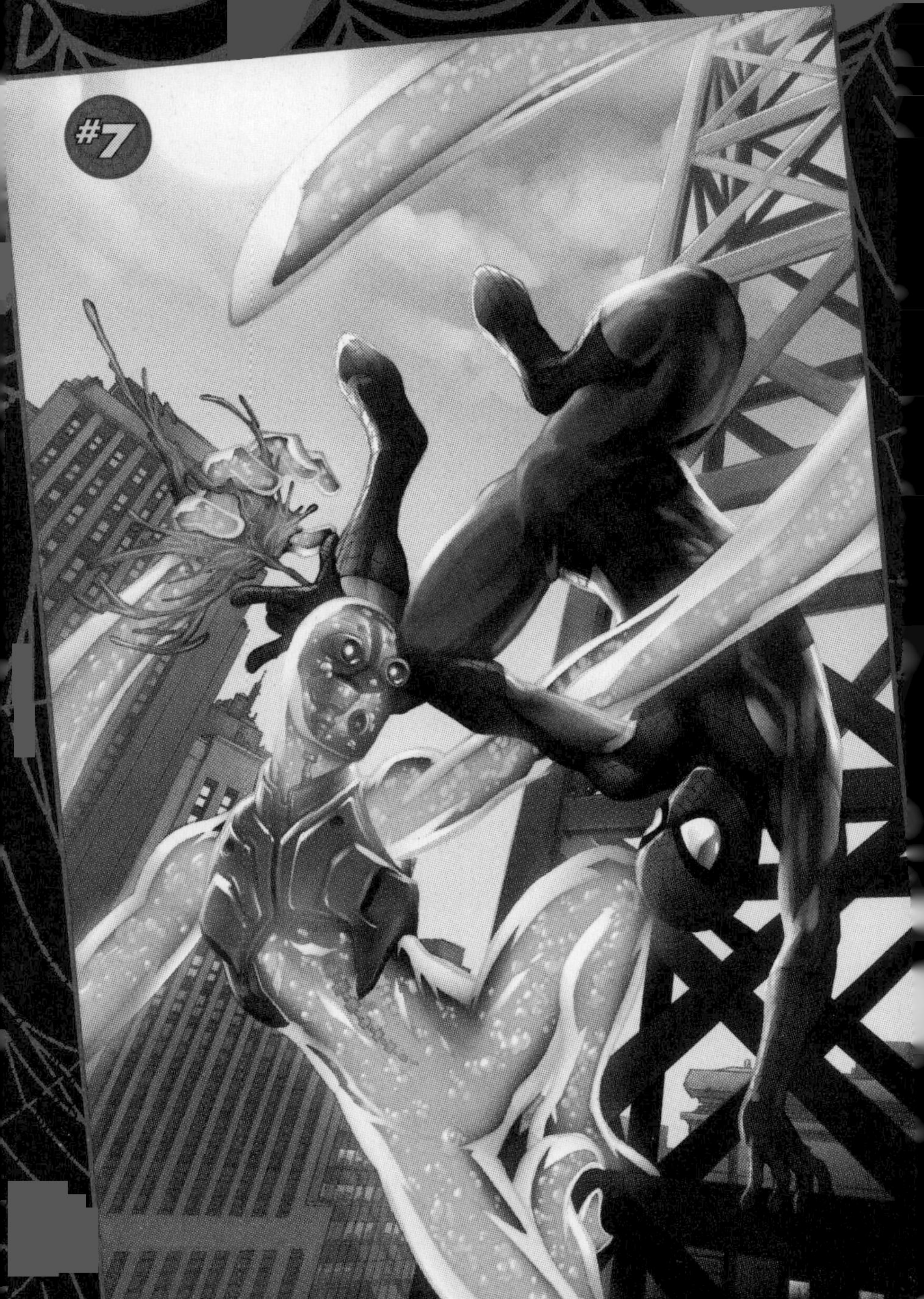
#7

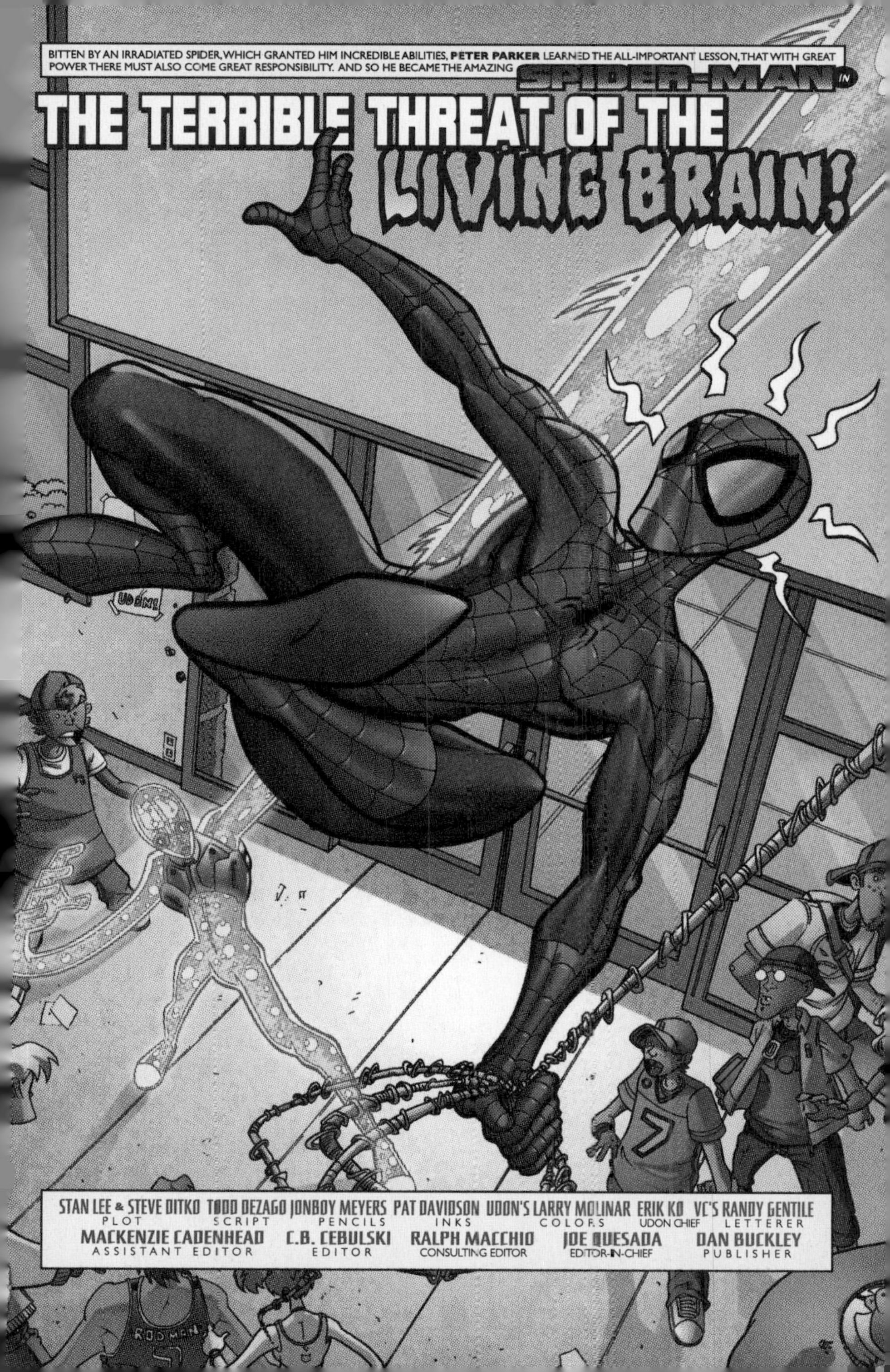
BITTEN BY AN IRRADIATED SPIDER, WHICH GRANTED HIM INCREDIBLE ABILITIES, PETER PARKER LEARNED THE ALL-IMPORTANT LESSON, THAT WITH GREAT POWER THERE MUST ALSO COME GREAT RESPONSIBILITY. AND SO HE BECAME THE AMAZING SPIDER-MAN IN
THE TERRIBLE THREAT OF THE LIVING BRAIN!
STAN LEE & STEVE DITKO PLOT
TODD DEZAGO SCRIPT
JONBOY MEYERS PENCILS
PAT DAVIDSON INKS
UDON'S LARRY MOLINAR COLORS
ERIK KO UDON CHIEF
VC'S RANDY GENTILE LETTERER
MACKENZIE CADENHEAD ASSISTANT EDITOR
C.B. CEBULSKI EDITOR
RALPH MACCHIO CONSULTING EDITOR
JOE QUESADA EDITOR-IN-CHIEF
DAN BUCKLEY PUBLISHER
7
RODMAN

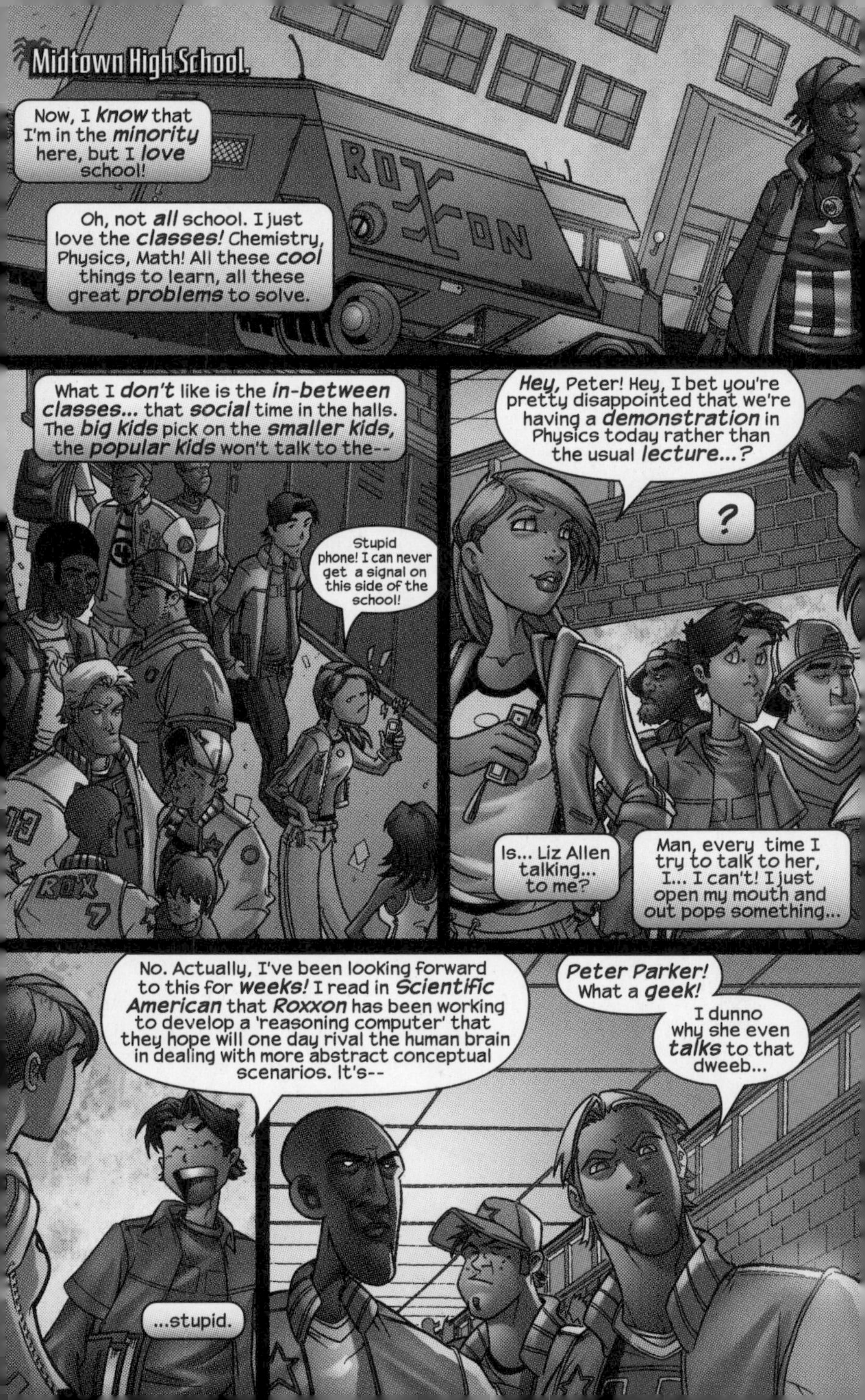
Midtown High School.
Now, I know that I'm in the minority here, but I love school!
Oh, not all school. I just love the classes! Chemistry, Physics, Math! All these cool things to learn, all these great problems to solve.
ROXXON
What I don't like is the in-between classes... that social time in the halls. The big kids pick on the smaller kids, the popular kids won't talk to the--
Stupid phone! I can never get a signal on this side of the school!
Hey, Peter! Hey, I bet you're pretty disappointed that we're having a demonstration in Physics today rather than the usual lecture...?
?
Is... Liz Allen talking... to me?
Man, every time I try to talk to her, I... I can't! I just open my mouth and out pops something...
No. Actually, I've been looking forward to this for weeks! I read in Scientific American that Roxxon has been working to develop a 'reasoning computer' that they hope will one day rival the human brain in dealing with more abstract conceptual scenarios. It's--
Peter Parker! What a geek!
I dunno why she even talks to that dweeb...
...stupid.

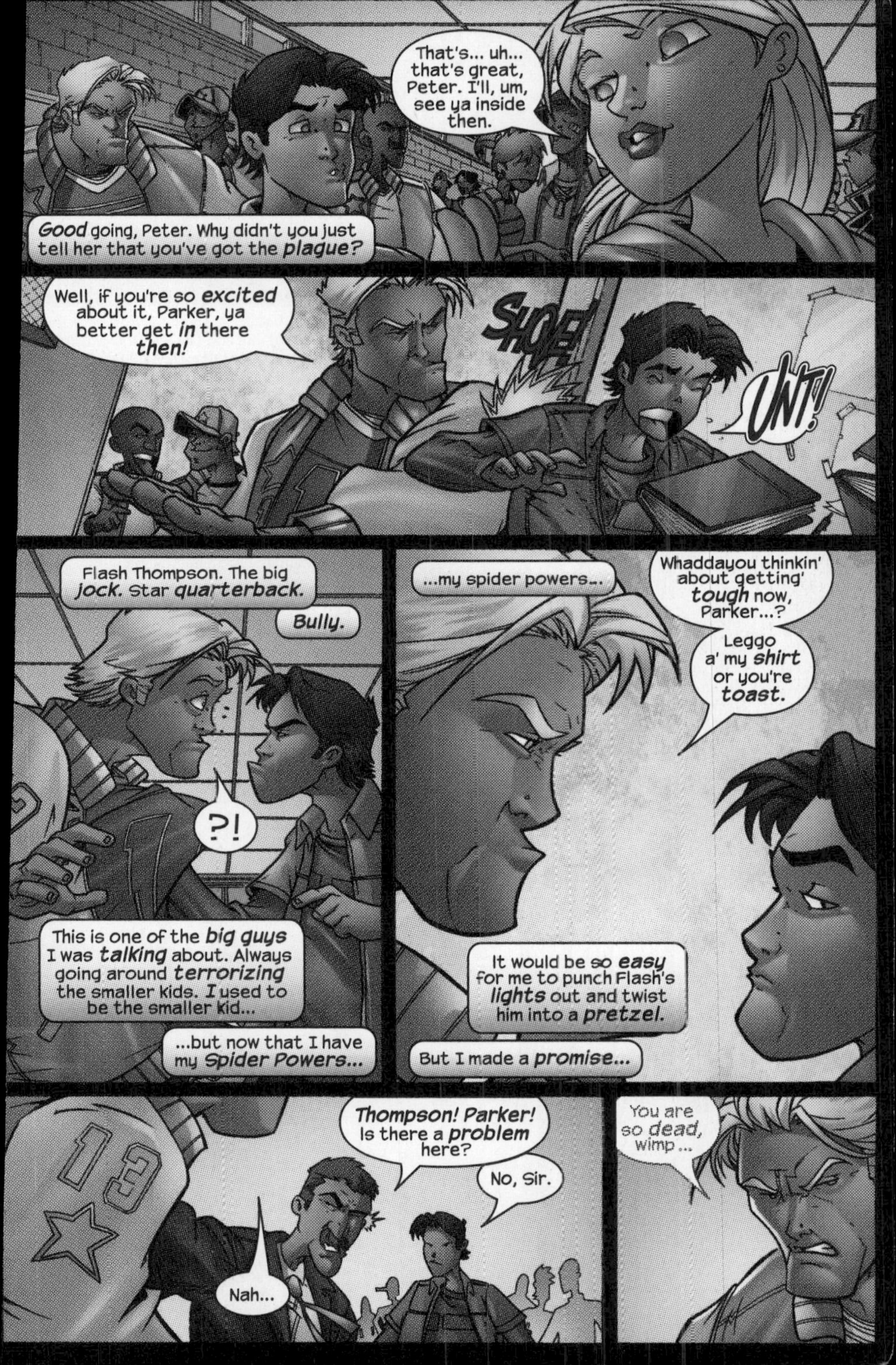
That's... uh... that's great, Peter. I'll, um, see ya inside then.
Good going, Peter. Why didn't you just tell her that you've got the plague?
Well, if you're so excited about it, Parker, ya better get in there then!
SHOVE!
UNT!
Flash Thompson. The big jock. Star quarterback.
Bully.
?!
This is one of the big guys I was talking about. Always going around terrorizing the smaller kids. I used to be the smaller kid...
...but now that I have my Spider Powers...
...my spider powers...
Whaddayou thinkin' about getting' tough now, Parker...?
Leggo a' my shirt or you're toast.
It would be so easy for me to punch Flash's lights out and twist him into a pretzel.
But I made a promise...
Thompson! Parker! Is there a problem here?
No, Sir.
Nah...
You are so dead, wimp...

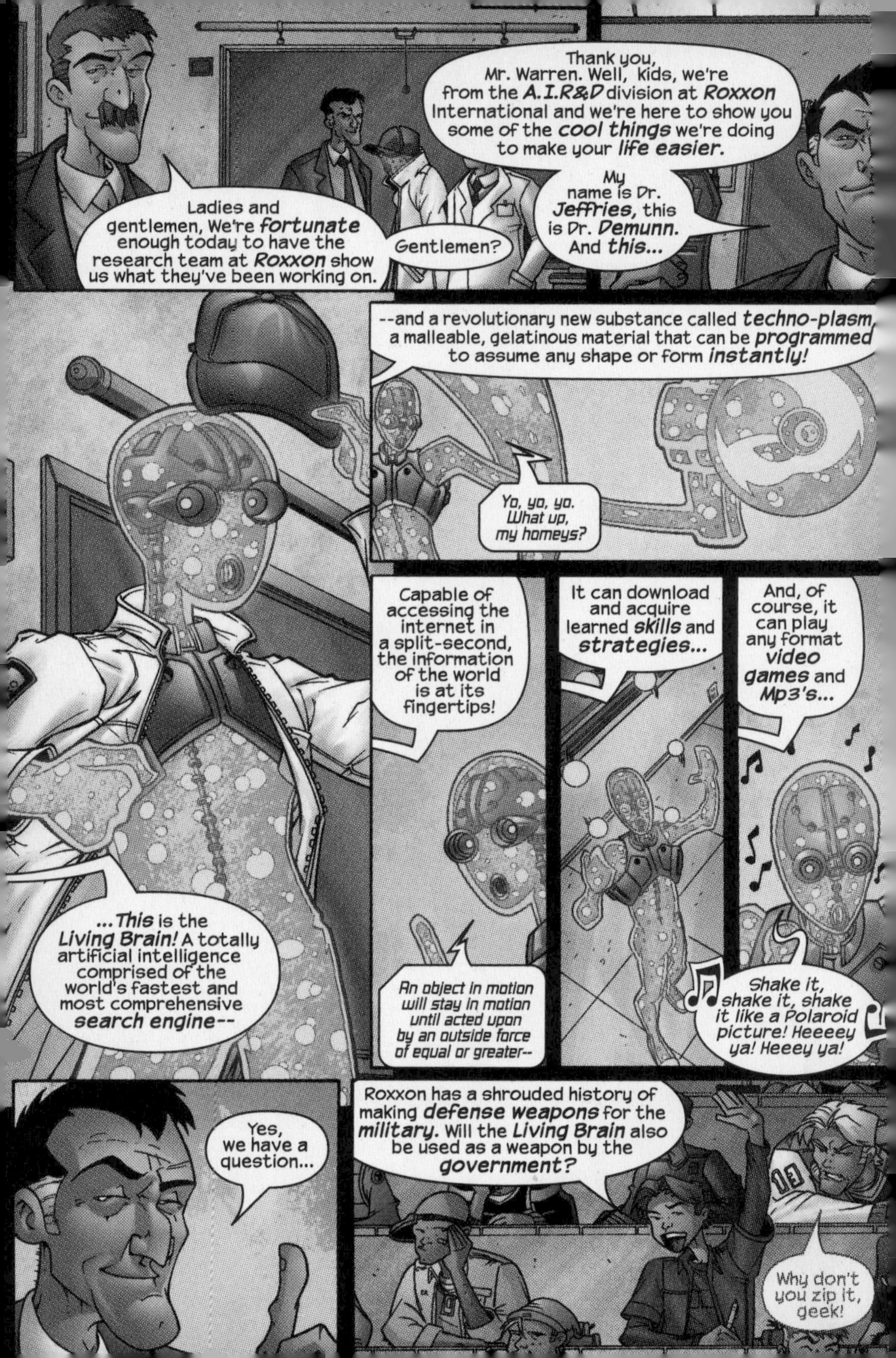
Ladies and gentlemen, We're fortunate enough today to have the research team at Roxxon show us what they've been working on.
Gentlemen?
Thank you, Mr. Warren. Well, kids, we're from the A.I.R&D division at Roxxon International and we're here to show you some of the cool things we're doing to make your life easier.
My name is Dr. Jeffries, this is Dr. Demunn. And this...
...This is the Living Brain! A totally artificial intelligence comprised of the world's fastest and most comprehensive search engine--
--and a revolutionary new substance called techno-plasm, a malleable, gelatinous material that can be programmed to assume any shape or form instantly!
Yo, yo, yo. What up, my homeys?
Capable of accessing the internet in a split-second, the information of the world is at its fingertips!
An object in motion will stay in motion until acted upon by an outside force of equal or greater--
It can download and acquire learned skills and strategies...
And, of course, it can play any format video games and Mp3's...
Shake it, shake it, shake it like a Polaroid picture! Heeeey ya! Heeey ya!
Yes, we have a question...
Roxxon has a shrouded history of making defense weapons for the military. Will the Living Brain also be used as a weapon by the government?
Why don't you zip it, geek!

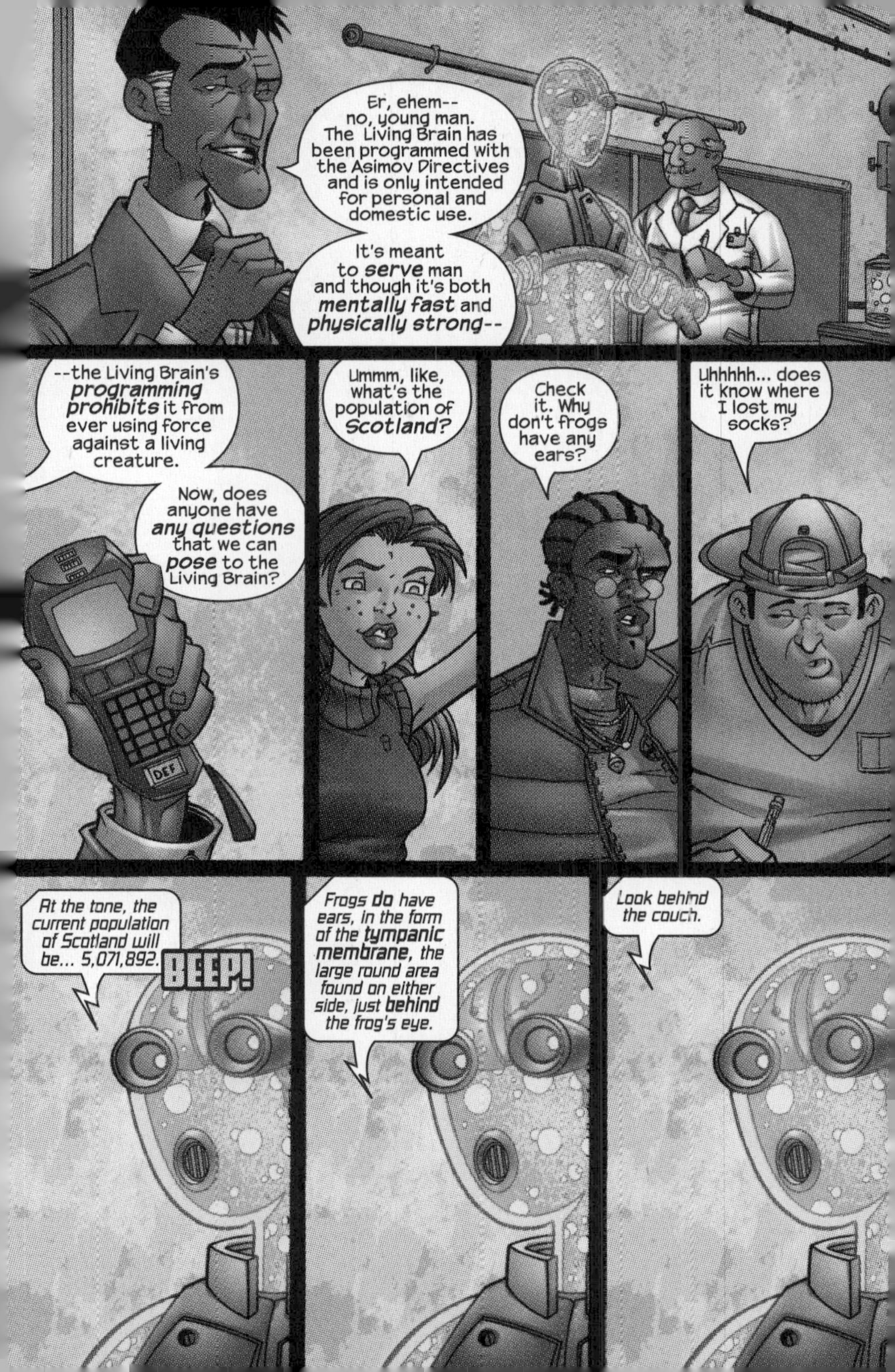

Er, ehem-- no, young man. The Living Brain has been programmed with the Asimov Directives and is only intended for personal and domestic use.
It's meant to serve man and though it's both mentally fast and physically strong--
--the Living Brain's programming prohibits it from ever using force against a living creature.
Now, does anyone have any questions that we can pose to the Living Brain?
DEF
Ummm, like, what's the population of Scotland?
Check it. Why don't frogs have any ears?
Uhhhhh... does it know where I lost my socks?
At the tone, the current population of Scotland will be... 5,071,892.
BEEP!
Frogs do have ears, in the form of the tympanic membrane, the large round area found on either side, just behind the frog's eye.
Look behind the couch.

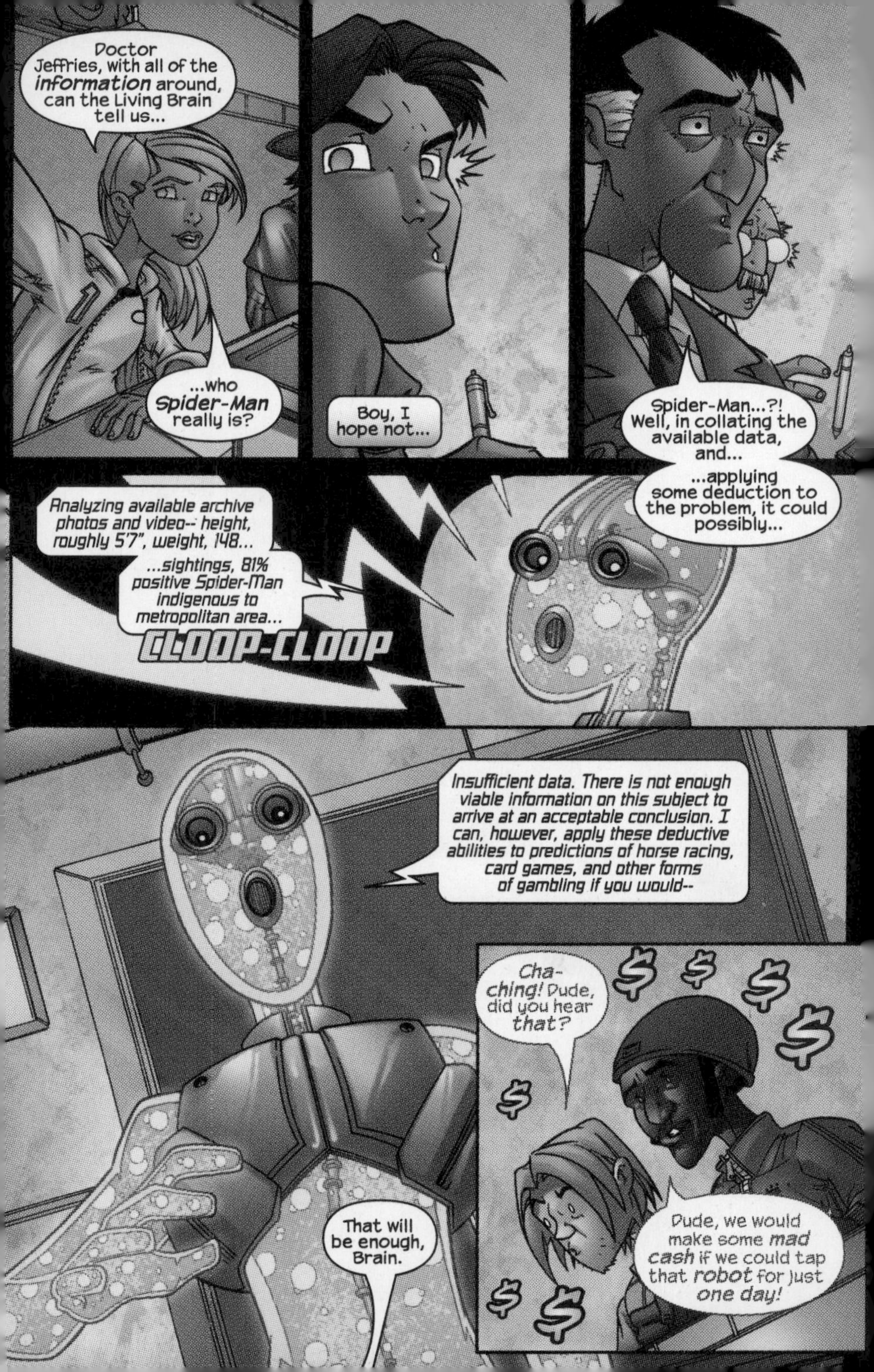

Doctor Jeffries, with all of the *information* around, can the Living Brain tell us...
...who *Spider-Man* really is?
Boy, I hope not...
Spider-Man...?! Well, in collating the available data, and...
...applying some deduction to the problem, it could possibly...
Analyzing available archive photos and video-- height, roughly 5'7", weight, 148...
...sightings, 81% positive Spider-Man indigenous to metropolitan area...
CLOOP-CLOOP
Insufficient data. There is not enough viable information on this subject to arrive at an acceptable conclusion. I can, however, apply these deductive abilities to predictions of horse racing, card games, and other forms of gambling if you would--
Cha-ching! Dude, did you hear *that*?
Dude, we would make some *mad cash* if we could tap that *robot* for just *one day!*
That will be enough, Brain.

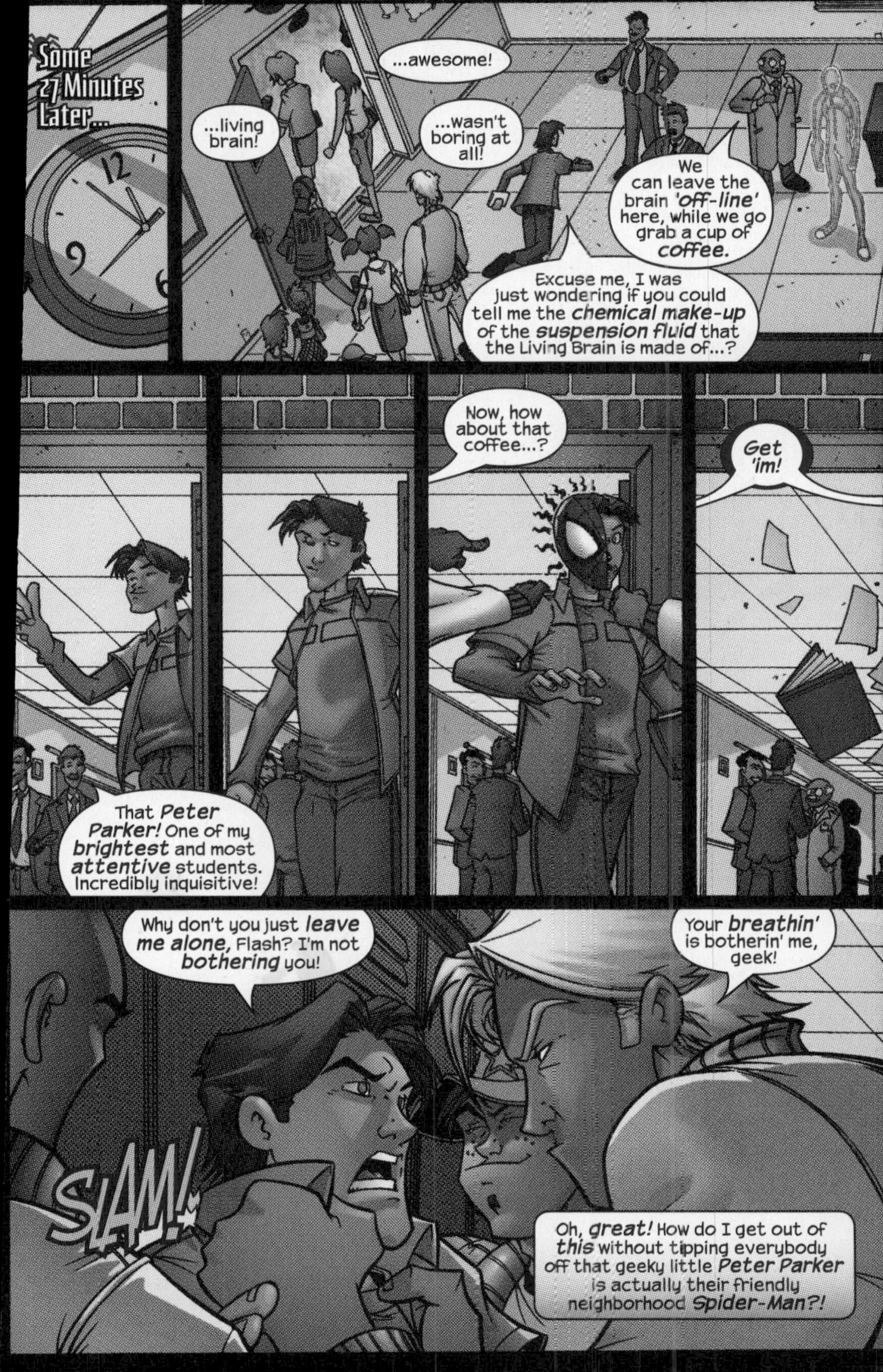

Some 27 Minutes Later...
...living brain!
...awesome!
...wasn't boring at all!
We can leave the brain 'off-line' here, while we go grab a cup of coffee.
Excuse me, I was just wondering if you could tell me the chemical make-up of the suspension fluid that the Living Brain is made of...?
That Peter Parker! One of my brightest and most attentive students. Incredibly inquisitive!
Now, how about that coffee...?
Get 'im!
Why don't you just leave me alone, Flash? I'm not bothering you!
Your breathin' is botherin' me, geek!
SLAM!
Oh, great! How do I get out of this without tipping everybody off that geeky little Peter Parker is actually their friendly neighborhood Spider-Man?!

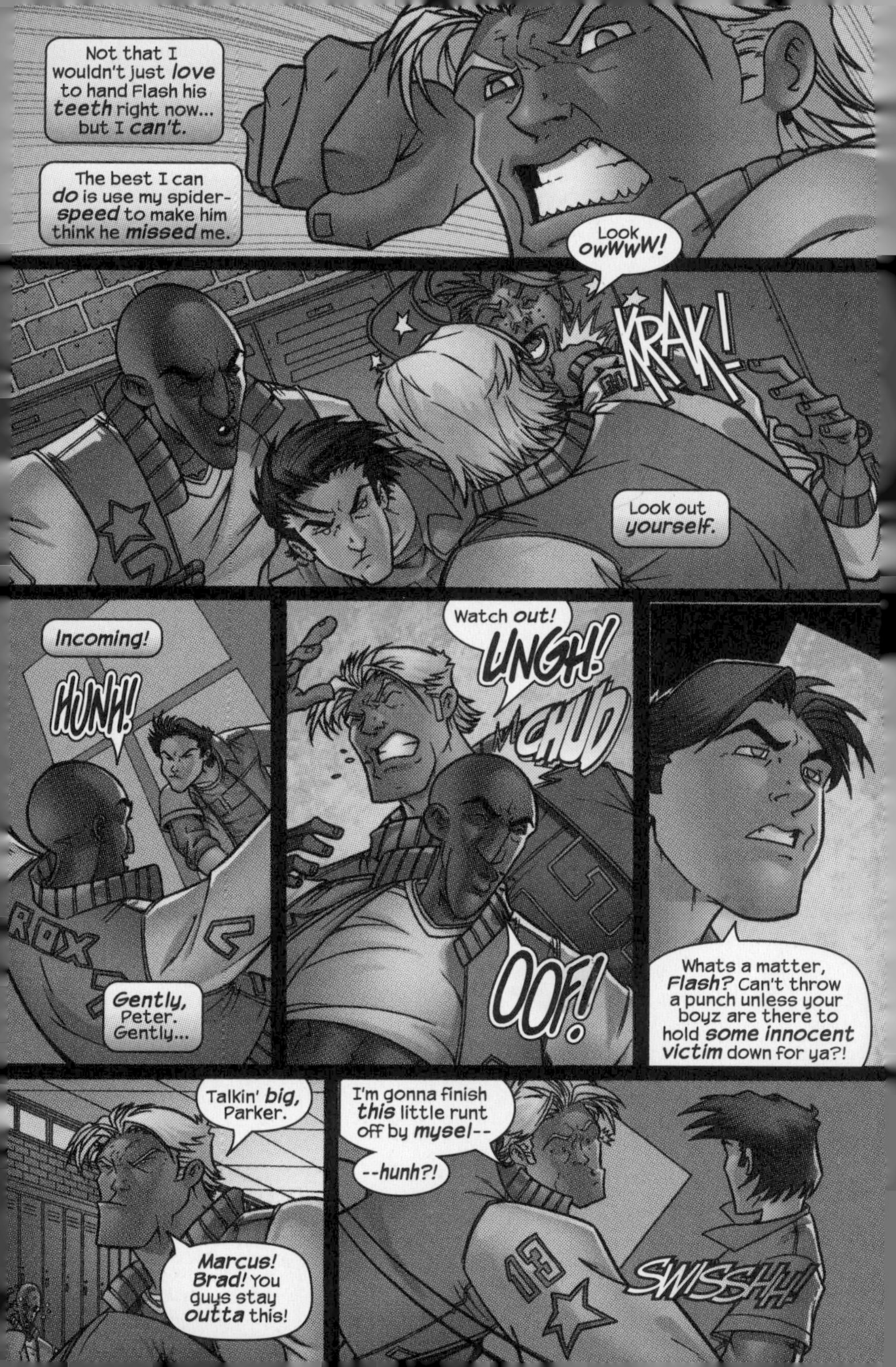
Not that I wouldn't just love to hand Flash his teeth right now... but I can't.
The best I can do is use my spider-speed to make him think he missed me.
Look owWWW!
KRAK!
Look out yourself.
Incoming!
HUNH!
Gently, Peter. Gently...
Watch out!
UNGH!
CHUD
OOF!
Whats a matter, Flash? Can't throw a punch unless your boyz are there to hold some innocent victim down for ya?!
Talkin' big, Parker.
Marcus! Brad! You guys stay outta this!
I'm gonna finish this little runt off by mysel--
--hunh?!
SWISSH!

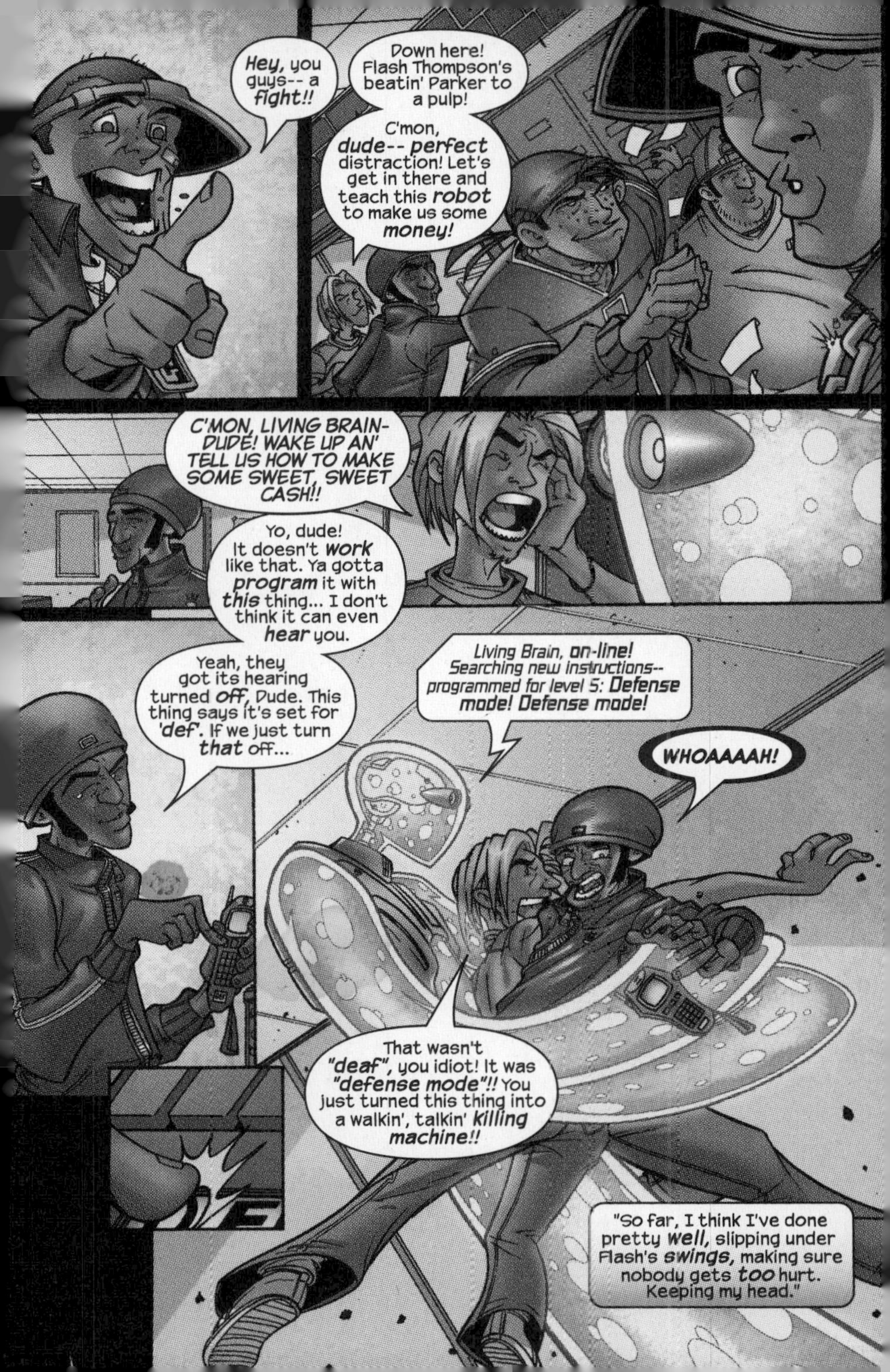
Hey, you guys-- a fight!!
Down here! Flash Thompson's beatin' Parker to a pulp!
C'mon, dude-- perfect distraction! Let's get in there and teach this robot to make us some money!
C'MON, LIVING BRAIN-DUDE! WAKE UP AN' TELL US HOW TO MAKE SOME SWEET, SWEET CASH!!
Yo, dude! It doesn't work like that. Ya gotta program it with this thing... I don't think it can even hear you.
Yeah, they got its hearing turned off, Dude. This thing says it's set for 'def'. If we just turn that off...
Living Brain, on-line! Searching new instructions-- programmed for level 5: Defense mode! Defense mode!
WHOAAAAH!
That wasn't "deaf", you idiot! It was "defense mode"!! You just turned this thing into a walkin', talkin' killing machine!!
"So far, I think I've done pretty well, slipping under Flash's swings, making sure nobody gets too hurt. Keeping my head."

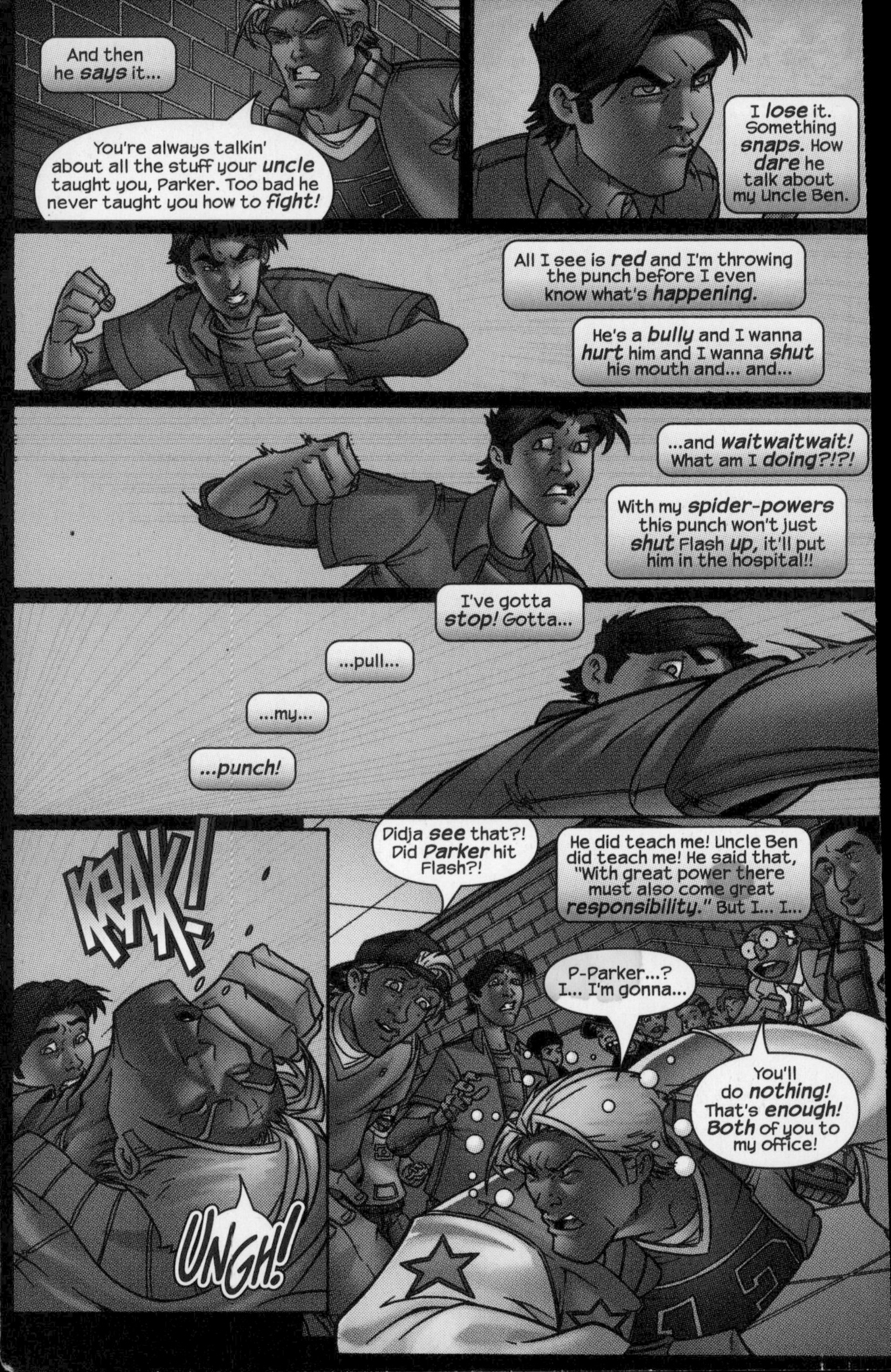
And then he *says* it...
You're always talkin' about all the stuff your *uncle* taught you, Parker. Too bad he never taught you how to *fight!*
I *lose* it. Something *snaps*. How *dare* he talk about my Uncle Ben.
All I see is *red* and I'm throwing the punch before I even know what's *happening.*
He's a *bully* and I wanna *hurt* him and I wanna *shut* his mouth and... and...
...and *waitwaitwait!* What am I *doing?!?!*
With my *spider-powers* this punch won't just *shut* Flash *up,* it'll put him in the hospital!!
I've gotta *stop!* Gotta...
...pull...
...my...
...*punch!*
KRAK!
UNGH!
Didja *see* that?! Did *Parker* hit Flash?!
He did teach me! Uncle Ben did teach me! He said that, "With great power there must also come great *responsibility.*" But I... I...
P-Parker...? I... I'm gonna...
You'll do *nothing!* That's *enough!* *Both* of you to my office!

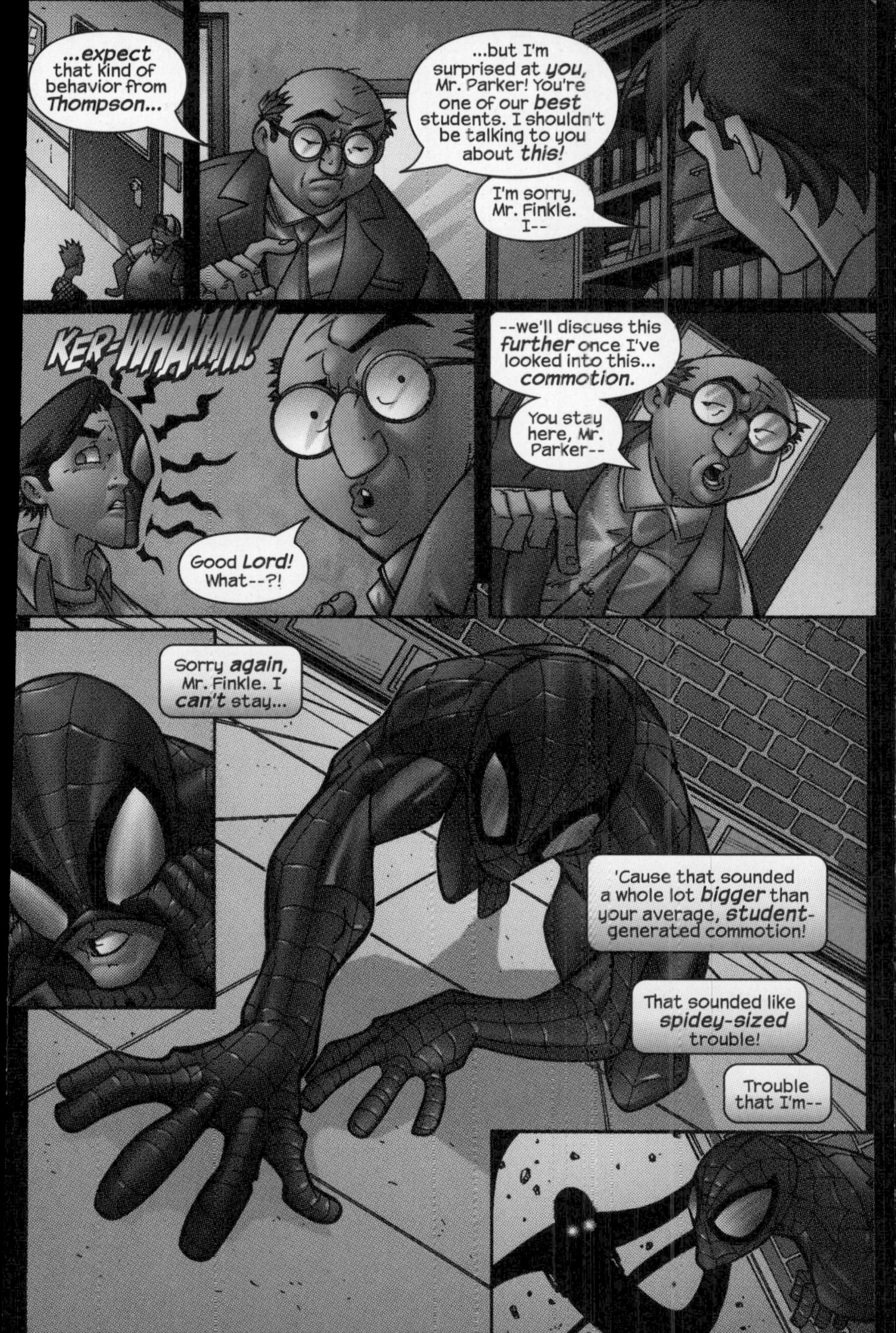
...expect that kind of behavior from Thompson...
...but I'm surprised at you, Mr. Parker! You're one of our best students. I shouldn't be talking to you about this!
I'm sorry, Mr. Finkle. I--
KER-WHAMM!
Good Lord! What--?!
--we'll discuss this further once I've looked into this... commotion.
You stay here, Mr. Parker--
Sorry again, Mr. Finkle. I can't stay...
'Cause that sounded a whole lot bigger than your average, student-generated commotion!
That sounded like spidey-sized trouble!
Trouble that I'm--

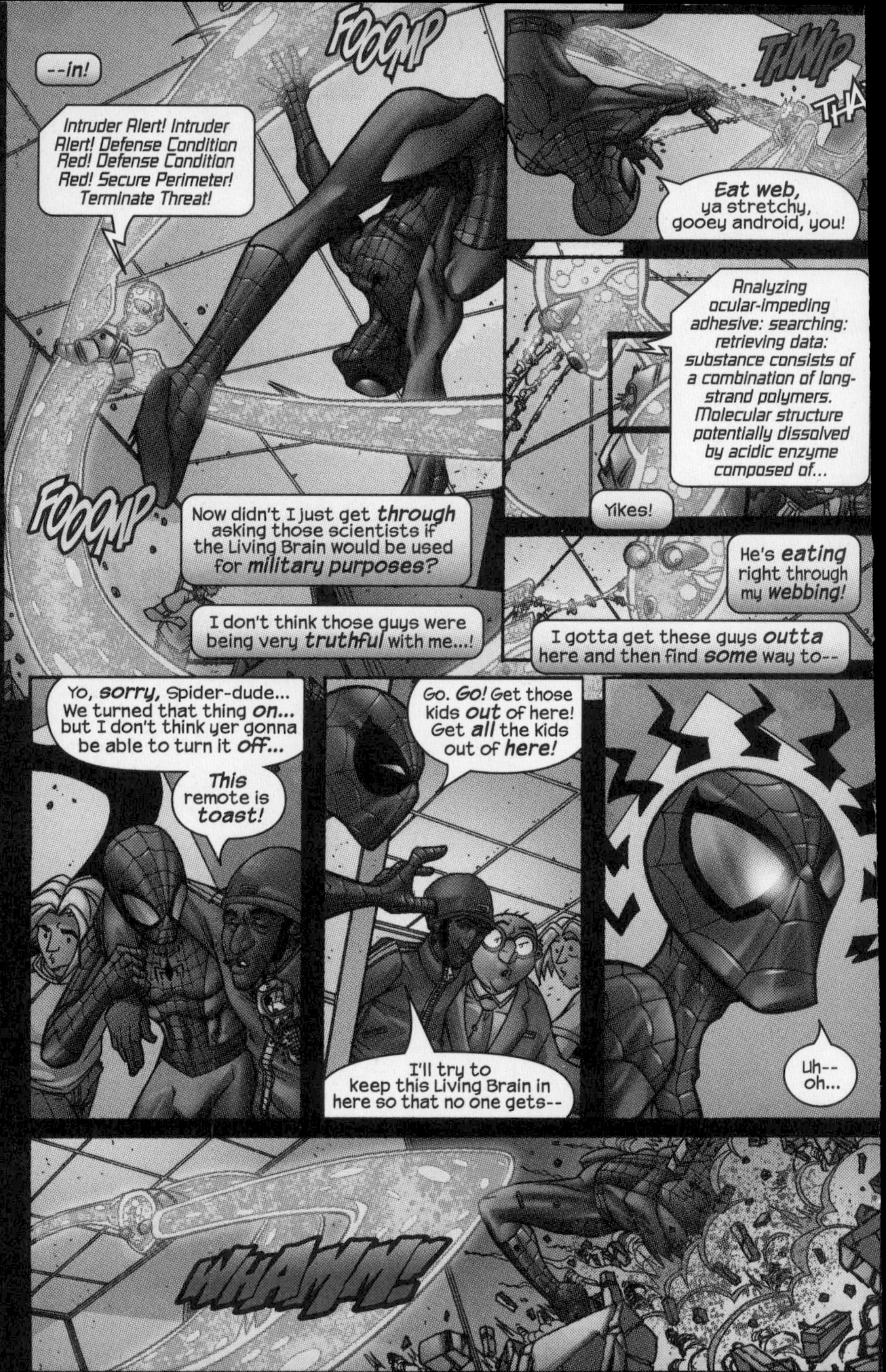
FOOOMP
--in!
Intruder Alert! Intruder Alert! Defense Condition Red! Defense Condition Red! Secure Perimeter! Terminate Threat!
FOOOMP
Now didn't I just get through asking those scientists if the Living Brain would be used for military purposes?
I don't think those guys were being very truthful with me...!
THWIP
THA
Eat web, ya stretchy, gooey android, you!
Analyzing ocular-impeding adhesive: searching: retrieving data: substance consists of a combination of long-strand polymers. Molecular structure potentially dissolved by acidic enzyme composed of...
Yikes!
He's eating right through my webbing!
I gotta get these guys outta here and then find some way to--
Yo, sorry, Spider-dude... We turned that thing on... but I don't think yer gonna be able to turn it off...
This remote is toast!
Go. Go! Get those kids out of here! Get all the kids out of here!
I'll try to keep this Living Brain in here so that no one gets--
Uh-- oh...
WHAMM!

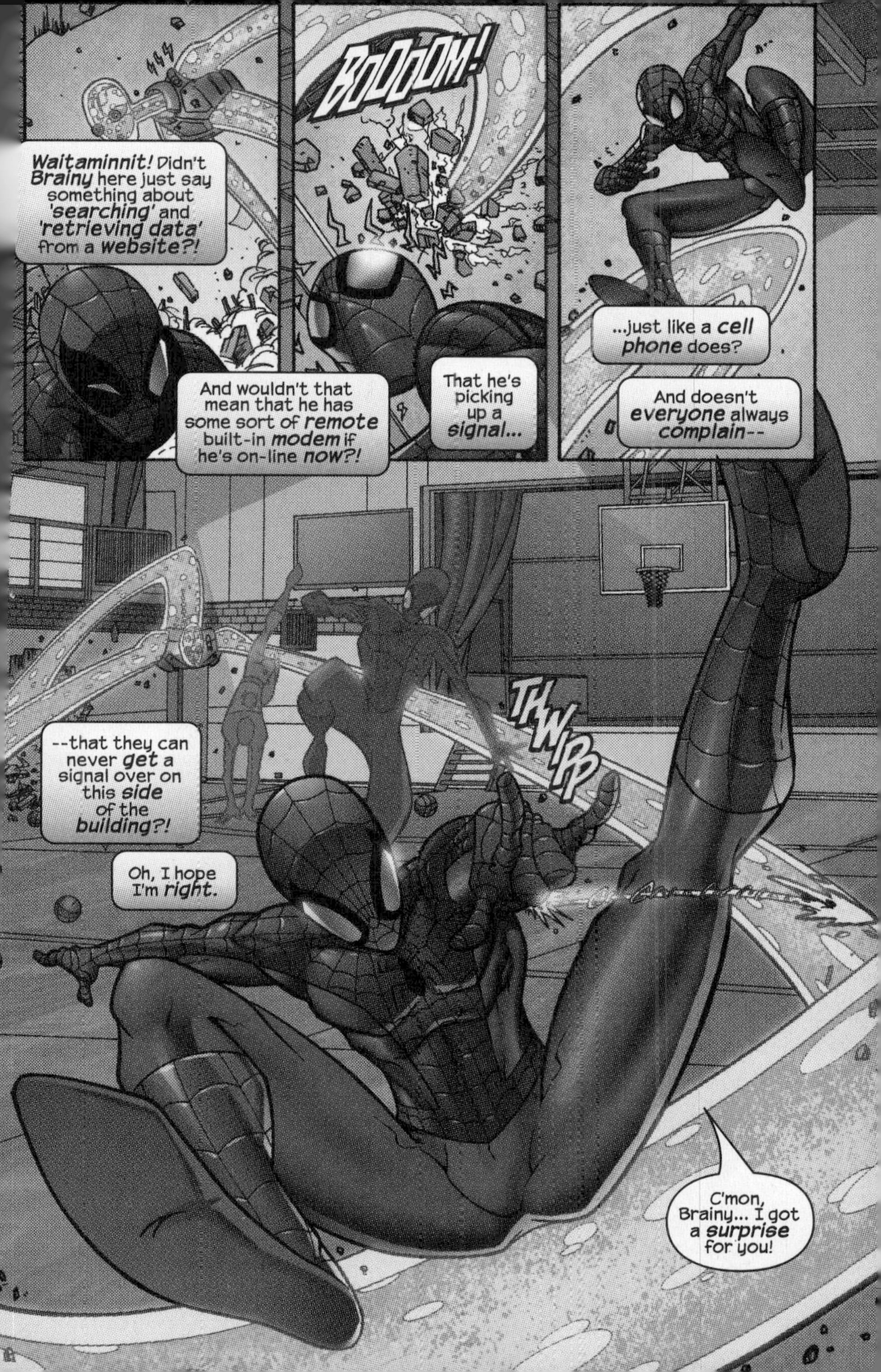

Waitaminnit! Didn't Brainy here just say something about 'searching' and 'retrieving data' from a website?!
BOOOOOM!
And wouldn't that mean that he has some sort of remote built-in modem if he's on-line now?!
That he's picking up a signal...
...just like a cell phone does?
And doesn't everyone always complain--
--that they can never get a signal over on this side of the building?!
Oh, I hope I'm right.
THWIPP
C'mon, Brainy... I got a surprise for you!

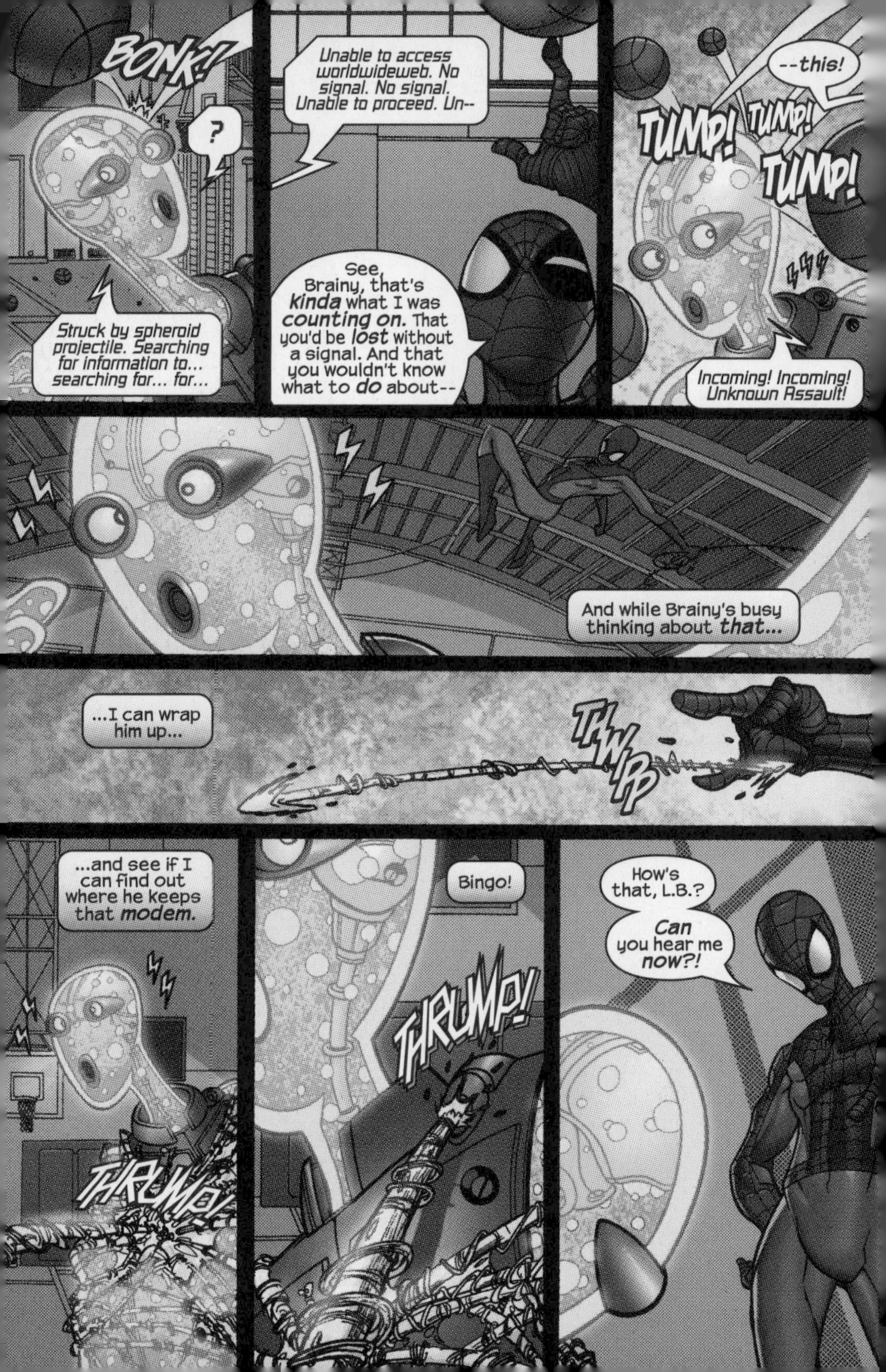
BONK?!
?
Struck by spheroid projectile. Searching for information to... searching for... for...
Unable to access worldwideweb. No signal. No signal. Unable to proceed. Un--
See, Brainy, that's kinda what I was counting on. That you'd be lost without a signal. And that you wouldn't know what to do about--
--this!
TUMP! TUMP! TUMP!
Incoming! Incoming! Unknown Assault!
And while Brainy's busy thinking about that...
...I can wrap him up...
THWIP
...and see if I can find out where he keeps that modem.
THRUMP!
Bingo!
THRUMP!
How's that, L.B.?
Can you hear me now?!

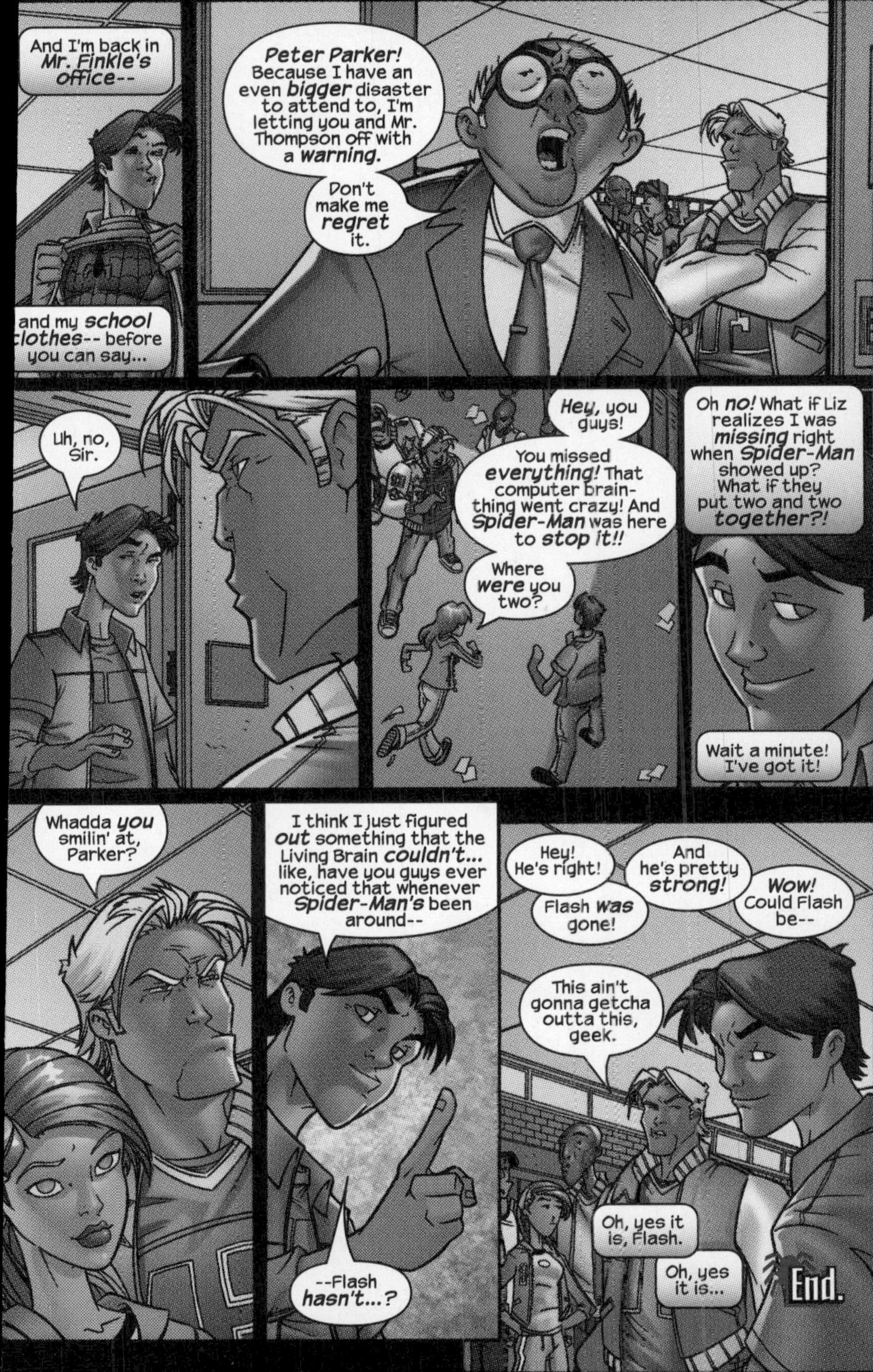
And I'm back in Mr. Finkle's office--
and my school clothes-- before you can say...
Peter Parker! Because I have an even bigger disaster to attend to, I'm letting you and Mr. Thompson off with a warning.
Don't make me regret it.
Uh, no, Sir.
Hey, you guys!
You missed everything! That computer brain-thing went crazy! And Spider-Man was here to stop it!!
Where were you two?
Oh no! What if Liz realizes I was missing right when Spider-Man showed up? What if they put two and two together?!
Wait a minute! I've got it!
Whadda you smilin' at, Parker?
I think I just figured out something that the Living Brain couldn't... like, have you guys ever noticed that whenever Spider-Man's been around--
--Flash hasn't...?
Hey! He's right!
Flash was gone!
And he's pretty strong!
Wow! Could Flash be--
This ain't gonna getcha outta this, geek.
Oh, yes it is, Flash.
Oh, yes it is...
End.

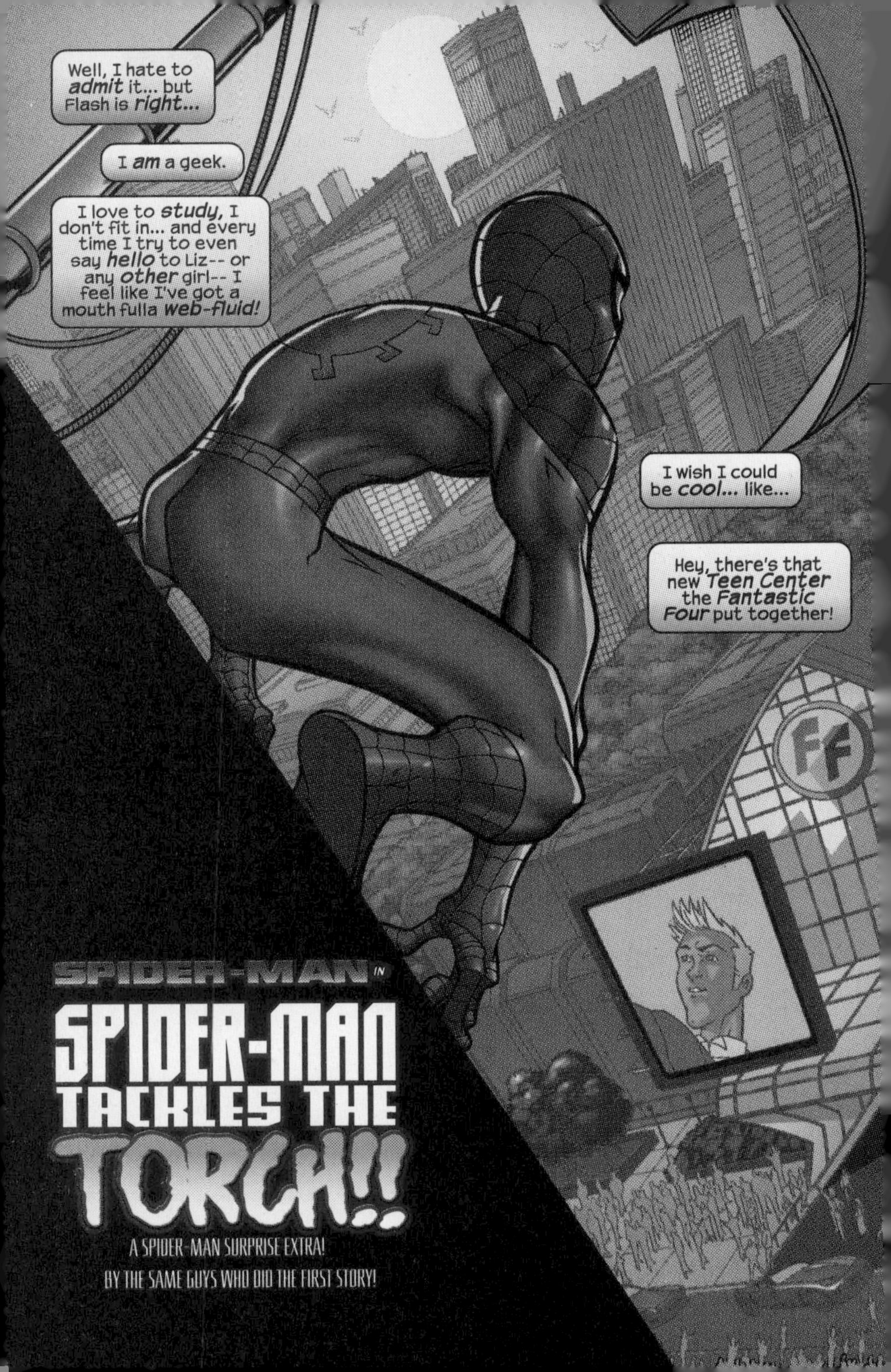

Well, I hate to admit it... but Flash is right...
I am a geek.
I love to study, I don't fit in... and every time I try to even say hello to Liz-- or any other girl-- I feel like I've got a mouth fulla web-fluid!
I wish I could be cool... like...
Hey, there's that new Teen Center the Fantastic Four put together!
FF
SPIDER-MAN IN
SPIDER-MAN TACKLES THE TORCH!!
A SPIDER-MAN SURPRISE EXTRA!
BY THE SAME GUYS WHO DID THE FIRST STORY!

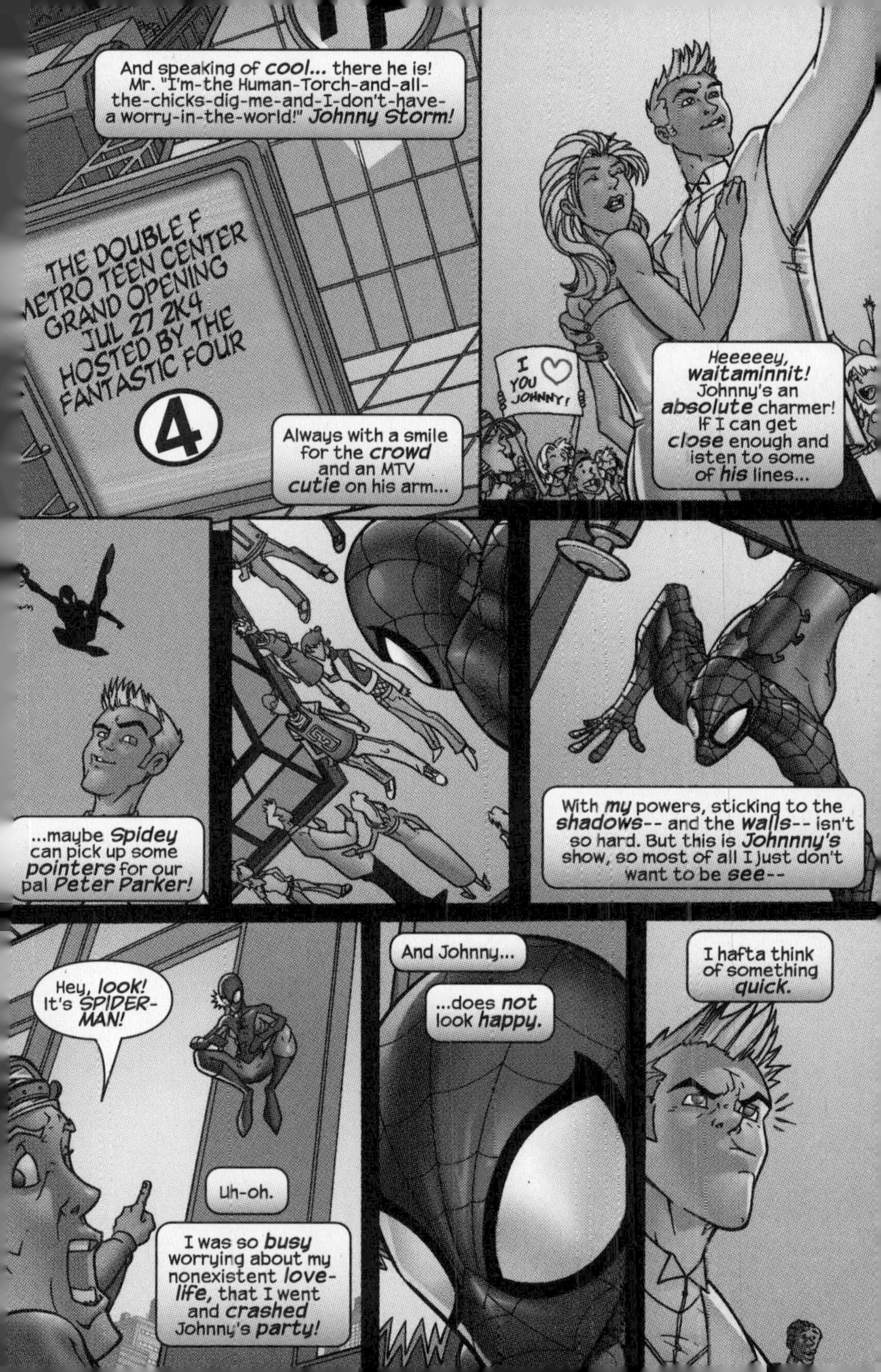

And speaking of cool... there he is! Mr. "I'm-the Human-Torch-and-all-the-chicks-dig-me-and-I-don't-have-a worry-in-the-world!" Johnny Storm!
THE DOUBLE F METRO TEEN CENTER GRAND OPENING JUL 27 2K4 HOSTED BY THE FANTASTIC FOUR
4
Always with a smile for the crowd and an MTV cutie on his arm...
I ♡ YOU JOHNNY!
Heeeeey, waitaminnit! Johnny's an absolute charmer! If I can get close enough and isten to some of his lines...
...maybe Spidey can pick up some pointers for our pal Peter Parker!
With my powers, sticking to the shadows-- and the walls-- isn't so hard. But this is Johnnny's show, so most of all I just don't want to be see--
Hey, look! It's SPIDER-MAN!
Uh-oh.
I was so busy worrying about my nonexistent love-life, that I went and crashed Johnny's party!
And Johnny...
...does not look happy.
I hafta think of something quick.

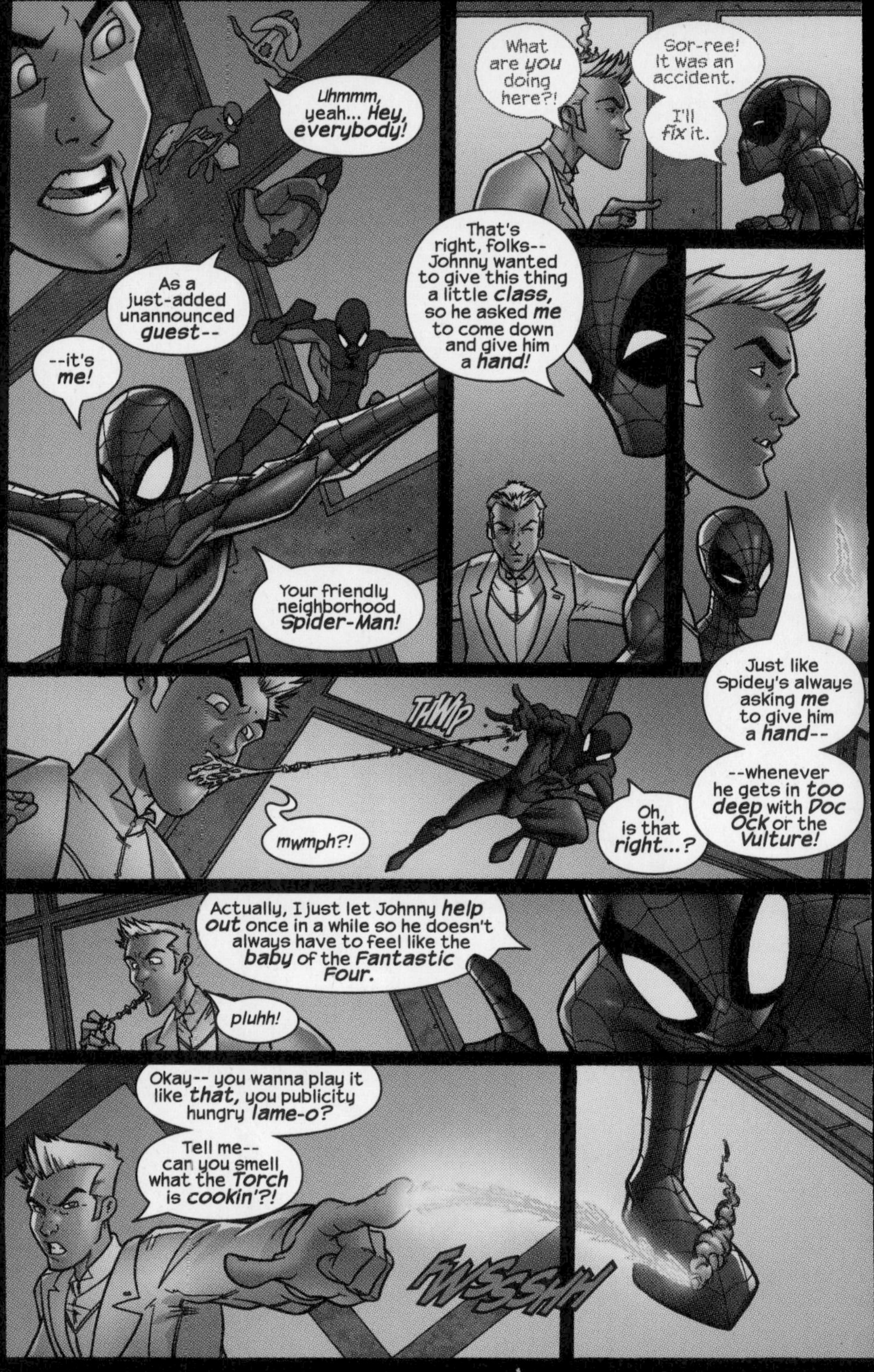

Uhmmm, yeah... Hey, everybody!
As a just-added unannounced guest--
--it's me!
Your friendly neighborhood Spider-Man!
What are you doing here?!
Sor-ree! It was an accident.
I'll fix it.
That's right, folks-- Johnny wanted to give this thing a little class, so he asked me to come down and give him a hand!
Just like Spidey's always asking me to give him a hand--
--whenever he gets in too deep with Doc Ock or the Vulture!
THWIP
mwmph?!
Oh, is that right...?
Actually, I just let Johnny help out once in a while so he doesn't always have to feel like the baby of the Fantastic Four.
pluhh!
Okay-- you wanna play it like that, you publicity hungry lame-o?
Tell me-- can you smell what the Torch is cookin'?!
FWSSSH

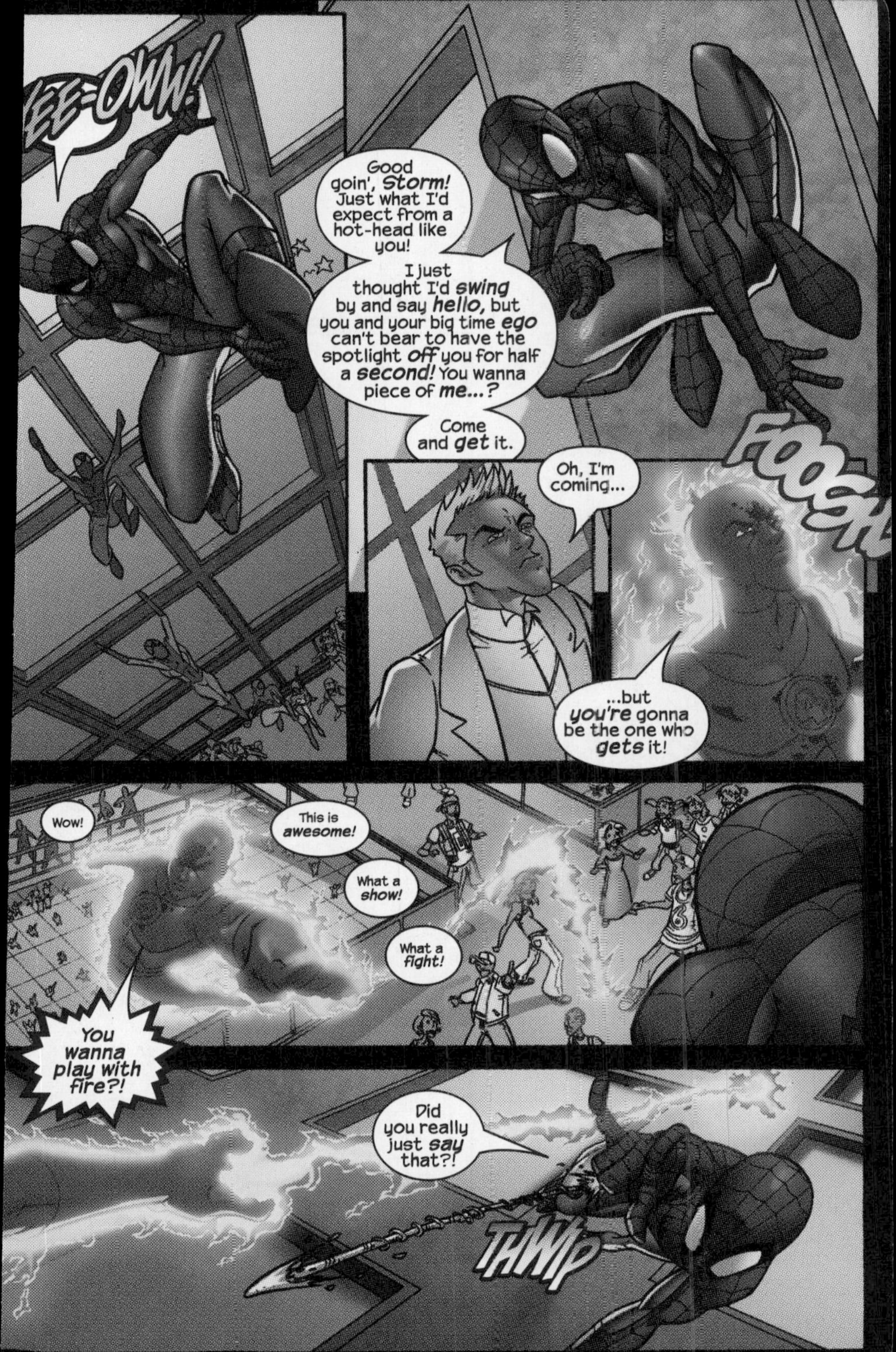

EE-OWW!
Good goin', Storm! Just what I'd expect from a hot-head like you!
I just thought I'd swing by and say hello, but you and your big time ego can't bear to have the spotlight off you for half a second! You wanna piece of me...?
Come and get it.
FOOSH
Oh, I'm coming...
...but you're gonna be the one who gets it!
Wow!
This is awesome!
What a show!
What a fight!
You wanna play with fire?!
Did you really just say that?!
THWIP

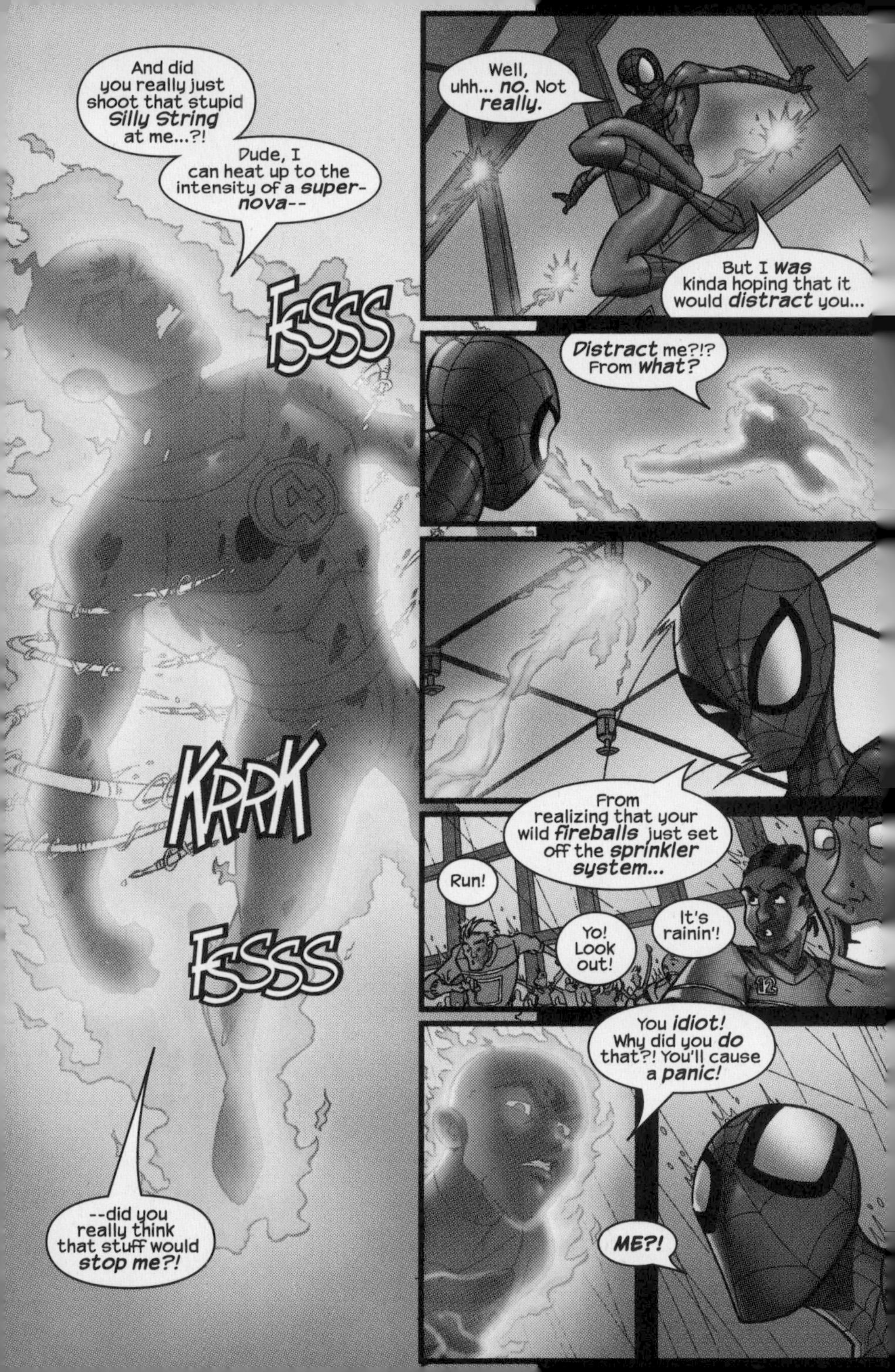

And did you really just shoot that stupid Silly String at me...?!
Dude, I can heat up to the intensity of a super-nova--
FSSSS
KRRK
FSSSS
--did you really think that stuff would stop me?!
Well, uhh... no. Not really.
But I was kinda hoping that it would distract you...
Distract me?!? From what?
From realizing that your wild fireballs just set off the sprinkler system...
Run!
Yo! Look out!
It's rainin'!
You idiot! Why did you do that?! You'll cause a panic!
ME?!

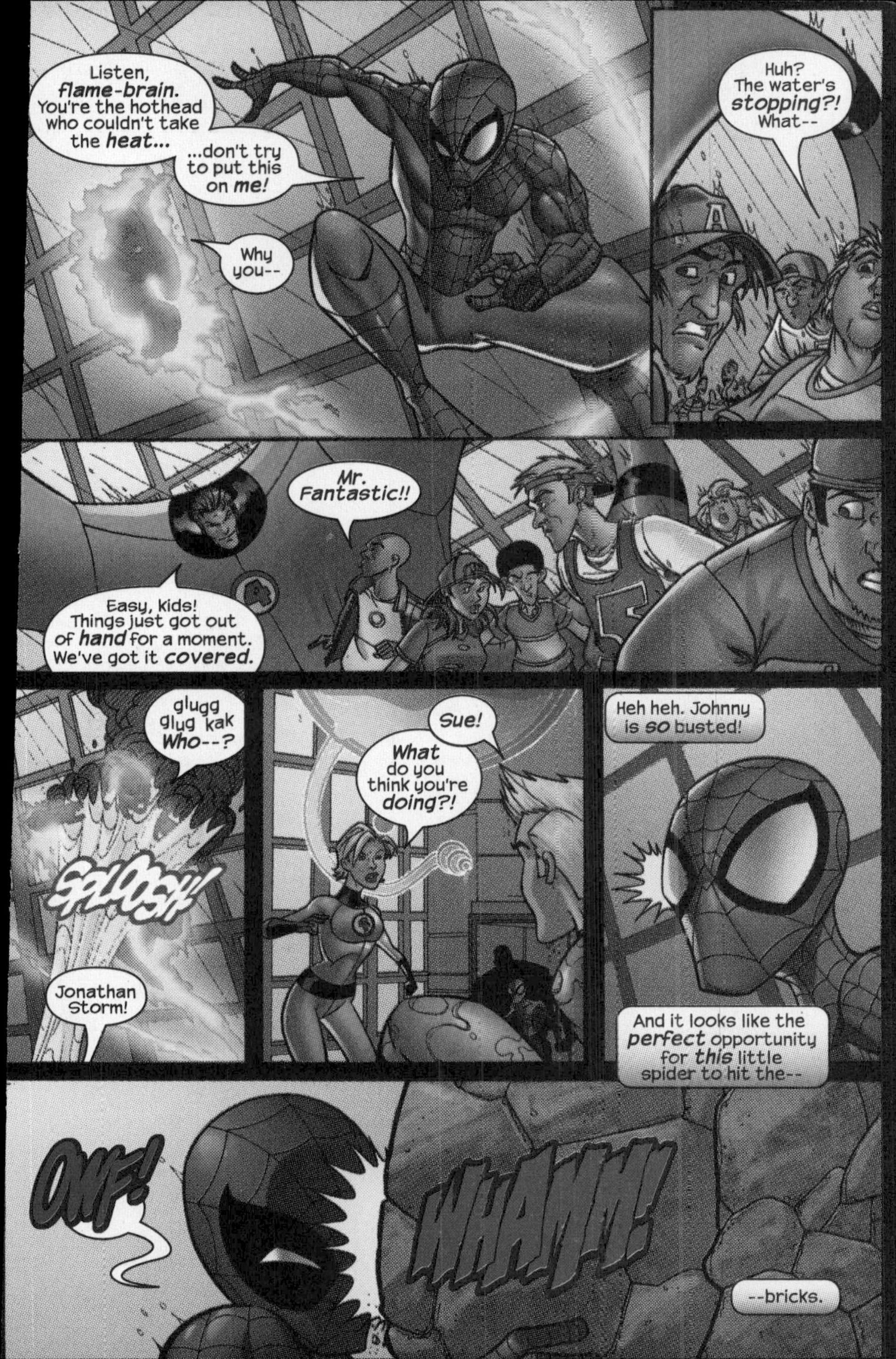
Listen, flame-brain. You're the hothead who couldn't take the heat...
...don't try to put this on me!
Why you--
Huh? The water's stopping?! What--
Mr. Fantastic!!
Easy, kids! Things just got out of hand for a moment. We've got it covered.
glugg glug kak Who--?
SPLOOSH!
Jonathan Storm!
Sue!
What do you think you're doing?!
Heh heh. Johnny is so busted!
And it looks like the perfect opportunity for this little spider to hit the--
OWF!
WHAMM!
--bricks.

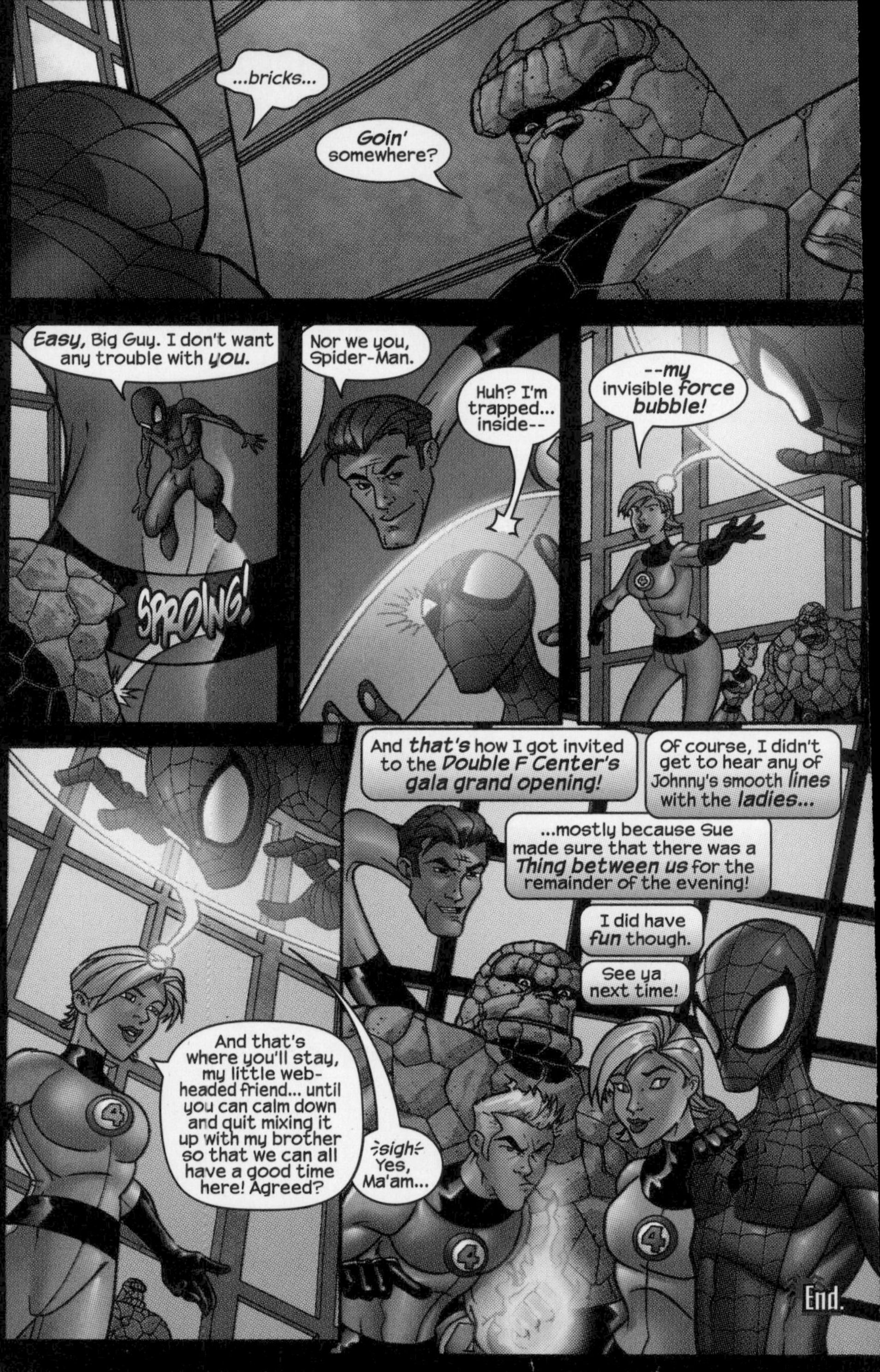

...bricks...
Goin' somewhere?
Easy, Big Guy. I don't want any trouble with you.
SPROING!
Nor we you, Spider-Man.
Huh? I'm trapped... inside--
--my invisible force bubble!
And that's where you'll stay, my little web-headed friend... until you can calm down and quit mixing it up with my brother so that we can all have a good time here! Agreed?
sigh Yes, Ma'am...
And that's how I got invited to the Double F Center's gala grand opening!
Of course, I didn't get to hear any of Johnny's smooth lines with the ladies...
...mostly because Sue made sure that there was a Thing between us for the remainder of the evening!
I did have fun though.
See ya next time!
End.

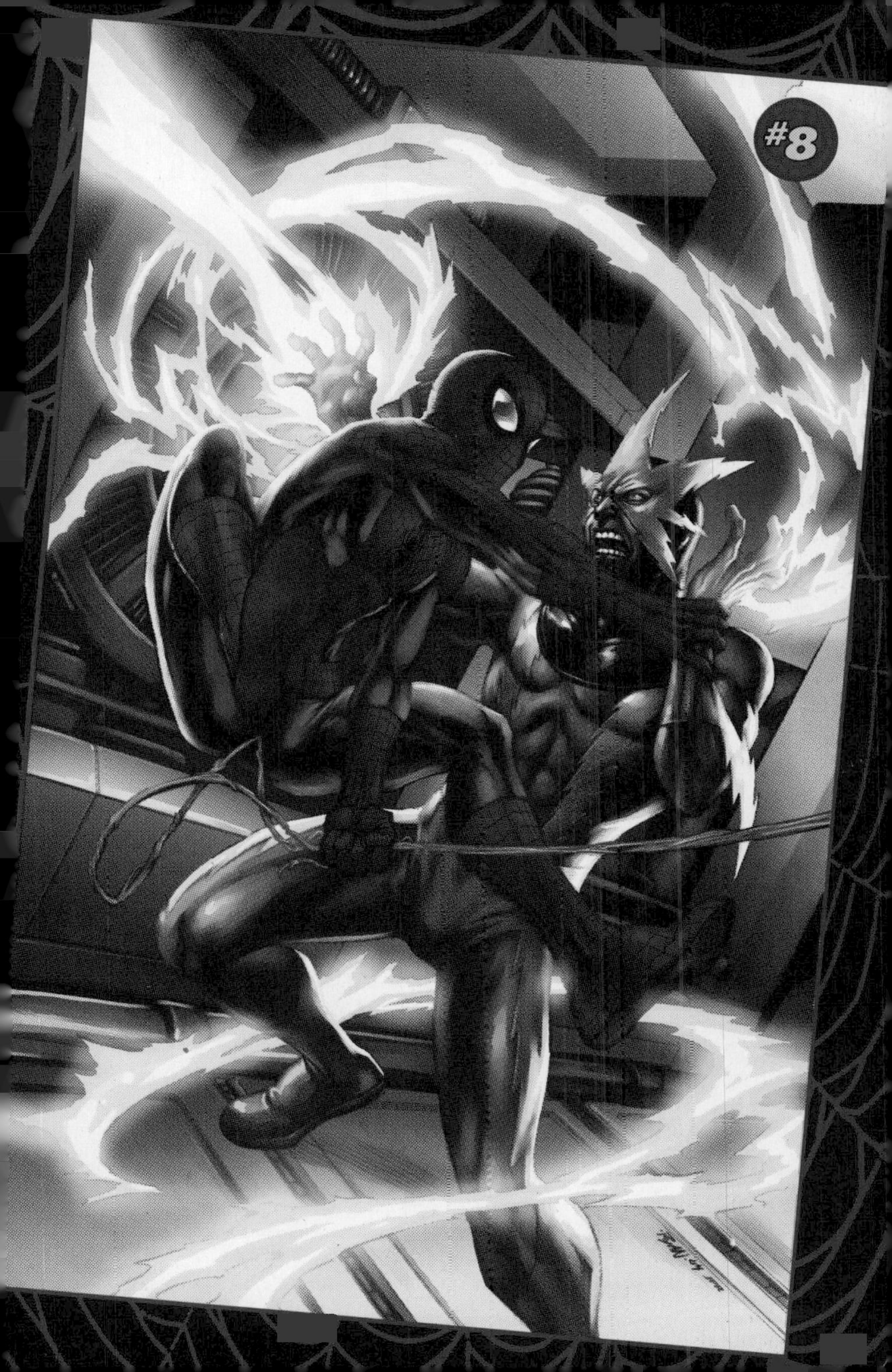
#8

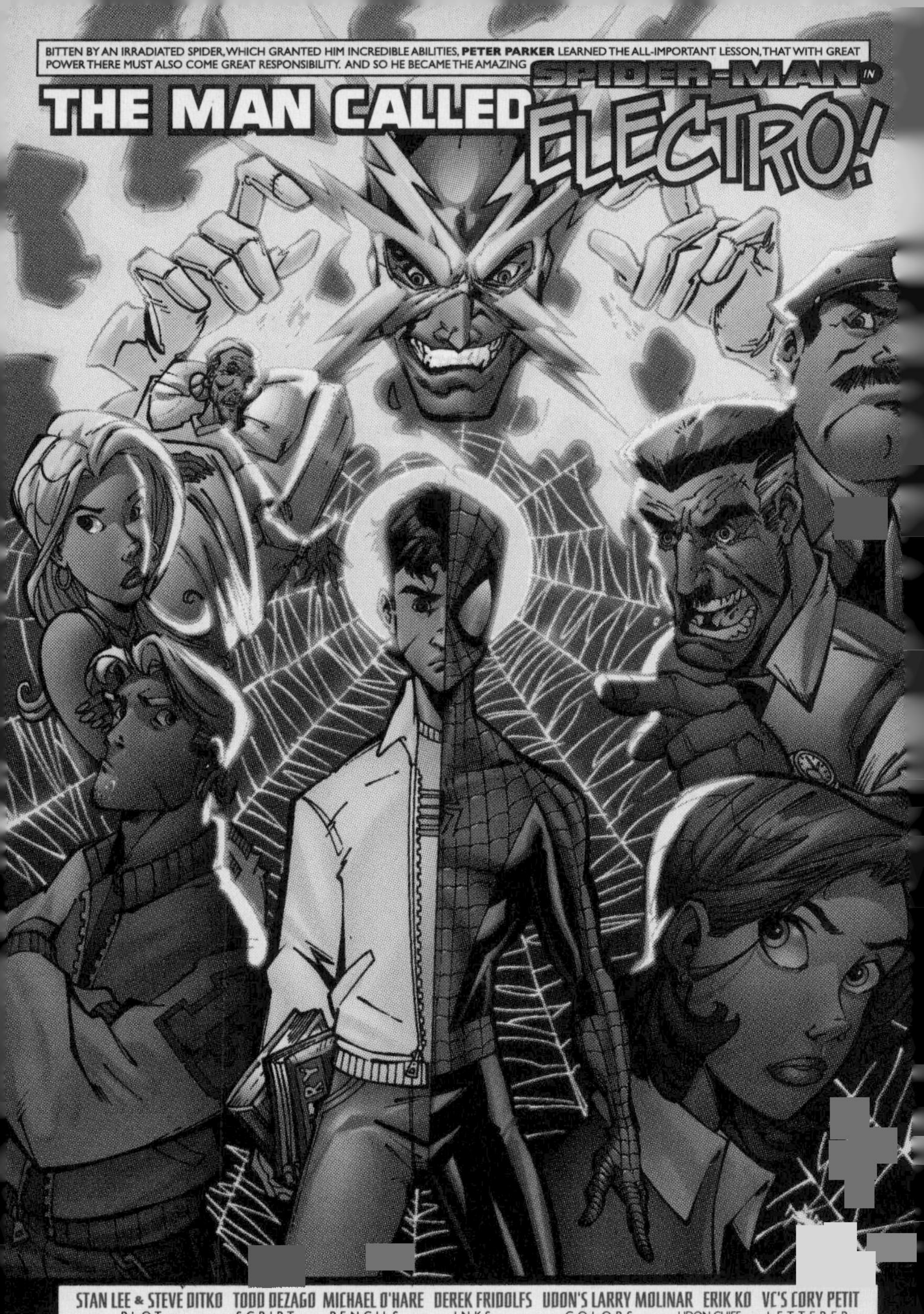
BITTEN BY AN IRRADIATED SPIDER, WHICH GRANTED HIM INCREDIBLE ABILITIES, PETER PARKER LEARNED THE ALL-IMPORTANT LESSON, THAT WITH GREAT POWER THERE MUST ALSO COME GREAT RESPONSIBILITY. AND SO HE BECAME THE AMAZING
SPIDER-MAN IN
THE MAN CALLED ELECTRO!

STAN LEE & STEVE DITKO PLOT · TODD DEZAGO SCRIPT · MICHAEL O'HARE PENCILS · DEREK FRIDOLFS INKS · UDON'S LARRY MOLINAR COLORS · ERIK KO UDON CHIEF · VC'S CORY PETIT LETTERER

MACKENZIE CADENHEAD ASSISTANT EDITOR · C.B. CEBULSKI EDITOR · RALPH MACCHIO CONSULTING EDITOR · JOE QUESADA EDITOR-IN-CHIEF · DAN BUCKLEY PUBLISHER

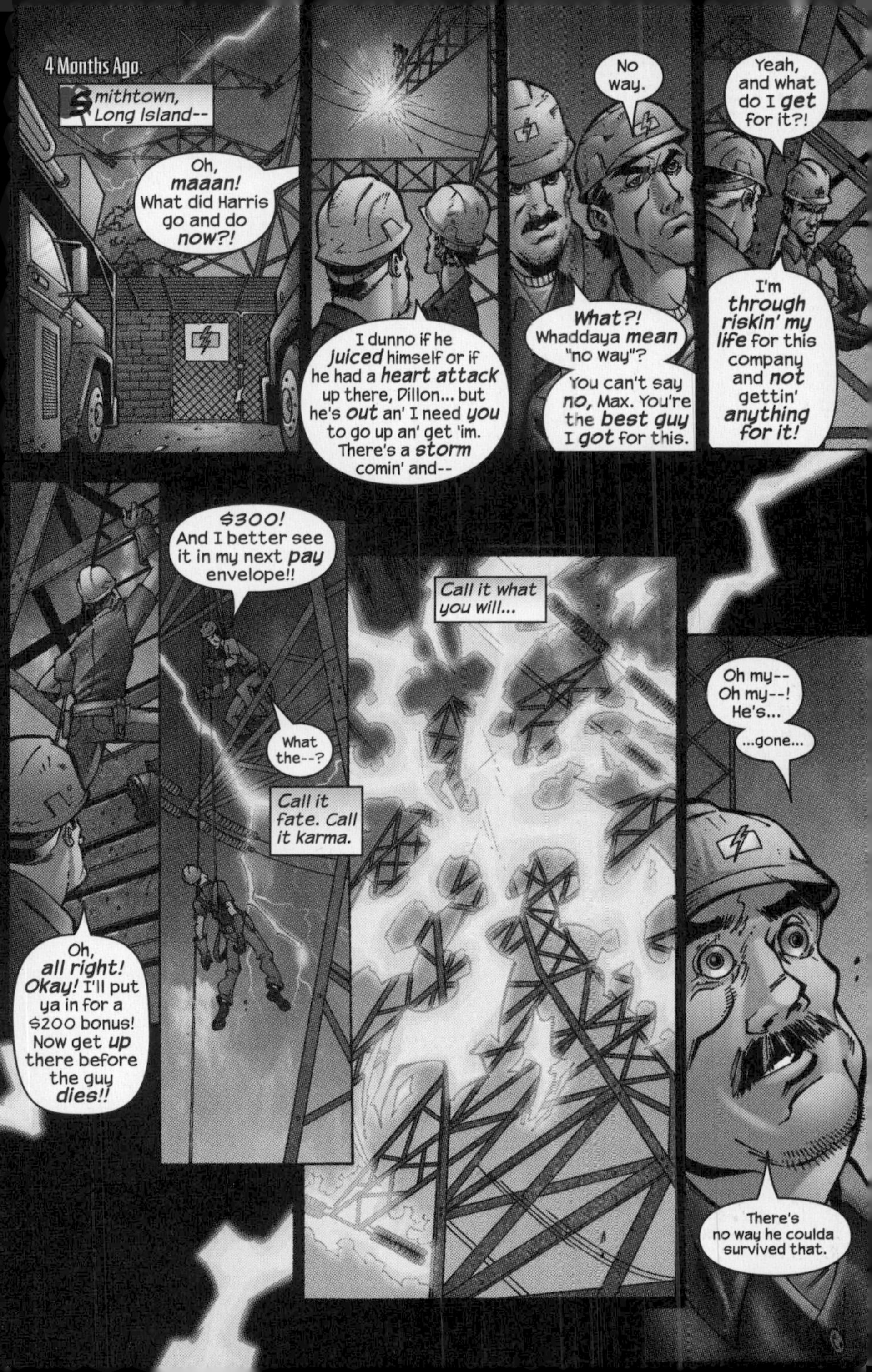
4 Months Ago.
Smithtown, Long Island--
Oh, maaan! What did Harris go and do now?!
I dunno if he juiced himself or if he had a heart attack up there, Dillon... but he's out an' I need you to go up an' get 'im. There's a storm comin' and--
No way.
What?! Whaddaya mean "no way"?
You can't say no, Max. You're the best guy I got for this.
Yeah, and what do I get for it?!
I'm through riskin' my life for this company and not gettin' anything for it!
Oh, all right! Okay! I'll put ya in for a $200 bonus! Now get up there before the guy dies!!
$300! And I better see it in my next pay envelope!!
What the--?
Call it fate. Call it karma.
Call it what you will...
Oh my-- Oh my--! He's...
...gone...
There's no way he coulda survived that.

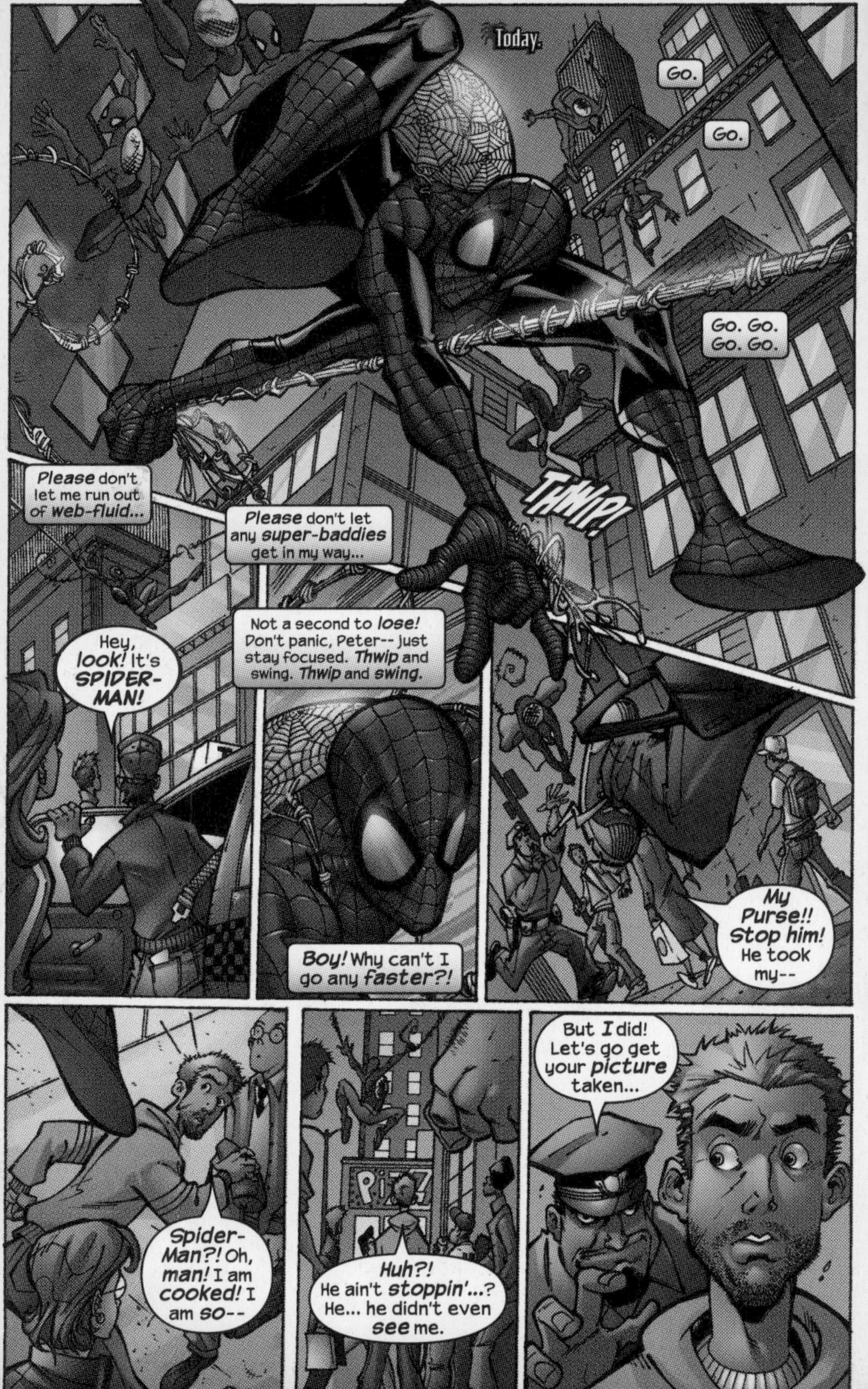
Today.
Go.
Go.
Go. Go. Go. Go.
Please don't let me run out of web-fluid...
Please don't let any super-baddies get in my way...
THWIP!
Hey, look! It's SPIDER-MAN!
Not a second to lose! Don't panic, Peter-- just stay focused. Thwip and swing. Thwip and swing.
Boy! Why can't I go any faster?!
My Purse!! Stop him! He took my--
Spider-Man?! Oh, man! I am cooked! I am so--
Huh?! He ain't stoppin'...? He... he didn't even see me.
But I did! Let's go get your picture taken...

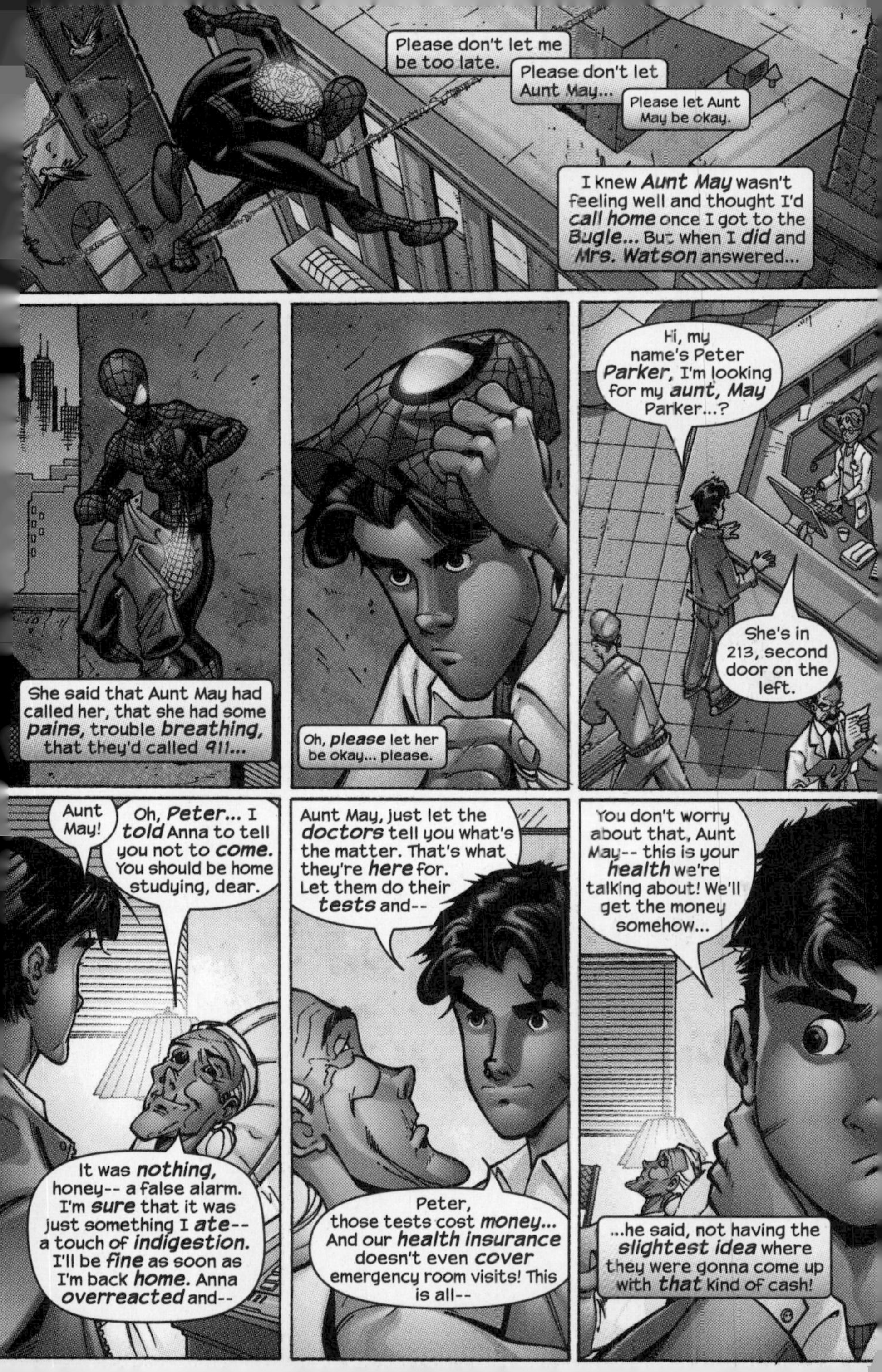
Please don't let me be too late.
Please don't let Aunt May...
Please let Aunt May be okay.
I knew Aunt May wasn't feeling well and thought I'd call home once I got to the Bugle... But when I did and Mrs. Watson answered...
She said that Aunt May had called her, that she had some pains, trouble breathing, that they'd called 911...
Oh, please let her be okay... please.
Hi, my name's Peter Parker, I'm looking for my aunt, May Parker...?
She's in 213, second door on the left.
Aunt May!
Oh, Peter... I told Anna to tell you not to come. You should be home studying, dear.
It was nothing, honey-- a false alarm. I'm sure that it was just something I ate-- a touch of indigestion. I'll be fine as soon as I'm back home. Anna overreacted and--
Aunt May, just let the doctors tell you what's the matter. That's what they're here for. Let them do their tests and--
Peter, those tests cost money... And our health insurance doesn't even cover emergency room visits! This is all--
You don't worry about that, Aunt May-- this is your health we're talking about! We'll get the money somehow...
...he said, not having the slightest idea where they were gonna come up with that kind of cash!

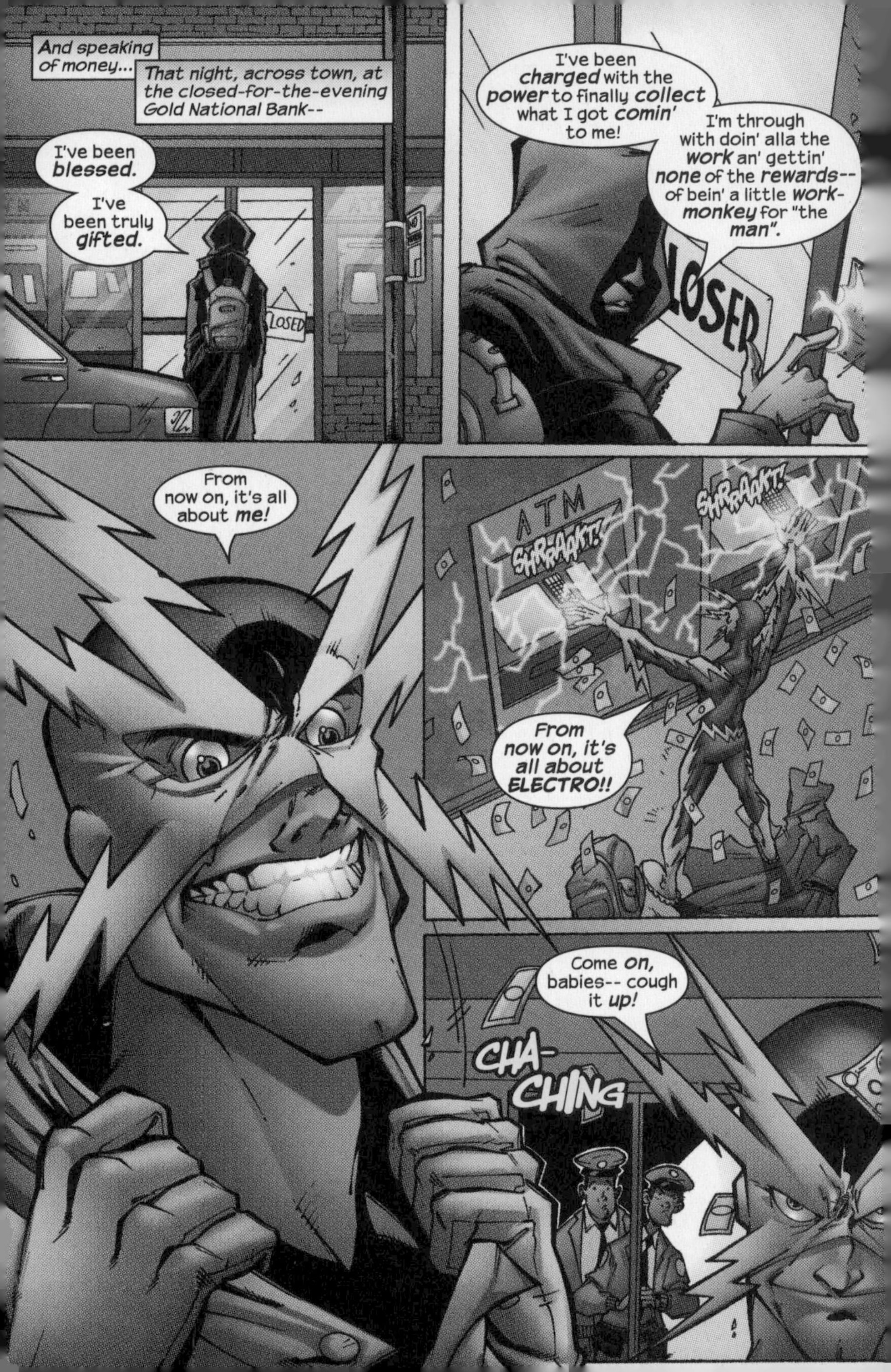
And speaking of money...
That night, across town, at the closed-for-the-evening Gold National Bank--
I've been blessed.
I've been truly gifted.
CLOSED
I've been charged with the power to finally collect what I got comin' to me!
I'm through with doin' alla the work an' gettin' none of the rewards-- of bein' a little work-monkey for "the man".
From now on, it's all about me!
ATM
SHRRAAKT!
SHRRAAKT!
From now on, it's all about ELECTRO!!
Come on, babies-- cough it up!
CHA-CHING

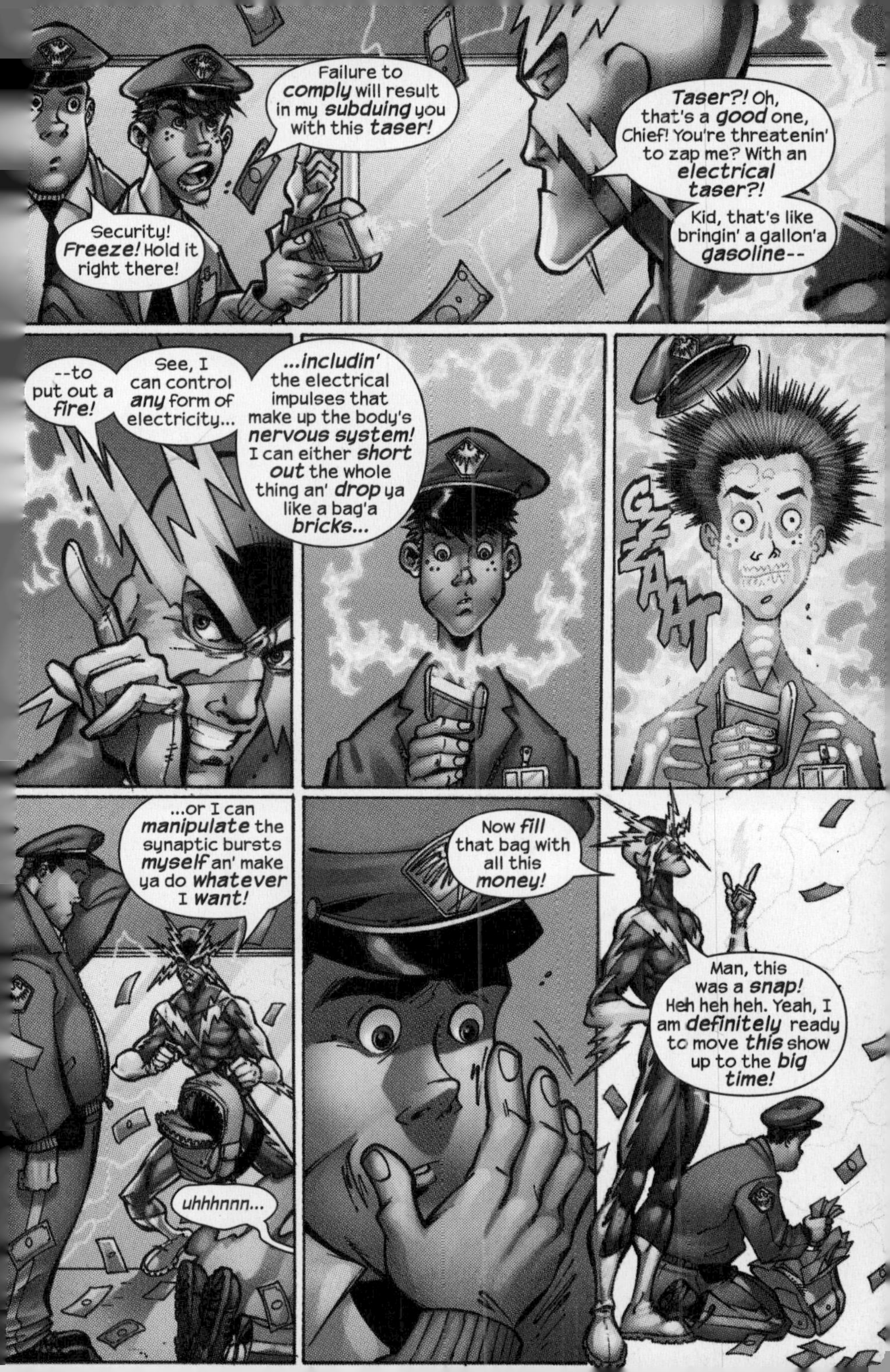
Failure to comply will result in my subduing you with this taser!
Security! Freeze! Hold it right there!
Taser?! Oh, that's a good one, Chief! You're threatenin' to zap me? With an electrical taser?!
Kid, that's like bringin' a gallon'a gasoline--
--to put out a fire!
See, I can control any form of electricity...
...includin' the electrical impulses that make up the body's nervous system! I can either short out the whole thing an' drop ya like a bag'a bricks...
GZZAAAT
...or I can manipulate the synaptic bursts myself an' make ya do whatever I want!
uhhhnnn...
Now fill that bag with all this money!
Man, this was a snap! Heh heh heh. Yeah, I am definitely ready to move this show up to the big time!

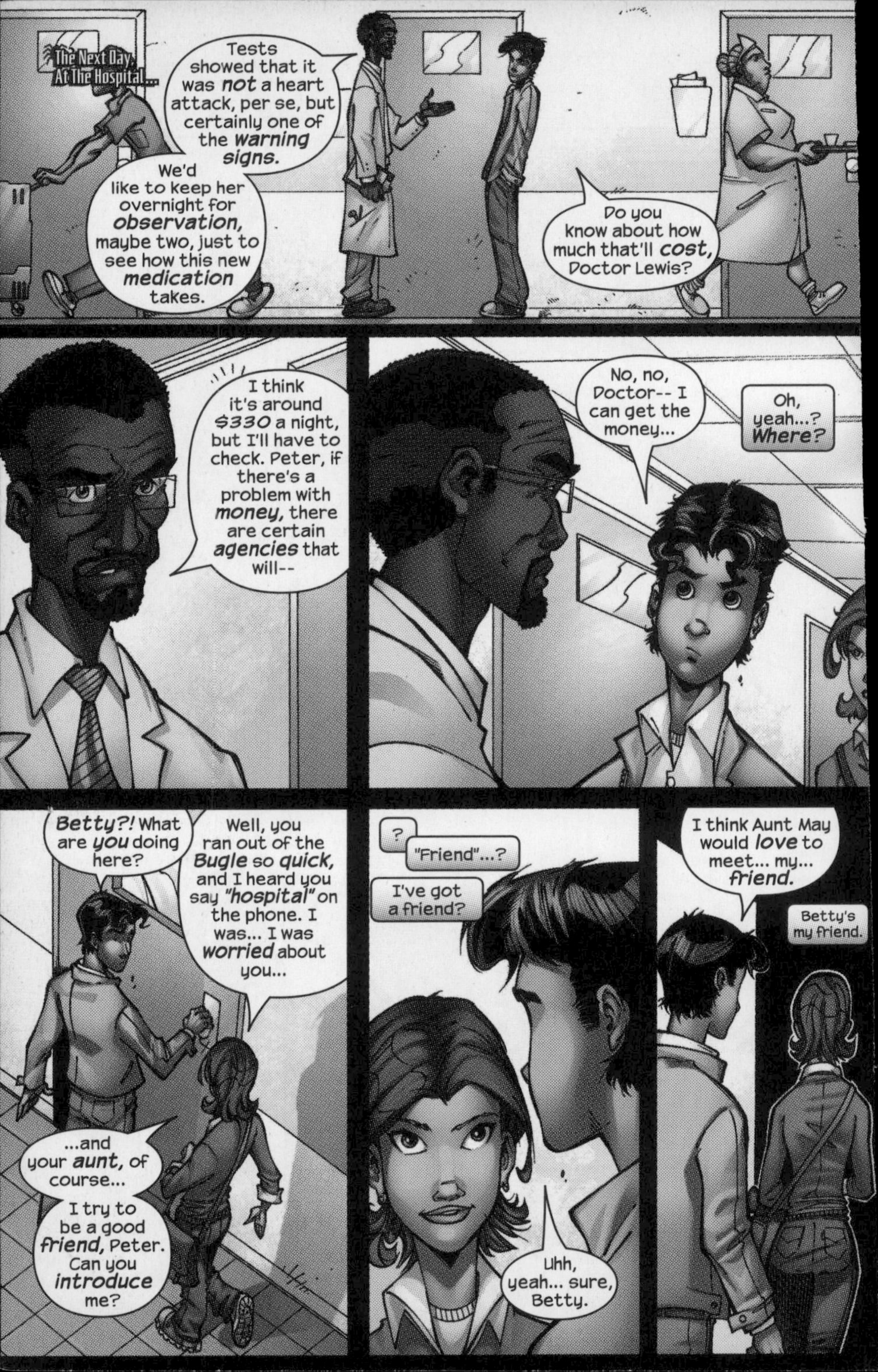
The Next Day, At The Hospital...
Tests showed that it was not a heart attack, per se, but certainly one of the warning signs.
We'd like to keep her overnight for observation, maybe two, just to see how this new medication takes.
Do you know about how much that'll cost, Doctor Lewis?
I think it's around $330 a night, but I'll have to check. Peter, if there's a problem with money, there are certain agencies that will--
No, no, Doctor-- I can get the money...
Oh, yeah...? Where?
Betty?! What are you doing here?
Well, you ran out of the Bugle so quick, and I heard you say "hospital" on the phone. I was... I was worried about you...
...and your aunt, of course...
I try to be a good friend, Peter. Can you introduce me?
?
"Friend"...?
I've got a friend?
Uhh, yeah... sure, Betty.
I think Aunt May would love to meet... my... friend.
Betty's my friend.

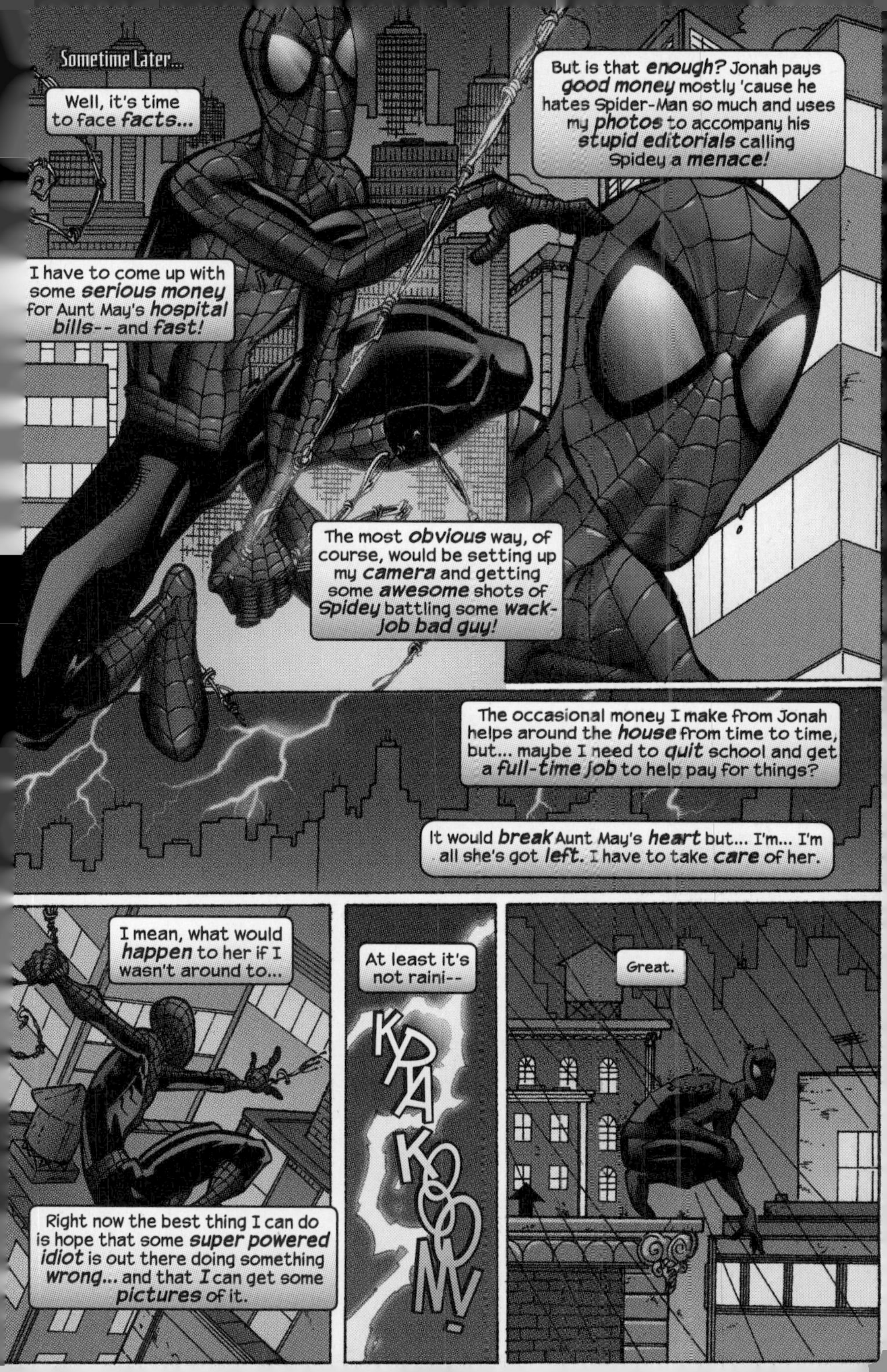
Sometime Later...
Well, it's time to face facts...
But is that enough? Jonah pays good money mostly 'cause he hates Spider-Man so much and uses my photos to accompany his stupid editorials calling Spidey a menace!
I have to come up with some serious money for Aunt May's hospital bills-- and fast!
The most obvious way, of course, would be setting up my camera and getting some awesome shots of Spidey battling some wack-job bad guy!
The occasional money I make from Jonah helps around the house from time to time, but... maybe I need to quit school and get a full-time job to help pay for things?
It would break Aunt May's heart but... I'm... I'm all she's got left. I have to take care of her.
I mean, what would happen to her if I wasn't around to...
Right now the best thing I can do is hope that some super powered idiot is out there doing something wrong... and that I can get some pictures of it.
At least it's not raini--
KRAKOOOM!
Great.

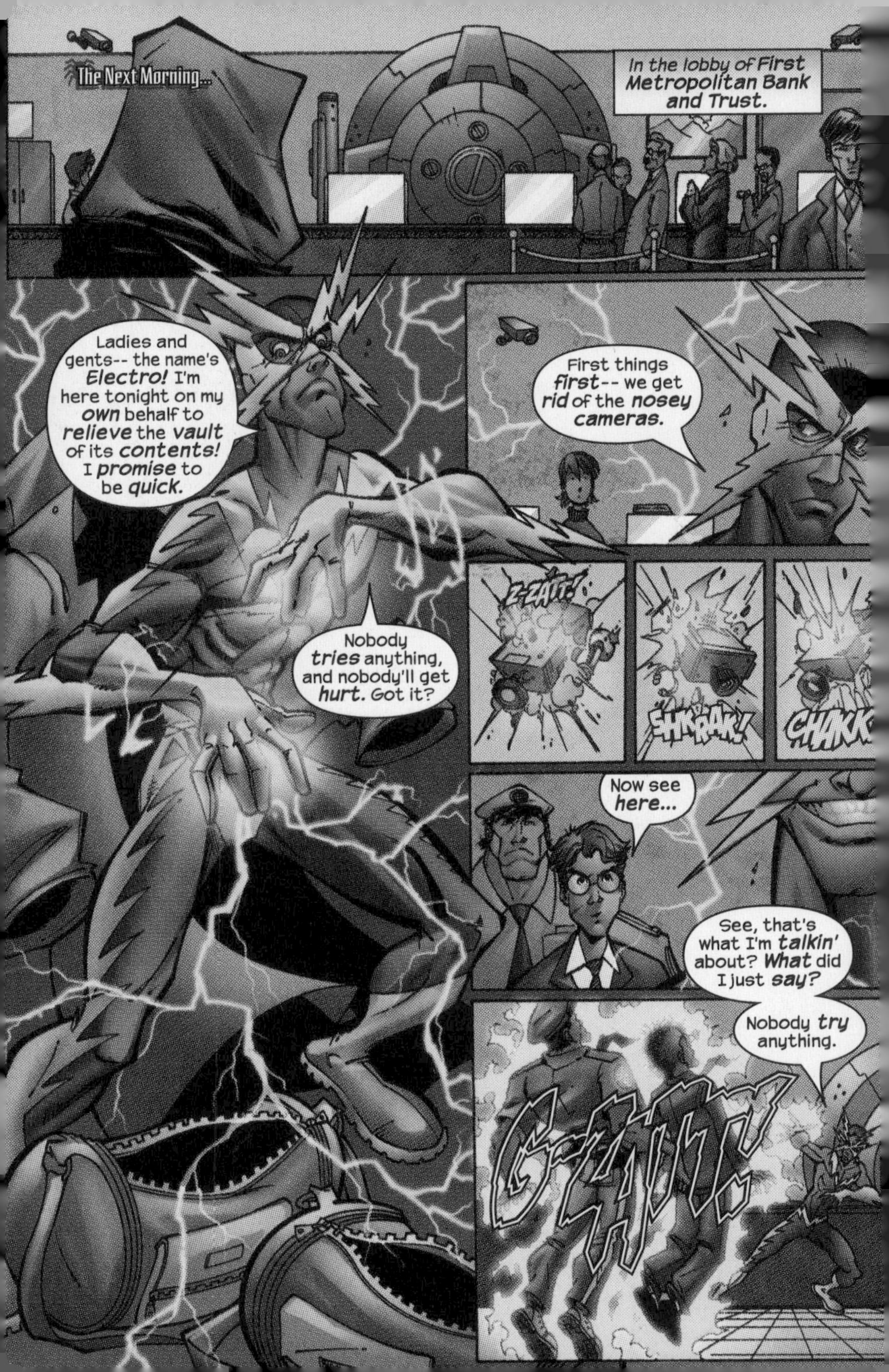
The Next Morning...
In the lobby of First Metropolitan Bank and Trust.
Ladies and gents-- the name's Electro! I'm here tonight on my own behalf to relieve the vault of its contents! I promise to be quick.
Nobody tries anything, and nobody'll get hurt. Got it?
First things first-- we get rid of the nosey cameras.
Z-ZAT!
SHKRAK!
Now see here...
See, that's what I'm talkin' about? What did I just say?
Nobody try anything.

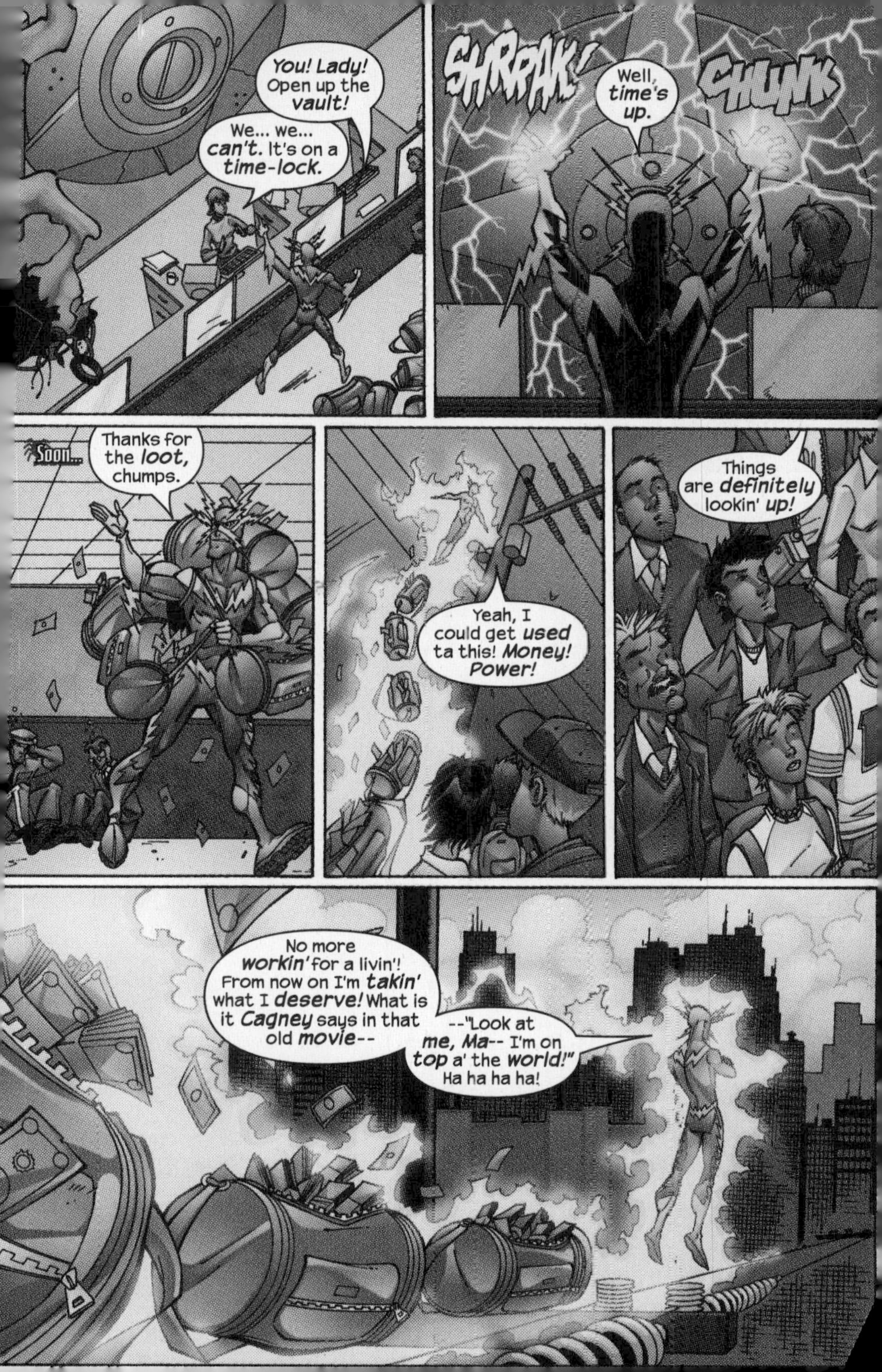
You! Lady! Open up the vault!
We... we... can't. It's on a time-lock.
SHRRAK!
Well, time's up.
CHUNK
Soon...
Thanks for the loot, chumps.
Yeah, I could get used ta this! Money! Power!
Things are definitely lookin' up!
No more workin' for a livin'! From now on I'm takin' what I deserve! What is it Cagney says in that old movie--
--"Look at me, Ma-- I'm on top a' the world!" Ha ha ha ha!

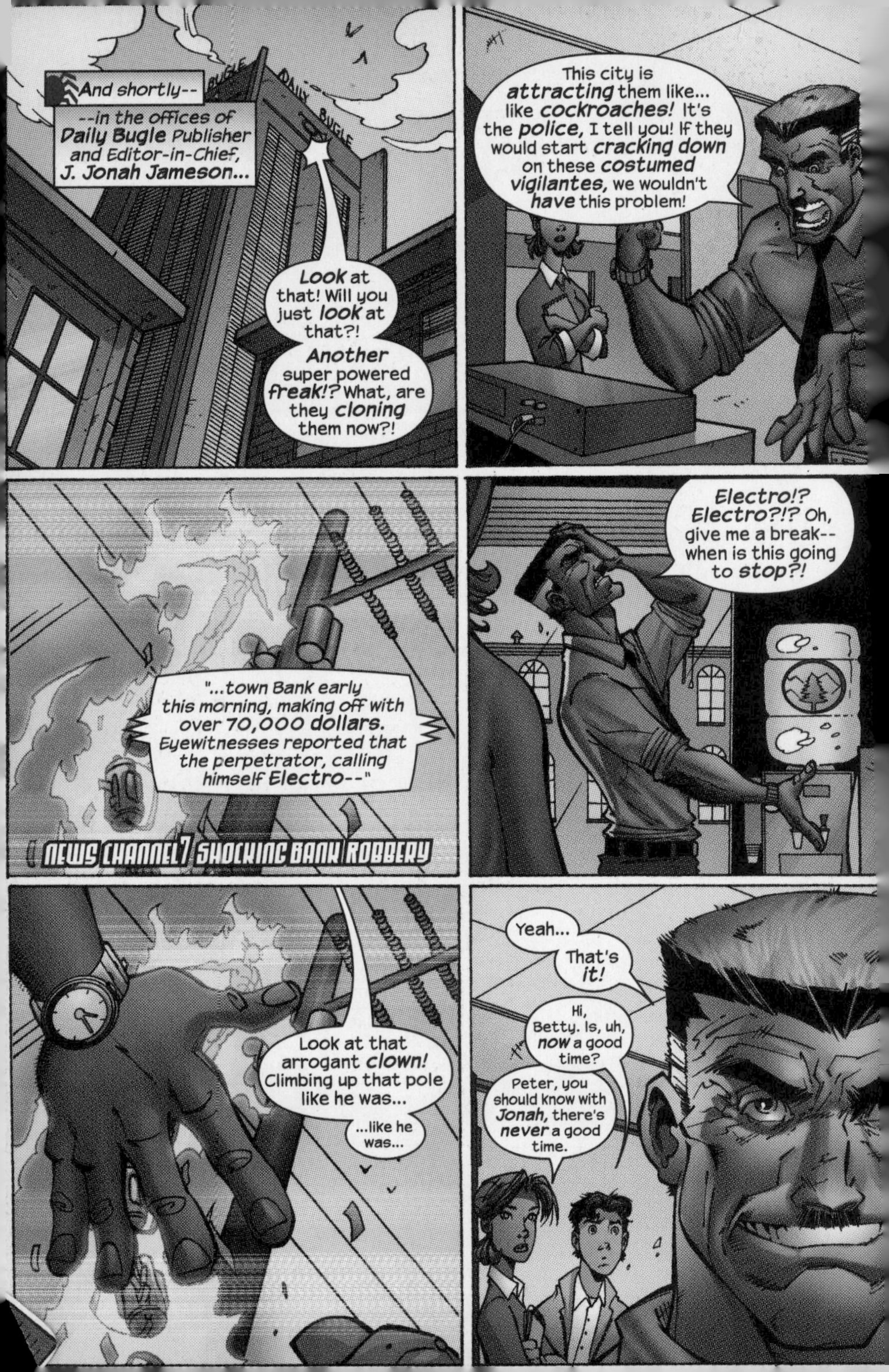

And shortly--
--in the offices of Daily Bugle Publisher and Editor-in-Chief, J. Jonah Jameson...
Look at that! Will you just look at that?!
Another super powered freak!? What, are they cloning them now?!
This city is attracting them like... like cockroaches! It's the police, I tell you! If they would start cracking down on these costumed vigilantes, we wouldn't have this problem!
"...town Bank early this morning, making off with over 70,000 dollars. Eyewitnesses reported that the perpetrator, calling himself Electro--"
NEWS CHANNEL 7 SHOCKING BANK ROBBERY
Electro!? Electro?!? Oh, give me a break--when is this going to stop?!
Look at that arrogant clown! Climbing up that pole like he was...
...like he was...
Yeah...
That's it!
Hi, Betty. Is, uh, now a good time?
Peter, you should know with Jonah, there's never a good time.

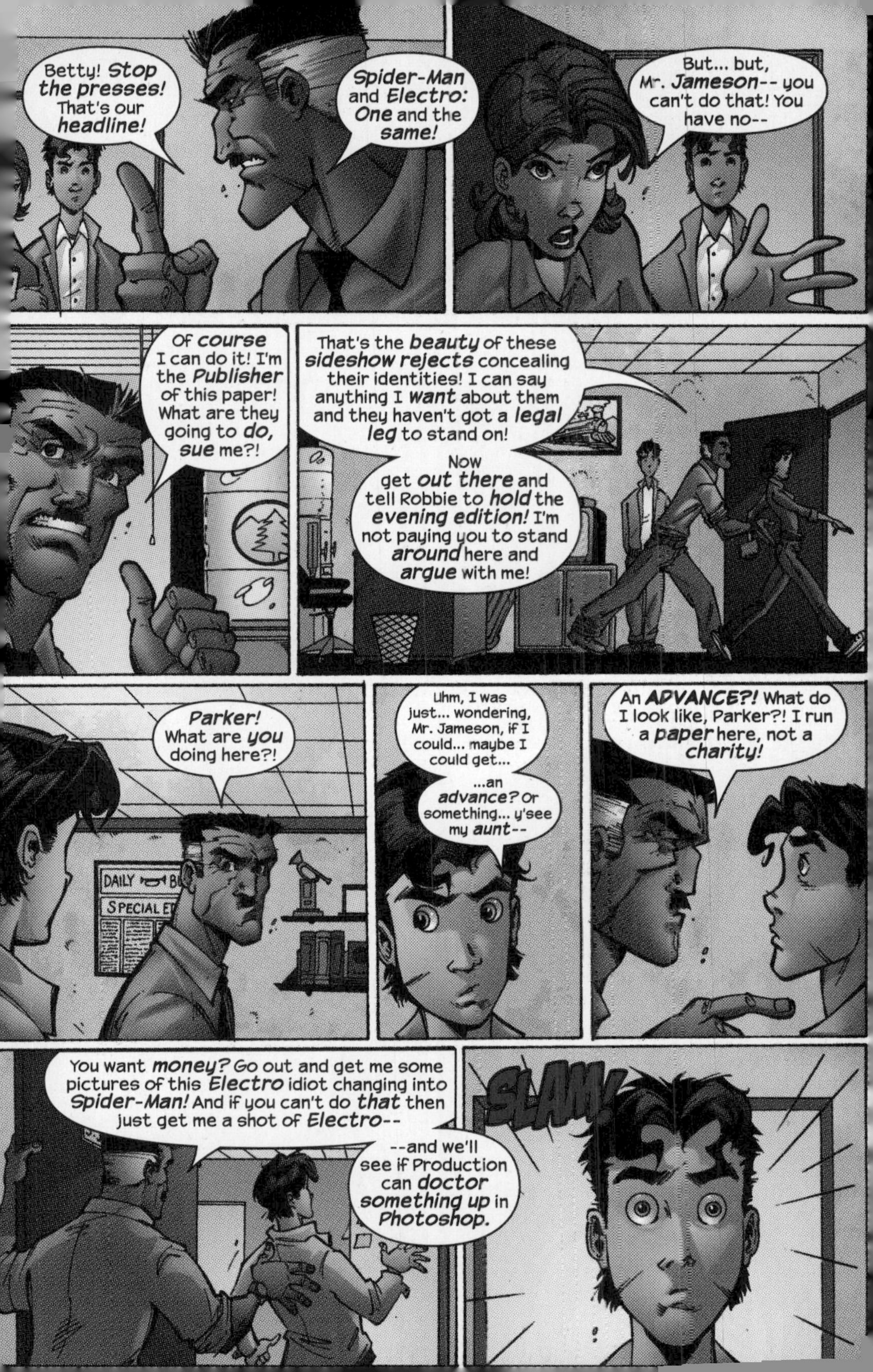
Betty! Stop the presses! That's our headline!
Spider-Man and Electro: One and the same!
But... but, Mr. Jameson-- you can't do that! You have no--
Of course I can do it! I'm the Publisher of this paper! What are they going to do, sue me?!
That's the beauty of these sideshow rejects concealing their identities! I can say anything I want about them and they haven't got a legal leg to stand on!
Now get out there and tell Robbie to hold the evening edition! I'm not paying you to stand around here and argue with me!
Parker! What are you doing here?!
DAILY BU
SPECIAL E
Uhm, I was just... wondering, Mr. Jameson, if I could... maybe I could get...
...an advance? Or something... y'see my aunt--
An ADVANCE?! What do I look like, Parker?! I run a paper here, not a charity!
You want money? Go out and get me some pictures of this Electro idiot changing into Spider-Man! And if you can't do that then just get me a shot of Electro--
--and we'll see if Production can doctor something up in Photoshop.
SLAM!

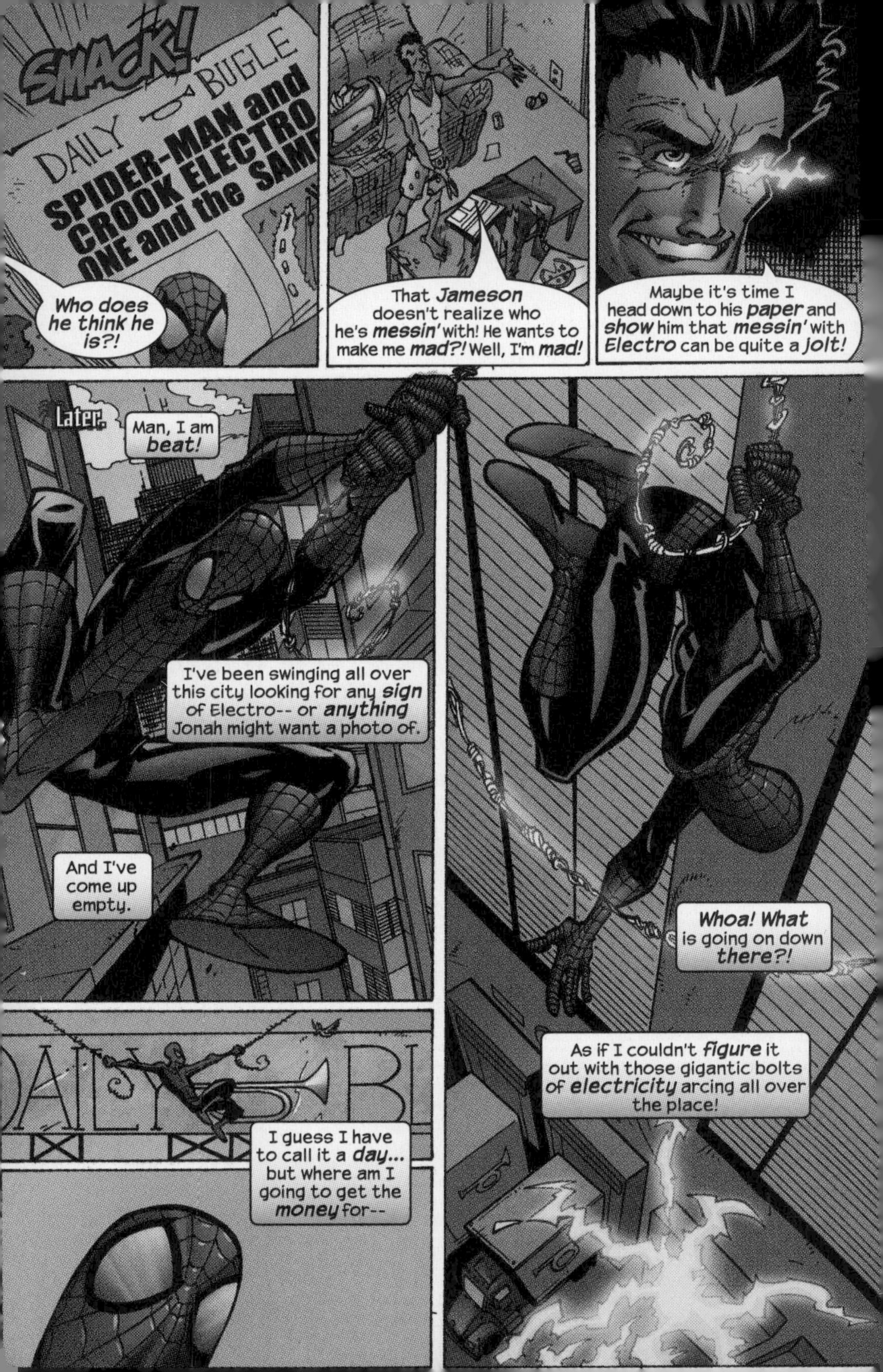
SMACK!
DAILY BUGLE
SPIDER-MAN and CROOK ELECTRO ONE and the SAM
Who does he think he is?!
That Jameson doesn't realize who he's messin' with! He wants to make me mad?! Well, I'm mad!
Maybe it's time I head down to his paper and show him that messin' with Electro can be quite a jolt!
Later.
Man, I am beat!
I've been swinging all over this city looking for any sign of Electro-- or anything Jonah might want a photo of.
And I've come up empty.
Whoa! What is going on down there?!
As if I couldn't figure it out with those gigantic bolts of electricity arcing all over the place!
I guess I have to call it a day... but where am I going to get the money for--

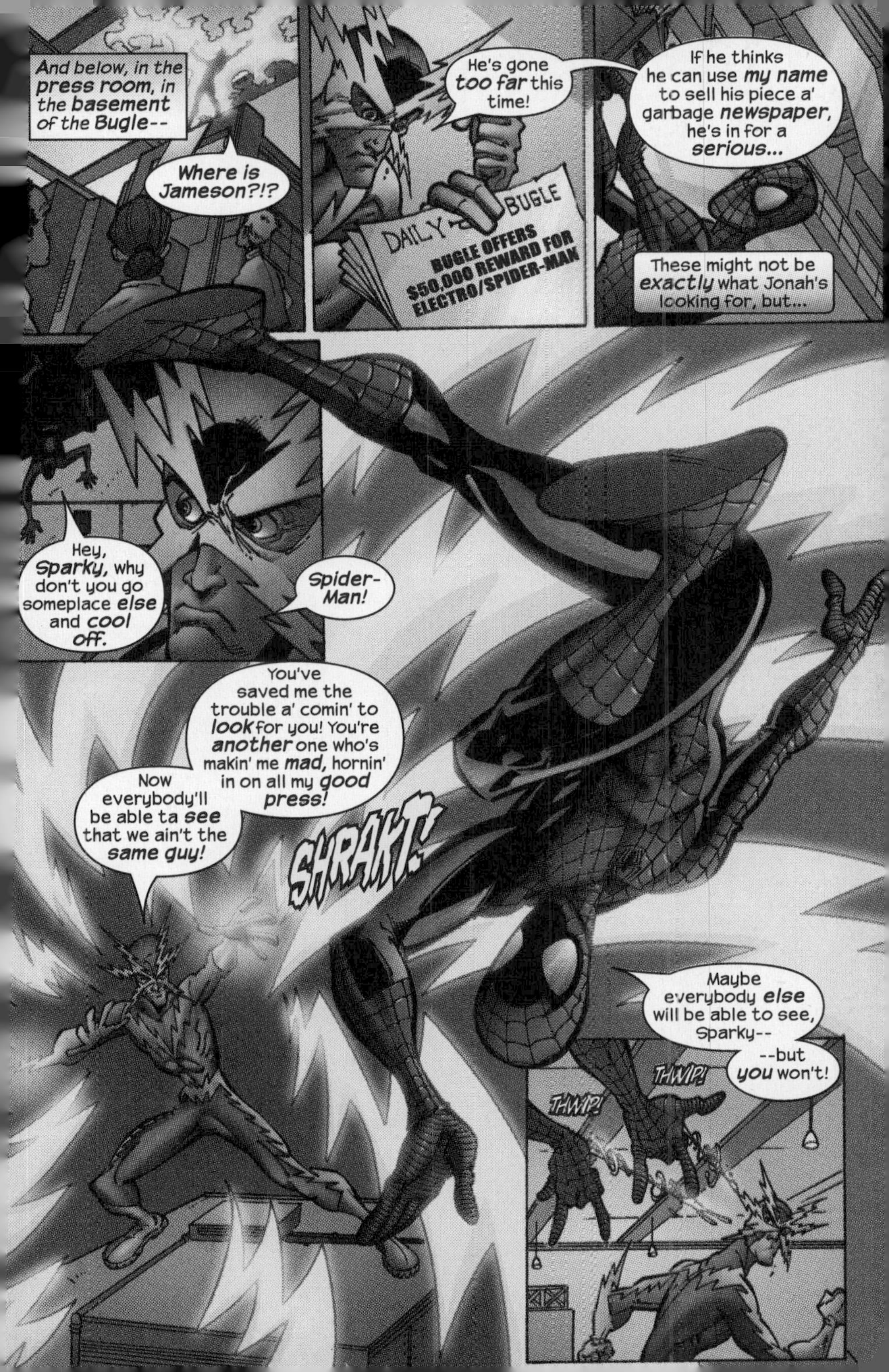

And below, in the press room, in the basement of the Bugle--
Where is Jameson?!?
He's gone too far this time!
DAILY BUGLE
BUGLE OFFERS $50,000 REWARD FOR ELECTRO/SPIDER-MAN
If he thinks he can use my name to sell his piece a' garbage newspaper, he's in for a serious...
These might not be exactly what Jonah's looking for, but...
Hey, Sparky, why don't you go someplace else and cool off.
Spider-Man!
You've saved me the trouble a' comin' to look for you! You're another one who's makin' me mad, hornin' in on all my good press!
Now everybody'll be able ta see that we ain't the same guy!
SHRAKT!
Maybe everybody else will be able to see, Sparky--
--but you won't!
THWIP!
THWIP!

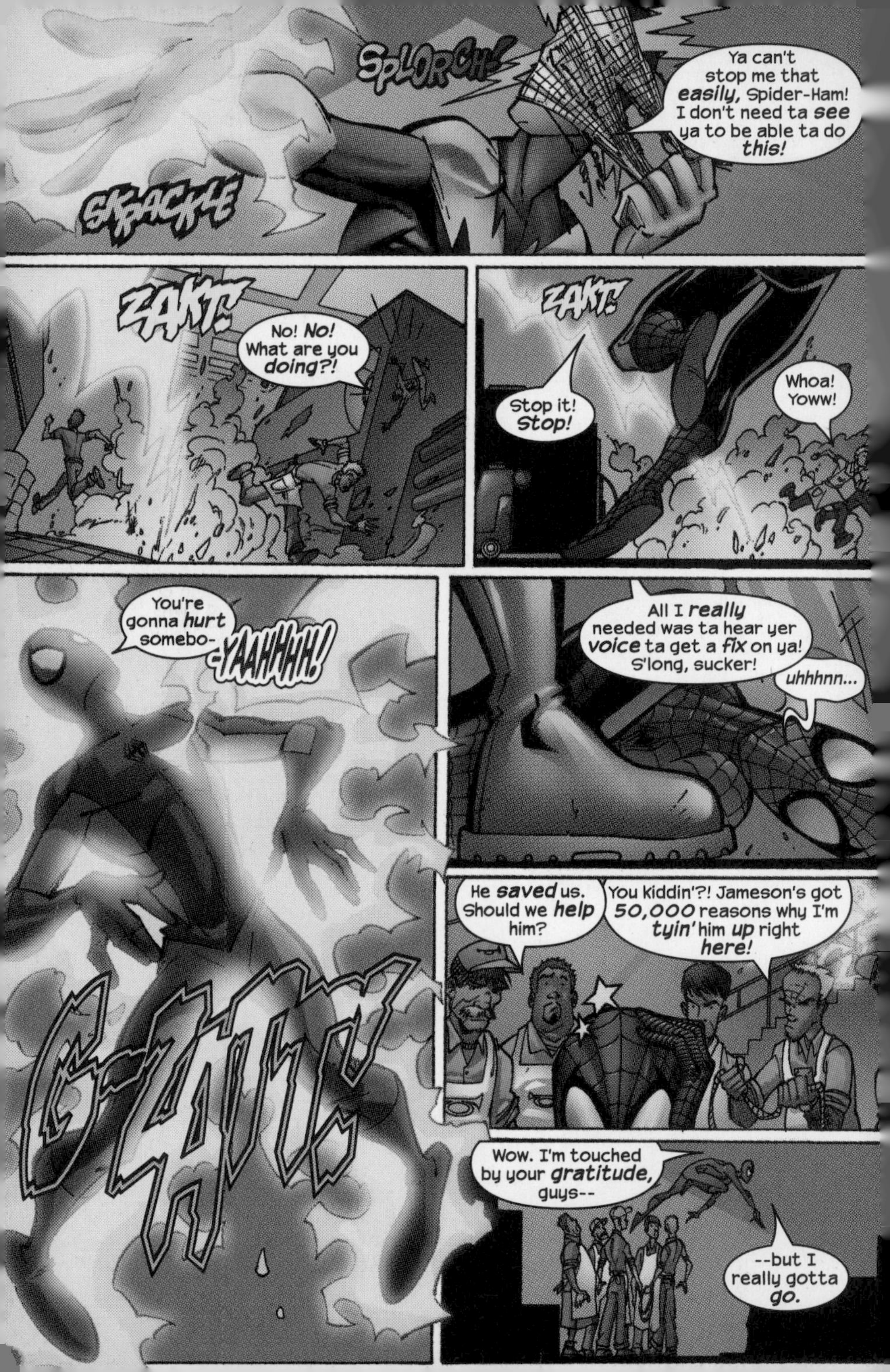
SPLORCH!
Ya can't stop me that easily, Spider-Ham! I don't need ta see ya to be able ta do this!
SKRACKLE
ZAKT!
No! No! What are you doing?!
ZAKT!
Stop it! Stop!
Whoa! Yoww!
You're gonna hurt somebo-
-YAAHHHH!
All I really needed was ta hear yer voice ta get a fix on ya! S'long, sucker!
uhhhnn...
He saved us. Should we help him?
You kiddin'?! Jameson's got 50,000 reasons why I'm tyin' him up right here!
Wow. I'm touched by your gratitude, guys--
--but I really gotta go.

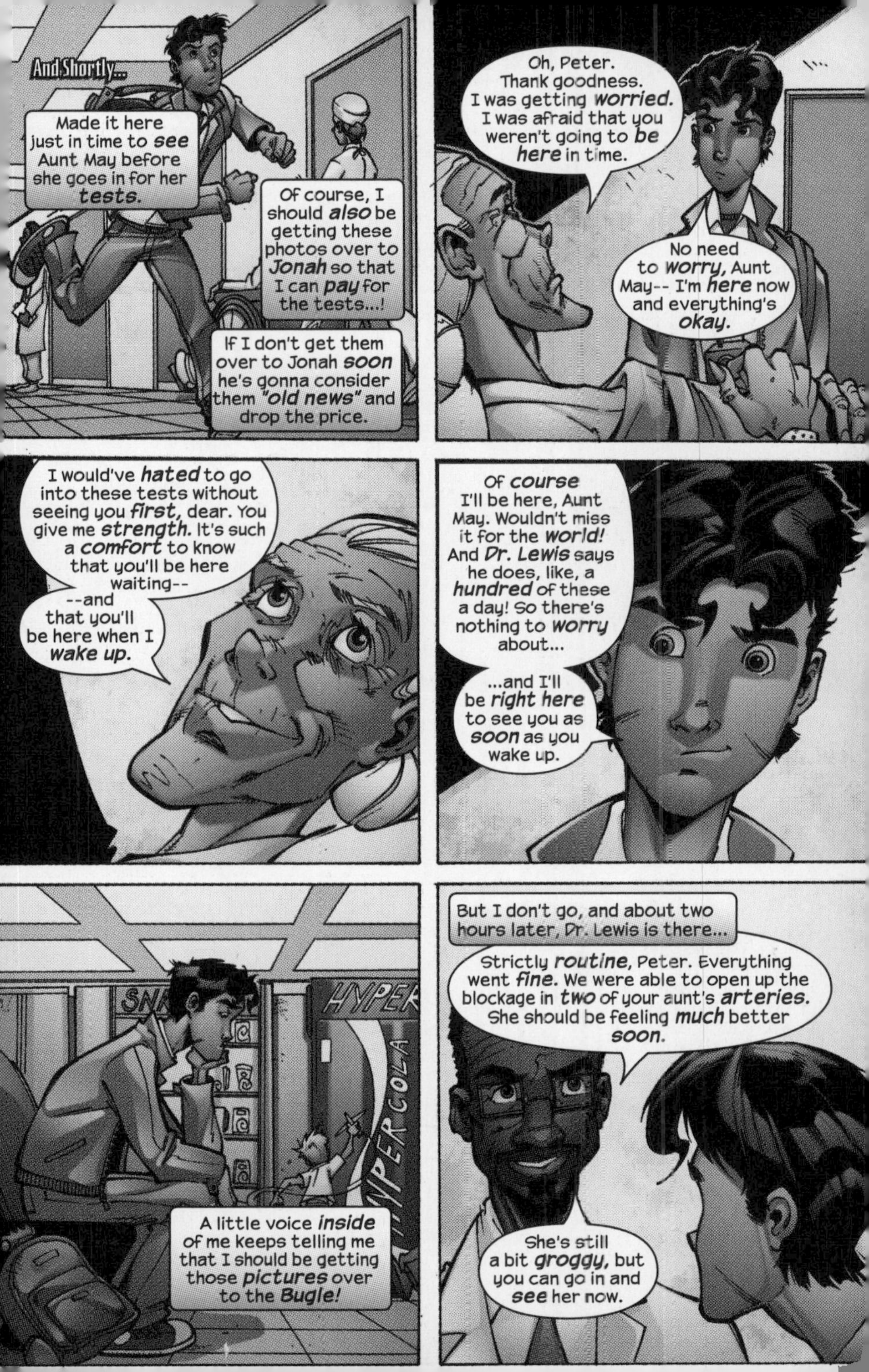
And Shortly...
Made it here just in time to see Aunt May before she goes in for her tests.
Of course, I should also be getting these photos over to Jonah so that I can pay for the tests...!
If I don't get them over to Jonah soon he's gonna consider them "old news" and drop the price.
Oh, Peter. Thank goodness. I was getting worried. I was afraid that you weren't going to be here in time.
No need to worry, Aunt May-- I'm here now and everything's okay.
I would've hated to go into these tests without seeing you first, dear. You give me strength. It's such a comfort to know that you'll be here waiting--
--and that you'll be here when I wake up.
Of course I'll be here, Aunt May. Wouldn't miss it for the world! And Dr. Lewis says he does, like, a hundred of these a day! So there's nothing to worry about...
...and I'll be right here to see you as soon as you wake up.
SNA
HYPER
HYPER COLA
A little voice inside of me keeps telling me that I should be getting those pictures over to the Bugle!
But I don't go, and about two hours later, Dr. Lewis is there...
Strictly routine, Peter. Everything went fine. We were able to open up the blockage in two of your aunt's arteries. She should be feeling much better soon.
She's still a bit groggy, but you can go in and see her now.

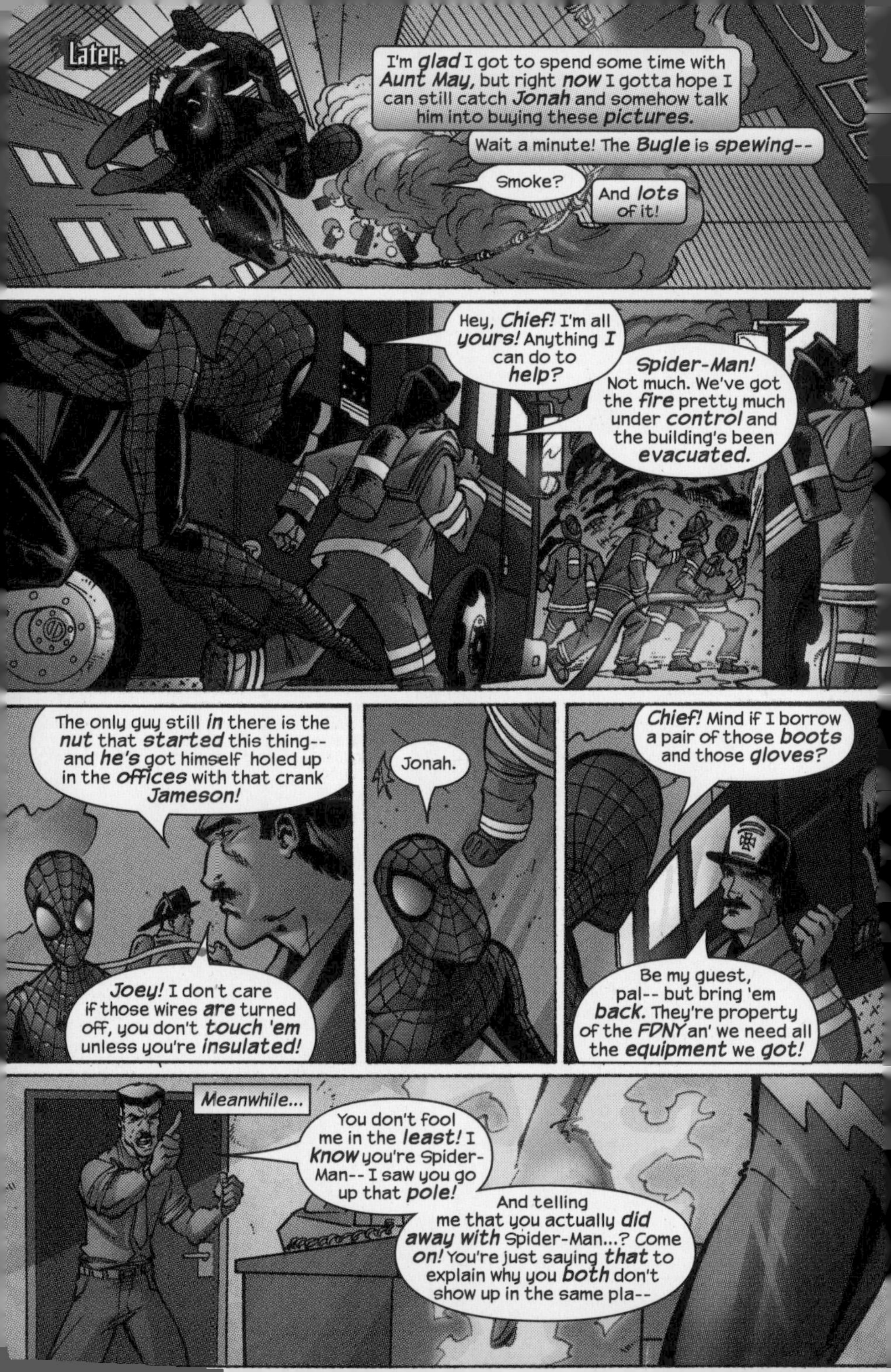
Later.
I'm glad I got to spend some time with Aunt May, but right now I gotta hope I can still catch Jonah and somehow talk him into buying these pictures.
Wait a minute! The Bugle is spewing--
Smoke?
And lots of it!
Hey, Chief! I'm all yours! Anything I can do to help?
Spider-Man! Not much. We've got the fire pretty much under control and the building's been evacuated.
The only guy still in there is the nut that started this thing-- and he's got himself holed up in the offices with that crank Jameson!
Joey! I don't care if those wires are turned off, you don't touch 'em unless you're insulated!
Jonah.
Chief! Mind if I borrow a pair of those boots and those gloves?
Be my guest, pal-- but bring 'em back. They're property of the FDNY an' we need all the equipment we got!
Meanwhile...
You don't fool me in the least! I know you're Spider-Man-- I saw you go up that pole!
And telling me that you actually did away with Spider-Man...? Come on! You're just saying that to explain why you both don't show up in the same pla--

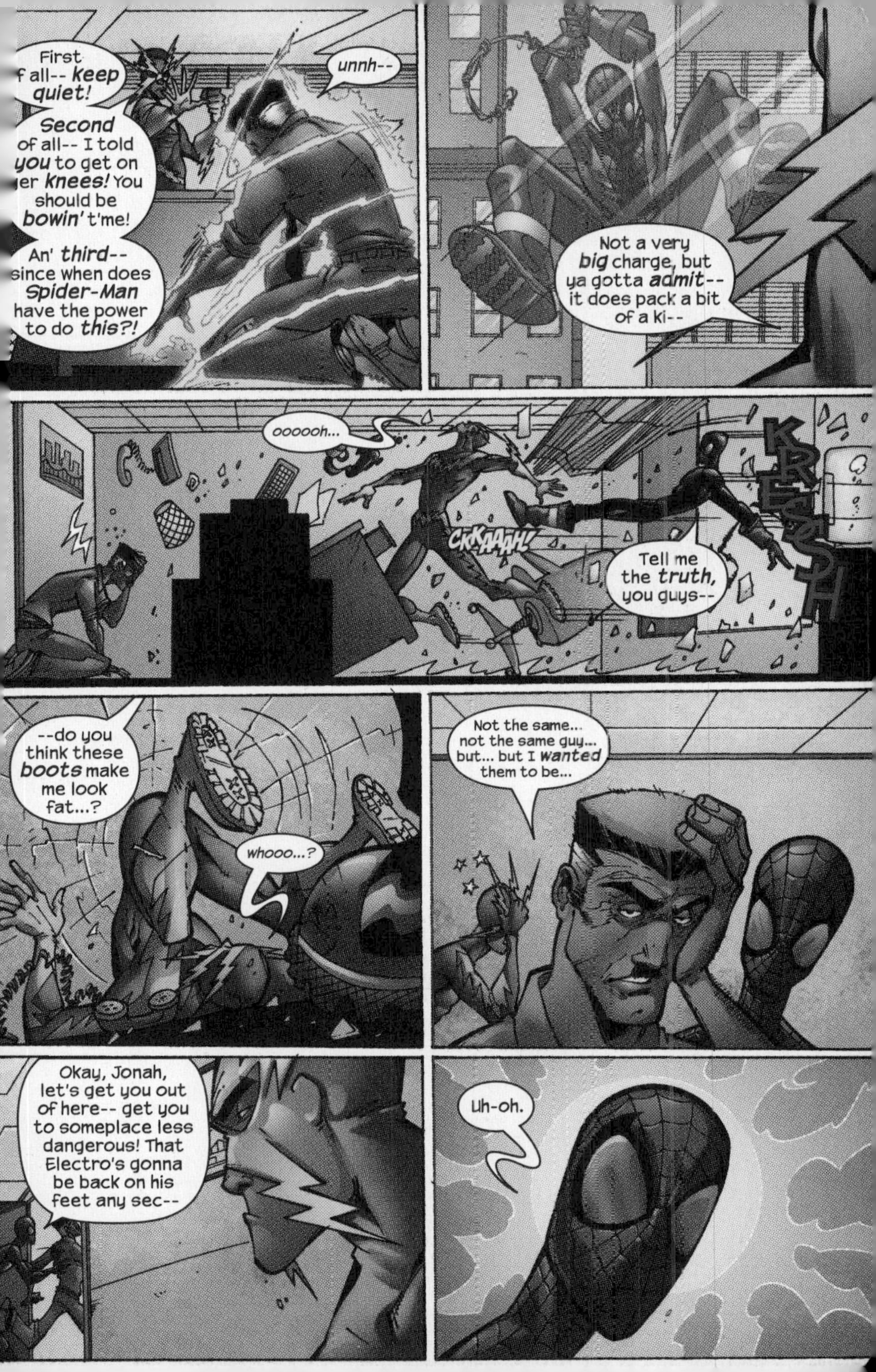

First -f all-- keep quiet!
Second of all-- I told you to get on -er knees! You should be bowin' t'me!
An' third-- since when does Spider-Man have the power to do this?!
unnh--
Not a very big charge, but ya gotta admit-- it does pack a bit of a ki--
oooooh...
KRESSSH
CKKAAAH!
Tell me the truth, you guys--
--do you think these boots make me look fat...?
whooo...?
Not the same... not the same guy... but... but I wanted them to be...
Okay, Jonah, let's get you out of here-- get you to someplace less dangerous! That Electro's gonna be back on his feet any sec--
Uh-oh.

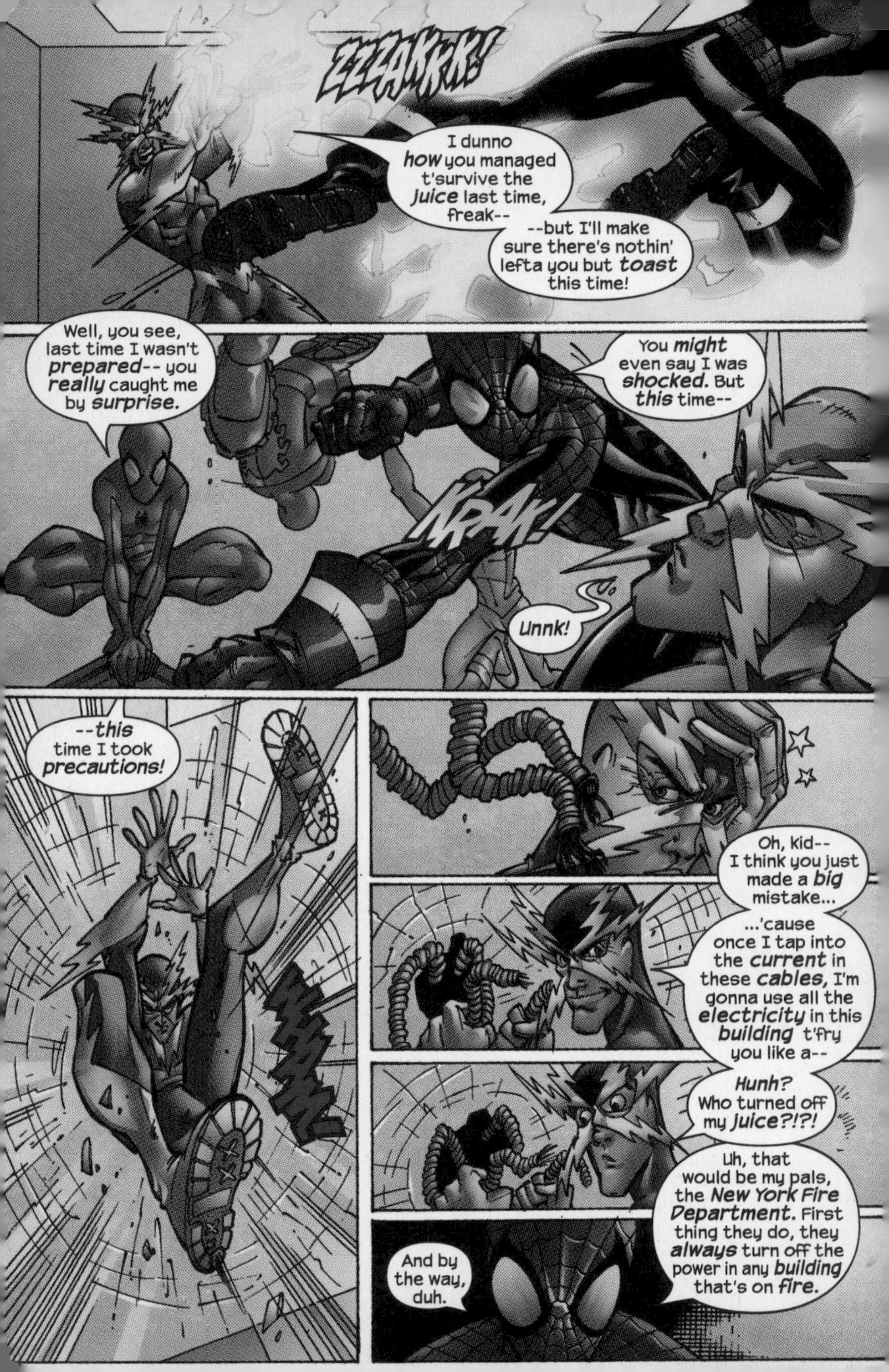
ZZZAKKK!
I dunno how you managed t'survive the juice last time, freak--
--but I'll make sure there's nothin' lefta you but toast this time!
Well, you see, last time I wasn't prepared-- you really caught me by surprise.
You might even say I was shocked. But this time--
KRAK!
Unnk!
--this time I took precautions!
Oh, kid-- I think you just made a big mistake...
...'cause once I tap into the current in these cables, I'm gonna use all the electricity in this building t'fry you like a--
Hunh? Who turned off my juice?!?!
Uh, that would be my pals, the New York Fire Department. First thing they do, they always turn off the power in any building that's on fire.
And by the way, duh.

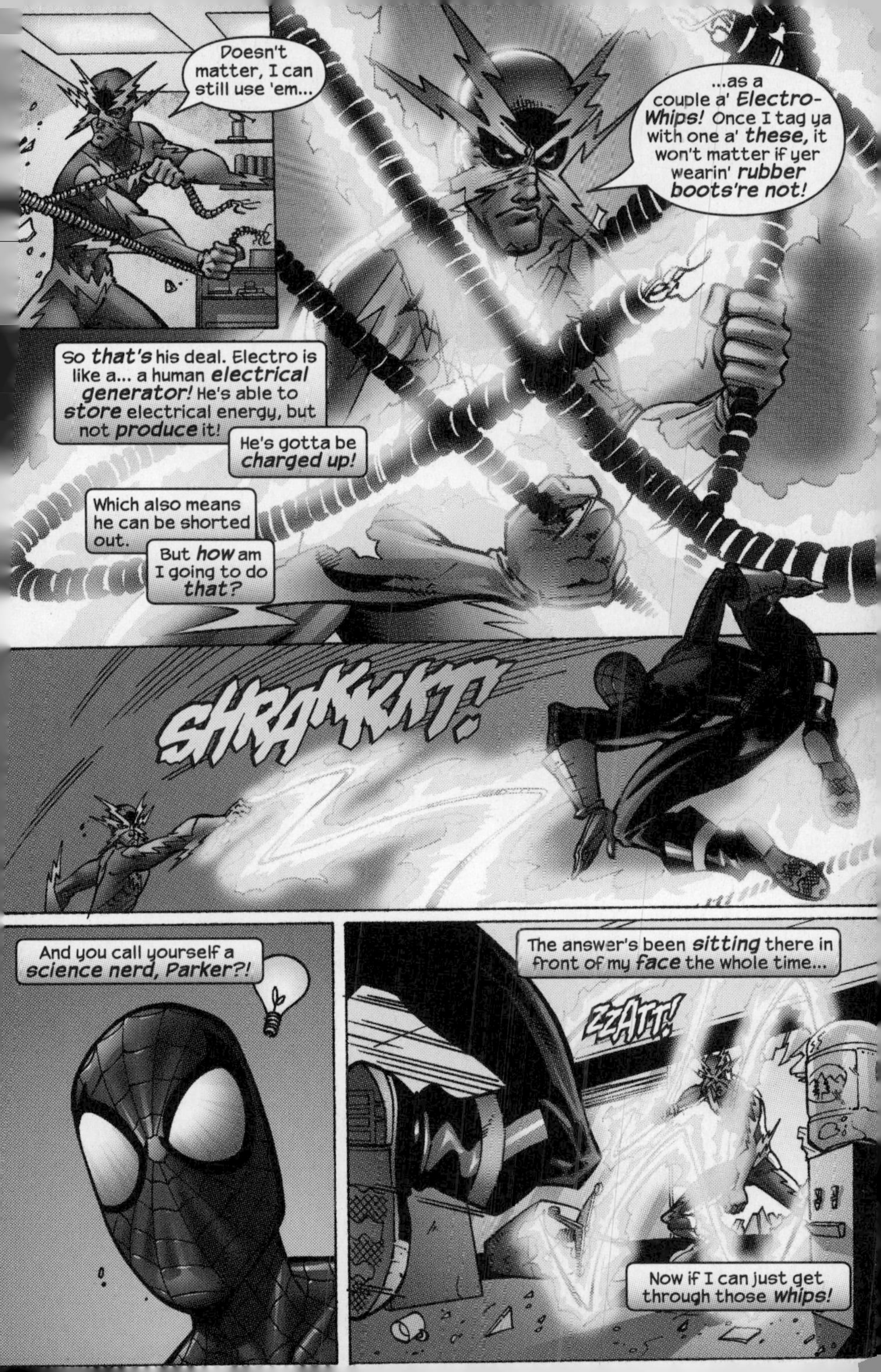
Doesn't matter, I can still use 'em...
...as a couple a' Electro-Whips! Once I tag ya with one a' these, it won't matter if yer wearin' rubber boots're not!
So that's his deal. Electro is like a... a human electrical generator! He's able to store electrical energy, but not produce it!
He's gotta be charged up!
Which also means he can be shorted out.
But how am I going to do that?
SHRAKKKT!
And you call yourself a science nerd, Parker?!
The answer's been sitting there in front of my face the whole time...
ZZATT!
Now if I can just get through those whips!

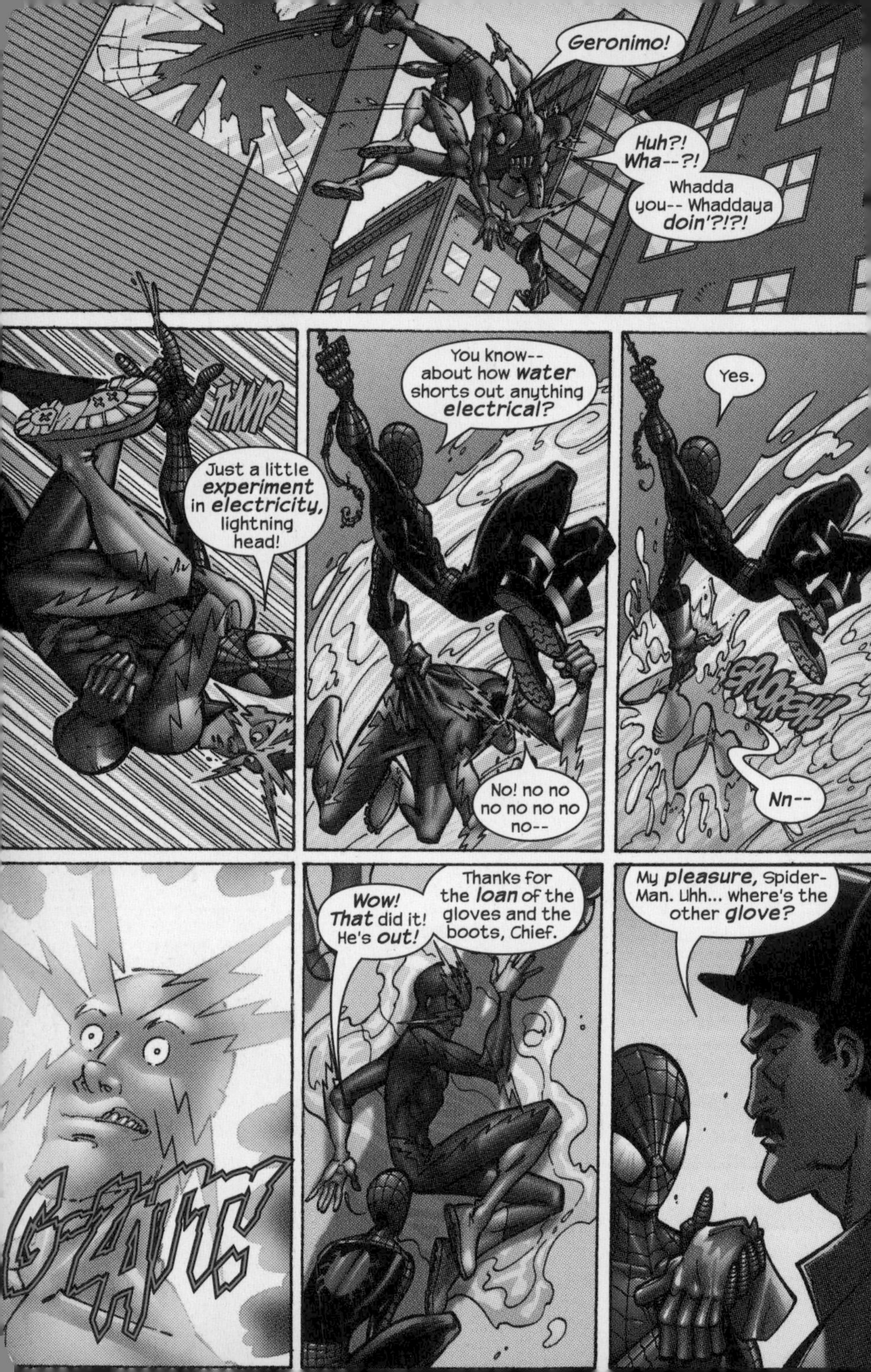
Geronimo!
Huh?! Wha--?!
Whadda you-- Whaddaya doin'?!?!
Just a little experiment in electricity, lightning head!
You know-- about how water shorts out anything electrical?
No! no no no no no no no--
Yes.
Nn--
Wow! That did it! He's out!
Thanks for the loan of the gloves and the boots, Chief.
My pleasure, Spider-Man. Uhh... where's the other glove?

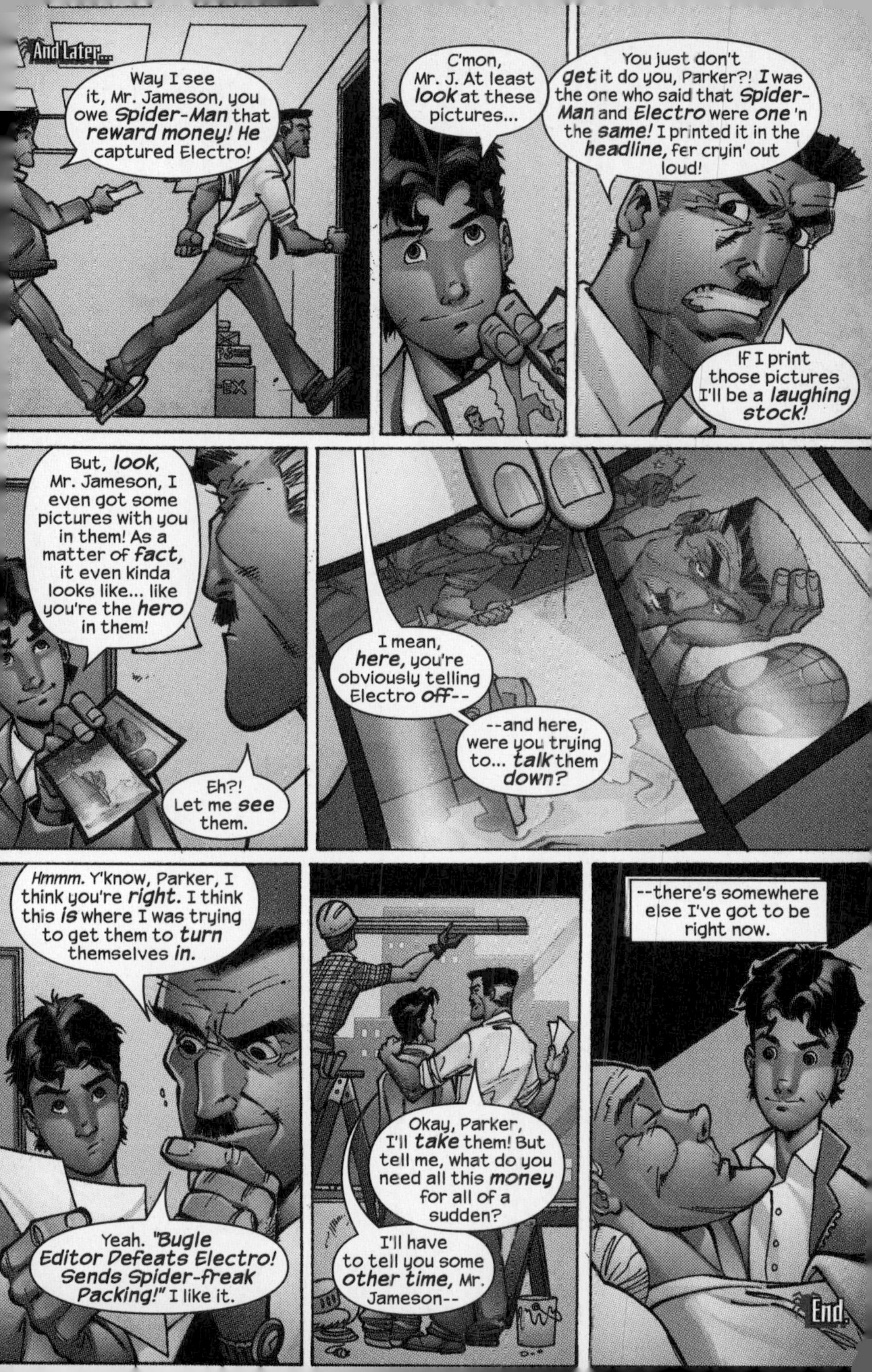
And Later...
Way I see it, Mr. Jameson, you owe Spider-Man that reward money! He captured Electro!
C'mon, Mr. J. At least look at these pictures...
You just don't get it do you, Parker?! I was the one who said that Spider-Man and Electro were one 'n the same! I printed it in the headline, fer cryin' out loud!
If I print those pictures I'll be a laughing stock!
But, look, Mr. Jameson, I even got some pictures with you in them! As a matter of fact, it even kinda looks like... like you're the hero in them!
Eh?! Let me see them.
I mean, here, you're obviously telling Electro off--
--and here, were you trying to... talk them down?
Hmmm. Y'know, Parker, I think you're right. I think this is where I was trying to get them to turn themselves in.
Yeah. "Bugle Editor Defeats Electro! Sends Spider-freak Packing!" I like it.
Okay, Parker, I'll take them! But tell me, what do you need all this money for all of a sudden?
I'll have to tell you some other time, Mr. Jameson--
--there's somewhere else I've got to be right now.
End.

Marvel Age Spider-Man Sketchbook

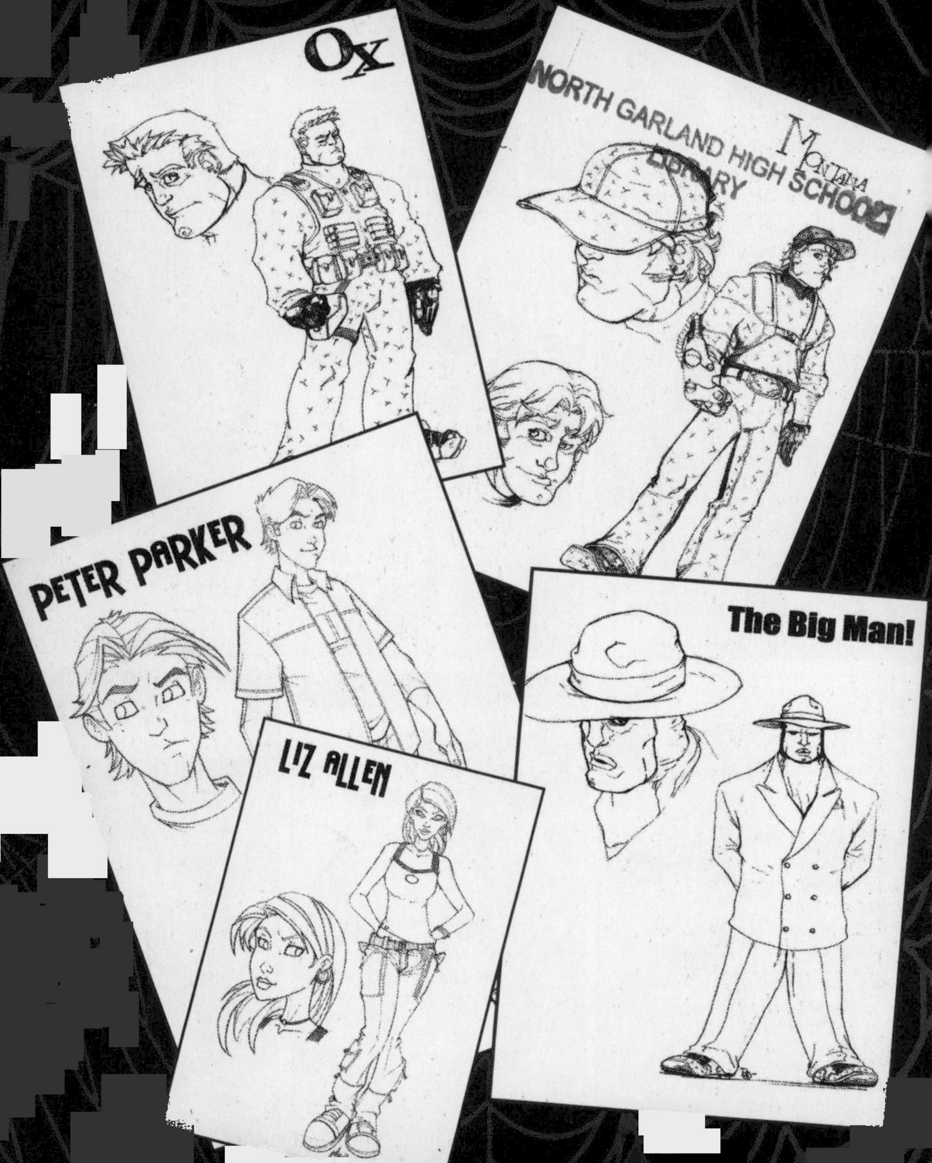
OX
MONTANA
PETER PARKER
LIZ ALLEN
The Big Man!